The story of Bela Gogos is a story of courage, hope, defiance and a lust for freedom, and it is a story of the Russian Gulag from a perspective I had never heard. This is a story that needs to be told.

The book is packed with action and surprises, right down to the last page. It is a must-read for everyone who really wants to understand the fate of the politically undesired in the Soviet Union and the Iron Curtain countries following the war. It is a story of human physical and spiritual survival under the most inhuman conditions.

—Bela Szalai
Grew up in communist-controlled Hungary.
IBM Senior engineer (ret.)

Youth Lost in Red Hell *is an incredible story of an incredible life. It is a story that needs to be told. I really found that I could not put it down. Reading it interfered with my entire Christmas weekend.*

Most of all, people need to know how the U.S. and Russia or any dictatorship differ, and how people suffer under dictatorial rule. It is a great time for such inspiration.

—George A. Hazelrigg
Author and National Science Foundation District Director

Bela, how do I say what a privilege it was to read your words, the story of your past, the story that made you who you are today? I was overwhelmed and could not stop reading until I finished. May you forever "fly free."

—Deborah Shelden
Historian

Despite the vague understanding that most Americans have of the Stalinist period in Russia and despite my own studies of Russian history, I find much of what you describe as new and informative, perhaps because it is so immediate. Thanks for sharing it . . .

—Barbara Hickingbottom
Attorney, living and practicing in California

YOUTH LOST
in
Red Hell

YOUTH LOST
in
Red Hell

Béla Gőgös

www.ivyhousebooks.com

Author's Note

In *Youth Lost in Red Hell*, there are no fictitious people or events.
However, the names of some people have been altered to prevent causing
embarrassment. For personal consideration, initials instead of names identify some people. If they are not named at all, it is only because human
memory has failed to preserve their names. But everything took place just
as described; it is the life of a Hungarian aviator.

PUBLISHED BY IVY HOUSE PUBLISHING GROUP
5122 Bur Oak Circle, Raleigh, North Carolina 27612
United States of America
919-782-0281
www.ivyhousebooks.com

ISBN 1-57197-372-9
Library of Congress Control Number: 2003104620

Printed in the United States of America

I dedicate my book as I have dedicated my life to my dear wife, Susan, and to all those nameless heroes who did not live to tell of the horrors of communist torture chambers. They gave their lives fighting Communism, demonstrating that oppression of totalitarian governments could not destroy the spirit of the people.

Contents

Foreword

Books written by historians provide the facts about World War II and its aftermath with varying degrees of accuracy. But they can't give the reader the personal perspective of one who actually lived through the devastation and suffered under the oppressive regime of a totalitarian government. *Youth Lost in Red Hell,* is much needed in post Cold War America. Historians of all generations and the general public will warmly receive this book, especially the "baby boomer" generation whose parents lived through the war and fought on its battlefields.

This book is the story of a personal journey, not a political polemic. As the author's journey unfolds, the coldness of totalitarianism is revealed in its relentless efforts to crush the author, physically and emotionally, with unimaginable brutality.

Youth Lost in Red Hell gives the reader the experiences of the author who survived a post World War II POW camp, torture chambers, prisons, and the infamous Soviet gulag masterminded by Lenin and implemented to its vicious extremes by Stalin.

The reader will get a glimpse of the author's Hungarian childhood, his early years, and schooling interrupted by the events of World War II. The war was hellish for everyone caught in its grasp, including the author. But his "Red Hell" began after the war, first as an air force pilot captured in the days following the end of the war, and then as a political prisoner sent to the gulag for taking part in the fight against Hungary's totalitarian government.

Opposition to Communism in the his native Hungary led to the author's arrest, imprisonment, torture, and subsequent relinquishment to the Soviet military authorities. The newly emerging Hungarian government, backed and controlled by the Kremlin and the occupying Red Army, didn't yet have the guts to stage the type of sham trial for him that would later become routine, when thousands of intellectuals and political and religious leaders were imprisoned or killed.

A Soviet military tribunal sentenced him and his fellow conspirators to twenty-five years in prison and labor camps. The sentence meant he would be sent to a place "from which there was no return," as they were told during their "trial."

The author's survival over the next ten years in Moscow's notorious Lubyanka prison and the Soviet gulag above the Arctic Circle is a testament to his unshakeable belief in a higher power, his strong will, and his ability to adapt in an inhumane environment.

As a countryman, fellow glider pilot, and friend for the past twenty-five years, I am grateful to Bela for letting us all know what life in "Red Hell" was like so that future generations will never forget.

Bela J. Szalai,
Pueblo, Colorado

Acknowledgments

I began writing this book many years ago with the intention of leaving my life story to my grandson, Kyle Bela, after I went to a better world. The original title was *The Life of a Hungarian Aviator.*

Encouraged by friends and family, I considered publishing it as a book to portray the horrors of life under communist governments. George Hazelrigg's persuasion and constructive critique after having read a draft of the book during his 2001 Christmas vacation convinced me to do just that.

Jim Kellett, Doug Hoffman, Caleb Hanson, and many others across the nation have read various drafts with critical eyes. Rachel Cartwright and Kitty Werner made excellent suggestions and finally, Hannah Kamenetsky applied the necessary scissors to arrive at the current, final version.

But there is always one person who, more than any other, becomes an indispensable participant of such a process. In this case, it has been my wife, Susan.

This page would not be complete without expressing my gratitude to many Americans who, in many encounters, taught me everything I know about the wonderful land of America.

Prologue

It's late November and the bitter cold has not yet settled in. But the trees are bare, the leaves having made their inevitable, silent journey to the earth, a tangible sign of the passage of time.

At the age of seventy-eight, I find myself looking back on my life, wondering where the time has gone, not just hours, but years. It seems like yesterday that I saw my wife, Susan, holding our baby in her arms. But that baby is now a grown woman. Where have the years gone?

It is strange to contemplate. Sometimes time seems to fly and other times its passage is cruelly slow. Why is that? I ask you. Do you know? In my life, I have known both the rush of joyful times and agonizing slowness of days so bleak that I could not stand another hour.

Now I find myself looking for answers to many questions such as these. They may seem simple and unimportant to you—but not to me. As I reflect back on my life and watch another autumn pass, I think these questions are what we live our lives to answer.

By now, you must be thinking that I'm old and senile. This is not so. I have a very clear and still very young mind, despite my feet of clay and hair that's white as snow. There was a day—and it seems not long ago—when my hair was as dark as the night and I was fast on my feet.

As I sit watching the sunset over the valley beyond my home, old memories overwhelm me. I think of what my father endured. Imagine being incarcerated without a trial. Imagine being imprisoned for doing something that you sincerely believe to be good and true to God. And I recall what I endured, more than eleven years of my youth stolen from me because I happened to live at a time and in a place where a government betrayed its own people, imprisoned millions, and let millions more die. You can only hope and pray to God Almighty that such a fate will never be yours. And you can read my story, and the stories of others who, like me, thanks to God, survived.

Introduction

This story begins late one night in the summer of 1948. I was an engineering student, preparing a class project when armed secret service agents burst into my apartment and arrested me for conspiracy against the Hungarian Communist government.

I had just been released only a few months earlier from the Soviet Union where I had spent almost three long years as a prisoner of war. Shortly after my return to Hungary, my homeland, I had been recruited into an underground anticommunist movement. Just months later, an agent provocateur led the Communist Secret Service to our group. Its members, including me, were arrested and charged with conspiracy and armed organization against the Hungarian Communist government.

Only weeks later, I found myself standing trial before a Soviet military court, facing the yawning chasm of Red Hell in the Soviet prison system. The sentence was twenty-five years of prison and forced labor. I was twenty-four years old.

I spent the next three years in solitary confinement in an eight-foot by four-foot cell in Lubyanka, Moscow's notorious central prison.

At the end of the third year, literally minutes from succumbing to a deep despair, a guard opened the door to my cell and led me deeper yet into Red Hell. To complete the remainder of my sentence, I was transported to the Soviet gulag at Inta/Vorkuta above the Arctic Circle where the line between life and death was razor thin and I struggled to survive killing cold, starvation, and hopelessness as a slave in a Soviet coal mine. Many of my fellow prisoners gave up the struggle.

Conditions in the camps improved somewhat following the death of Joseph Stalin in 1953, and with the help of friends and occasional acts of kindness by our Russian guards, I managed to survive there on the formidable Arctic tundra.

I was released after eight years. A free man for the first time since 1948, I witnessed the heroic Hungarian uprising and joined a political maneuver against the Communists. It wasn't long before I was advised to flee, however, just steps ahead of Hungarian and Soviet Secret Police.

With the help of friends, I joined others in search of freedom. Just yards from the Austrian border, only quick thinking and resourcefulness saved us from being sent back to Hungary—or a worse fate.

From Vienna, I secured passage on a ship to Canada, leaving behind friends and loved ones to sail toward the second chapter in my life.

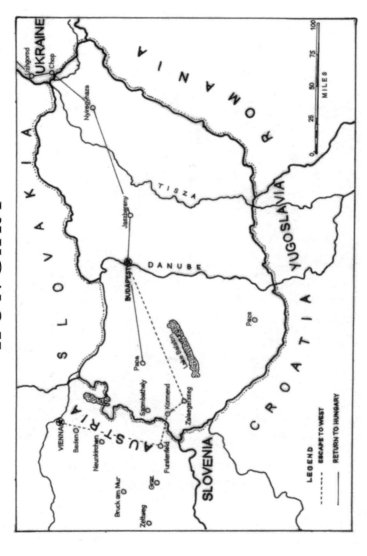

**JOURNEY TO "RED HELL" AND
RETURN TO FREEDOM**

1

How It All Began:
Communist Rule in Hungary
(1948)

Few are willing to brave the disapproval of their fellows, the censure of their colleagues, the wrath of their society. Moral courage is a rarer commodity than bravery in battle or great intelligence. Yet it is the one essential vital quality for those who seek to change a world that yields most painfully to change.

Robert F. Kennedy

Aftermath of the End of World War II

On 9 May 1945, the Second World War ended with Hungary on the losing side and occupied by the Russian Army. During the siege of Budapest and throughout the following weeks, Russian troops freely looted the city and the smaller towns and villages they overran. They entered practically every house—poor and rich alike—raping women of all ages, including nuns in convents. Those who resisted were shot as "offenders."

Hungary had been under Communist rule once before during the 133-day Bolshevik Red Terror regime of Bela Kun in 1919. The second rising of the Red Star in the wake of the Russian occupation in 1945 produced far greater horrors. Its cataclysmic proportions are often compared with the Mongolian invasion of 1241-1242.

After the Russian military conquest of Hungary, under the leadership of Matyas Rakosi, a group of Muscovite Hungarians was sent to complete the political takeover. The Hungarian Muscovites had high hopes that by the fall of 1945—the time set for the general election—they would have a winning hand.

Their confidence seemed justified for several reasons. The Communist Party enjoyed the support of the Soviet Army. They claimed credit for the land reform enacted by the communist-dominated interim government in March 1945 that distributed more than three million acres among landless peasants. The Party also emphasized the sanctity of private ownership as a prop to induce both big and small capitalists to rebuild their shops and factories and to increase production. Last but not least, the communists succeeded in wrestling control of the Federation of Hungarian Labor from the Social Democrats.

The campaign was a clever one and Rakosi and his cohorts were sure of victory against their weakly organized opponents in the national election set for 4 November 1945. They felt so confident of victory that in Budapest, they moved the date of the municipal election two weeks ahead of the national vote. A victory in Budapest would be the overture to an overwhelming communist victory nationwide.

Things, however, did not work out as planned. Budapest, believed to be a "Red City" reinforced by an industrial belt with a proletarian electorate, voted against the communists by giving the agrarian Small Landholders' Party more than fifty percent of the total vote. The Communist-Socialist ticket won only forty-three percent of the vote. More than anyone else, it was Bela Kovacs who helped engineer this victory for the Small Landholders.

The second blow, delivered to the national electorate on 4 November 1945, was even more devastating. The Small Landholders won the election by a significant margin.

Hungary's rejection of Communism under the shadow of Soviet military created a worldwide sensation that focused attention on the resistance of the Magyars against Communism.

But in a coup-like interference in Hungary's domestic affairs in 1947, the Russians arrested Bela Kovacs and deported him to Russia as an "anti-Soviet spy." Following his arrest, members of the old regime—statesmen, former officers of the Hungarian Army, lawyers, and even students—were systematically arrested in great numbers and incarcerated. Many of them were sentenced to ten to fifteen years of prison. Others were executed or sent to the Soviet gulag, from which many never returned.

Summer 1947

I had been an officer and pilot in the Hungarian Air Force, which no longer existed—and a Soviet POW for two and a half years. After my release from a Soviet POW camp, I needed emotional and physical strength and strong willpower to pick up the pieces of my life and build my future.

During my years at the Air Force Academy, I had nurtured a desire to earn a degree in aeronautical engineering. Under the newly formed communist government, however, this was impossible. The aeronautical industry in Hungary had been destroyed during the war and the Soviet invasion that followed. Consequently, the need for aeronautical engineers was reduced to a low level. Also, applicants had to pass a stringent screening based on their political background, and acceptance was dependent on the approval of the Communist Party. As a former officer in the Hungarian Air Force, I had no chance of being accepted. So, I decided to pursue electrical engineering at Jozsef Nador Technical University in Budapest, the only university in Hungary that offered an engineering degree.

To meet the deadline for enrollment in the fall semester, I immediately left for Budapest from my hometown of Papa, 110 miles to the southwest. After passing the entrance exam, I enrolled for the fall semester in the engineering program. At the end of the day, tired and exhausted, I went to see my uncle's family in their downtown apartment.

My uncle, Dez, and his wife, Jolan, owned and operated a small restaurant across the street from their apartment. Dez had been trained as a waiter and worked for a restaurant as a head-waiter until 1939. By then, he had gained enough experience and saved enough money so that he and Aunt Jolan could open a restaurant of their own. They put in long hours working from dawn to dusk.

One day, Dez didn't return from his daily marketing trip. Later, the family learned that the Russians grabbed him on a Budapest street, a common occurrence during their occupation of Hungary. He probably was shipped to a POW camp in Russia with thousands of others of his unfortunate country-men. His family never found out what happened to him; they only know that he never returned.

After my uncle's disappearance, Aunt Jolan carried on, but the communists eventually took the restaurant business away from her.

Aunt Jolan lived with their two children, Leslie, age twenty, an X-ray technician, and Eva, age thirteen, a high school student.

When I returned from two and a half years' imprisonment in a Soviet POW camp, I didn't even have enough money to rent a small room. "You stay with us and we'll share with you whatever we have until you earn enough money to be able to support yourself," Aunt Jolan said.

So I settled in and became a member of her family. I either walked or took a streetcar to classes at the university every day.

Our apartment was located on the first floor of a large complex in the financial center of the city. The entrance was reached through a courtyard. All the rooms opened onto a small hallway that led from the front door. Here, the members of the family and guests hung their coats and left their umbrellas on rainy days.

Facing the entrance was a bathroom, the kitchen was on the right, and on the left was a relatively large (fifteen square feet) room used as both a living room and bedroom. There were two sofas that could be used as beds. One was for Aunt Jolan and Eva and the other was for Leslie. My bed was a small cot in the kitchen. The room also contained two chairs and a large concert piano used by the children. I stored my books and notes on top of the piano where I also did my drawings. There wasn't a table in the apartment.

Leslie, to supplement his meager salary, formed a five-member band. On weekends, the band played at dance halls and coffee shops. They practiced on weekdays, sometimes late into the night. I usually waited to do my homework until after the band had finished practicing and the family had retired for the night.

11 March 1948

I had two visitors, Baki, a former fellow officer in the Hungarian Air Force, and a man with him whom I didn't know. He introduced himself as Kassai, a former officer in the Counter Intelligence Division of the Army.

"We've just arrived from Vienna. You can still see the Austrian dust on our boots," Baki said. "We got your address from Apponyi."

Apponyi was a descendent of a noble family. His grandfather had been the secretary of state after World War I and represented Hungary at the Peace Treaty of Trianon in 1920 at the Grand Trianon Palace in Versailles, France.

Young Apponyi was a fellow officer in the Hungarian Air Force and a good friend of mine. When the Russians occupied Hungary, his squadron was transferred to Germany. At the end of the war, he took up residency in Munich where he felt he could contribute more toward forming a resistance operation against the Hungarian government. In Munich, he met my uncle, a general in the Hungarian Army, and they organized an underground anticommunist movement, which didn't have a name since it was still in its infancy.

The plan was for Apponyi to sneak back into Hungary and set up a skeleton organization in large cities in the western part of the country. During one of his visits, he recruited me to be the central contact between him and others in various cities. My main duty was to maintain communications between our men inside Hungary and those stationed abroad. Because of this, I knew everyone involved.

"We just had a meeting with him in Vienna and he gave us your address and asked me to pick up whatever information you have," Baki said.

"I don't know what you are talking about," I said suspiciously.

"Aren't you the pivotal point in Apponyi's anticommunist movement?" Baki asked.

"I still do not know what you are referring to," I replied.

Noticing my reluctance to talk about my relationship with Apponyi, Kassai pulled a pistol from his pocket and threw it in the air a few times, saying, "We are going to fight and kill those damned communists, aren't we?"

The two men left after a brief visit. The next day, 12 March, Baki came back to my apartment. Most of our conversation revolved around mutual friends. Apponyi's name didn't come up.

During our conversation, I noticed Baki observing me closely. He seemed to sense that I wouldn't give away anything about the movement or my role in it.

"When is Apponyi coming to see you again?" he asked.

I gave no reply. Baki left, but returned late in the afternoon on the same day.

"I'm working on a machine design project that is due on Tuesday," I told him. "I have to finish it today because on Monday, I plan to travel to Papa to visit relatives and friends. They are expecting me."

"I'll give you a ride to Papa and back to Budapest," Baki replied. "If you accept my offer, I will be here at 7 A.M. on Monday morning."

I accepted.

When he was ready to leave, I escorted him to the street. As we walked, he looked behind him and warned, "Watch out! There is a secret service agent following and observing us." He grabbed my arm. "Don't look back."

We stopped and the man walked past us, but not before I had a chance to look at his face, an image that is carved in my memory. He seemed young—I guessed him to be in his mid-twenties—with curly black hair. His expression was menacing, reminding me of characters in old spy movies. Judging by his elegant, well-tailored suit, he could have been taken for a foreign diplomat.

15 March 1948

Budapest was celebrating, recalling the uprising of 1848 when the Hungarian people fought and won their freedom from their Habsburg oppressors. The mood was jubilant and the newspapers were extolling the glories of that earlier uprising, drawing a parallel between "the two revolutions."

Their attempts at drawing a parallel were a stretch, however. Under this new regime, we had "freedom"—freedom of thought, freedom of speech and religion, and freedom of press. But our newly found freedom, granted by a "considerate and understanding" Moscow, would ultimately have the "proper" limits set on it.

For me, 15 March 1948 has a special significance. It marked the beginning of my imprisonment in "Red Hell."

I had just finished a major project, an engineering drawing in ink, due on the following day in my Machine Design class. Three large drawings (1 1/2 feet by 2 1/2 feet) that counted as fifty percent of the final mark had to be submitted during the semester. It took approximately one hundred hours to complete each drawing. The professor himself checked each drawing and if it didn't meet his standards, he drew a large X on it in red ink. The drawing would have to be redrawn and resubmitted by a new deadline that was usually tight.

The rejection rate for the first submittal was high. If two intersecting lines were not well defined—as seen under a magnifying glass—it was reason enough for rejection. After the professor checked and graded the work, he put the drawings on a shelf outside his door to be picked up by the students.

My heart was pounding as I searched the pile for my drawing and it almost stopped when I saw the large X extending from one corner to the other. I picked it up, rolled it into a small cylinder, placed it in a cylindrical carrier case, and headed home.

During my forty-five-minute trip on the streetcar, I worked out plans and schedules to meet the new deadline, just two weeks away. I knew that to complete the drawing by the deadline, I would have to put in fifty hours of work each week. I still had to continue with my regular workload of attending lectures and studying. I wasn't sure if I had the willpower to redo the drawing or if I'd just drop the whole thing. But that wouldn't be me. In a short time, my mind was made up—full speed ahead.

Tired and ready for bed, I was alone in the apartment as I drew the final lines on my project, proud of the quality I'd achieved. I was sure it would be accepted. Aunt Jolan and Eva were away on a weekend trip to Aunt Jolan's relatives. Leslie was sleeping over at the home of some friends.

At 5:00 A.M., incessant pounding on the apartment door dragged me from a sound sleep. Had it been 1944 instead of 1948, I would have thought it was the milkman. But because of the political situation, I was sure it was the secret service, and my heart began to pound in fear.

Before I could reach the door, two uniformed agents broke it down and stormed in brandishing machine guns. One stopped long enough to read aloud a warrant for my arrest while the other ransacked my belongings. He examined everything. He pulled books off the shelves, yanked out drawers and dumped the contents on the floor, and tossed around my photographs and technical drawings.

He gathered up handfuls of things to take with him like cherished photographs of my childhood and family. Valuable wartime aviation pictures, books, and technical drawings were thrown around like confetti. My pilot logbook was taken from the top of the piano, with the cover on the floor and the inside pages torn out, and put on the pile to be used as evidence against me.

The drawing I had finished early that morning lay on the floor. The agents were trampling it with their dirty boots, competing with each other to see who could destroy more of my possessions.

I looked at my drawing lying facedown on the floor and tried to think of a way to salvage it—if it was at all possible. *If no more damage is done to it,* I thought, *I can restore it to near the original condition. I may be able to clean the back and explain to my professor what happened and hope he will accept it,* I told myself.

Then one of the secret service agents lifted the drawing to see what was on the other side. When he realized he couldn't understand it, he ripped it down the middle and threw the two pieces to the floor. Though tears trickled from my eyes as a dull pain ran through my body, my mind continued working to formulate another plan to save my work.

Then one of the agents in front of me held a submachine gun against my chest. I grabbed it, hoping he would shoot and kill me.

Then there was blackness.

I don't know how long I lay on the floor unconscious. When I came to, they grabbed me, stuffed a piece of dirty cloth into my mouth, blindfolded me, and cuffed my hands behind my back.

Quickly, so my neighbors wouldn't know what had happened to me, they dragged me through the courtyard to the street and into a waiting vehicle. This was their "modus operandi." The engine was running and the windows were darkened. The driver at the wheel was ready to go. The police didn't want anyone catching a glimpse of the unfortunate prisoners inside. It was the typical routine of the Hungarian Secret Service when kidnapping innocent citizens. They pushed me in and knocked me out with a well-aimed blow. There was stinging pain and then darkness.

Water splashed my face. I came out of darkness to see one of the secret service agents pouring water over my head. He had removed the blindfold and pulled the stinking rag from my mouth. I quickly looked around and assessed my situation.

I was in a large basement with a long row of doors. Between the doors, other prisoners were sitting on chairs facing the wall. Still, I was able to recognize them from behind. They were former fellow officers from the Hungarian Air Force—each of them a contact person in our anticommunist organization in my hometown or in Szombathely, a large city in the part of western Hungary known as Transdanubia.

Only Apponyi, the central figure in the anticommunist movement, and I knew who the other members of the movement were. The fact that these contacts were arrested before me aroused my suspicion that Apponyi was the traitor who sold us out. I found the idea hard to believe. But if not him, then who was the traitor?

I vowed to find the real traitor at any cost. Since I believe a higher power guides and controls our lives, I believed He would see that justice was done. But, even though I forgave the traitor and wouldn't seek revenge, I at least wanted to face him and say, "I know that you are the one who betrayed us."

Later, I found out that during the weekend of March 15, the secret service arrested more people than they had cells for, and had to hold the overflow in the corridor.

The secret service believed me to be the central figure in a nationwide anticommunist organization. They instructed the guards to keep a close eye on me because I might have the "superpower" to escape from their hands and take my information to my contacts outside Hungary.

I was rudely undressed, my pockets searched, my shoelaces and belt removed. They took away every item they found in my pockets, even my handkerchief.

Then I was ordered to dress. One of the guards took me upstairs on an elevator, opened a padded door, and pushed me into a room. Inside, uniformed secret servicemen, the inquisitors, sat at a table and threw names at me—names I had never heard before.

A piece of paper with red writing on it was pushed in front of me.

"Red is a good color for today! Yes?" a guard commented, looking pleased. "Now, sign it!"

The code of honor that I had learned and practiced in the air force surfaced in my mind. *No matter how they torture you, never sign anything and never mention anyone's name.* I refused to sign.

Suddenly, a fist came from nowhere, then more. I hit the floor and clenched my teeth as boots and fists pummeled my body. Still, I refused to cooperate. Using rubber clubs, the secret service agents beat me into unconsciousness.

When I awoke and peered through my swollen eyelids, I found myself lying on a cot in a small cell. A thin, white-faced, broken-looking young man stood watching me anxiously. Each waited for the other to speak. I had no idea where I was or who he was. My mind was still cloudy from the beating. I expected more of the same.

After what seemed an eternity, the young man broke the silence. He was there under the same circumstances as I. He assured me that we were alone and eagerly asked me questions about the "outside." He wanted to know what the political situation was inside and outside Hungary since his arrest a year earlier.

I wanted to know everything about our situation. He said we were at KATPOL (Military Political Institution) and I became all too aware of what the future there would hold for me.

The following days were quiet and uneventful, but every night after falling asleep, I was awakened by the "gentle nudge" of a machine gun. With my hands bound behind my back, I was walked through a dark corridor in the basement to the elevator. A soldier with a submachine gun followed.

The monotonous sound of the elevator motor frightened me. The higher it rose, the harder my heart would beat. The elevator stopped quietly. As the cage door opened at the third floor, I heard moans and screams of other prisoners.

At the end of the corridor, the guard ordered me to face the wall so I wouldn't be able to identify my torturers. I was led into the room, then kicked and beaten from behind. This was a warning of what I could expect in the next few minutes, but my indignation against unjust and brutal treatment was stronger than the physical pain. Those beatings were the daily routine and with each new interrogation, they introduced new, more vicious forms of torture.

Usually, simultaneous interrogations were conducted day and night on the dreaded third floor. Victims waiting in the corridor for their turn were ordered to face the wall so they couldn't recognize other victims entering and emerging from the interrogation chamber. In spite of this, I managed to see the faces of the other victims among my eight fellow officers. One of them was Baki, wearing his old uniform and moving about freely. He quickly turned around to hide his face from me. I immediately realized that he must be one of the traitors.

Later, Joco, a high school friend and also a conspirator, saw Berger, his fellow officer in the air force, as he left the interrogation room with no one guarding him. Berger accompanied Baki to my home and introduced himself as Kassai. This indicated to us that he was a traitor as well.

After my last beating, the secret service agents outlined the charge against me as having a leading role in organizing armed secret groups against the communist regime in case the Western nations decided to send their troops in.

This was a possibility in those days, according to our movement leaders and men stationed in Austria, university students and former air force officers with whom I had had contact.

The members didn't know each other, nor were they even aware of each other. As a result, the secret service caught only twelve of us even though a large part of the population was taking part in the anticommunist organization.

In our group, there were six former air force officers, a lawyer, a former cadet in a military school, four people from a small village near the Austrian-Hungarian border, a veterinarian, a professional officer in the Army Counter Intelligence Division, and Laci and Mary, a married couple who owned a mill and a large estate. This property ownership, in the eyes of the communists, was reason enough to eliminate someone and break up a happy marriage.

Eleven of us were handed over to the Soviets while Mary was transferred to a central jail in Budapest. Being pregnant didn't elicit considerate treatment by the Hungarian communists. Many years later, I learned that despite her advanced pregnancy, she was put in an ordinary cell with common criminals. She gave birth to a daughter with no medical assistance. The baby was taken away immediately and put into the jail's "nursery."

Mary was reunited with her baby a few months later and shortly after, they were released. But the harsh treatment during the last months of Mary's pregnancy took its toll and the criminally negligent "care" had lasting effects on the baby; she was physically disabled for the rest of her life.

Because my main duty was to maintain communications between members in Hungary and members stationed abroad, I knew everyone involved. So, I was the one the secret service sought to obtain information from.

The two missing officers, Baki and Kassai—agents provocateurs—had served as contacts between our home base in Hungary and members abroad. Besides myself, these two were the only ones who could identify our men operating in other locations. Through these traitors, the secret service knew I was the one who could supply them with all the information they needed—if they could make me talk. I knew they would try every one of their heinous methods to succeed.

On my third night in captivity, I was awakened as usual at 1 A.M. Fear enveloped me. By now, I knew too well the meaning of dragging a prisoner from his cot at that time of night—another session of questioning and torture on the dreaded third floor.

The guard roughly pushed me into a dimly lit room with no windows. The setting of the room and the expressions of my torturers indicated something more vicious than usual was about to happen. In one corner was an iron pole about three feet high with a chain attached to it. In the opposite corner sat an unlit floodlight. In the semi-darkness, men with beads of sweat on their faces stood in a circle around the iron pole.

Sweat trickled down my body and my heart pounded as I gathered what little strength I had left. I would not surrender to these animals. *No*, I repeated over and over in my mind. *They will not break me down, these vicious hired killers. Ideals and honesty must be stronger than bloody rubles. I must keep strength and mantra.*

They chained me to the pole. The floodlight snapped on, blinding me with its powerful light. Then the questioning began. It seemed unending. I prayed for the inevitable torture to begin to relieve the built up tension inside me. The veins in my forehead throbbed as if they would burst any second. I turned my thoughts inward, to my mother, my family, and my friends.

When I thought I could take no more, the first blow came—then another and another.

I don't remember what happened after that.

I regained consciousness back in my cell as my young cell-mate wiped the blood from my injured face and arm. My entire body ached. A two-foot chain bound together my right leg and left arm. Surprisingly, I felt relatively well; the tension had eased and the dull pain throughout my body gave me an almost delightful feeling.

Several days later, on Holy Thursday, I was freed from the chains and led out for yet another interrogation.

This time, the questioning was short and to the point and there was no physical violence. My investigators were in a hurry to begin their Easter holiday. They didn't believe in God or Easter, but they still wanted their holiday.

When the interrogation was done, the leader ordered, "Until further notice, solitary confinement for this prisoner."

I spent my Easter holiday in my new "home," a two-foot by three-foot windowless cell in the bowels of the prison. Holy Week brought to mind the story in the Bible. Perhaps it was the thought of the death of Christ on the cross that helped me bear the mental and physical pain of those lonely, dark days.

As punishment during solitary confinement, I was forced to stand day and night. A guard standing outside my cell made sure I kept to the rules. Food and water were withheld. My first day in this cage passed without much difficulty. I was not hungry. But by dawn the next day, I was suffering from extreme thirst. That day, I meditated. I believe that helped me bear the fatigue, hunger, and thirst a little more.

On Saturday, I experienced a sharp pain in my legs and by that afternoon, they were swollen to twice their normal size. On Easter Sunday morning, I couldn't bear the excruciating pain any longer. My entire body was drenched with sweat. What little strength I had was gone. I dropped unconscious to the floor.

When I came to, I still didn't feel well. I had lost all sense of time and there was no difference between night and day. It was all one long hell. It seemed as if I had been unconscious only a few minutes—not nearly a long enough reprieve from my suffering. But I knew that I had been lying on the floor for several hours because there was a new guard standing over me. I could also hear food being distributed in the upstairs cells.

My new guard soon decided that I had had enough of my "comfortable" position on the floor and forced me to my feet to continue my punishment. At times, I was drenched with sweat. At other times, cold chills shivered up my spine in the tiny, airless cell. By this time, my fourth day without food, water, or rest, I felt no fatigue or hunger, just an unbearable thirst. My body swelled, my skin cracked, dried, and peeled off in long strips. The slightest movement caused severe pain.

On Monday morning, the investigator ordered his men to bring me up to him. I had no strength left and couldn't bend my badly swollen legs. I had to be carried. When we got upstairs to the interrogation room, I was told to sit down. A bowl of freshly cooked macaroni, my favorite food, was placed in front of me.

"If you tell us all you know, you can eat as much as you like," the investigator said.

By this time, food had no attraction for me. I was too weak to even lift a fork to my mouth. Once again, I refused to talk.

What happened after this, I don't recall. I regained consciousness and opened my eyes a day and a half later. I was back in my cell and a fellow prisoner was watching me. He fed me and gave me water to drink. The pain in my legs was still almost unbearable, but while I slept, my body had begun to return to its normal size.

A day or so later, my interrogators tried again. This time, they used a different method. They threatened to torture my loved ones in front of me until I was willing to talk. They didn't arrest my mother, but they brought in the wife of one of my friends. She was eight months pregnant and in her presence, they continued their interrogation.

The questioning went on like this for weeks. At the end of their second unsuccessful month, they came up with yet another new method. A thick bundle of papers were placed in front of me. The papers contained my alleged confessions. I was given a choice to either sign the confessions, which I knew would be signing my death warrant, or go to Vienna for them to convince two of my Air Force colleagues living in Austria to return to Hungary. Their guarantee that I would return to Hungary was my mother. If I accepted the assignment, I would be a free man.

Naturally, I didn't agree to either of their proposals. Instead, I again asked to be granted a face-to-face confrontation with the two former Air Force officers turned traitors. Since I had first recognized them, they had done everything to avoid a face-to-face meeting with me. I couldn't have done much more than express my contempt for their betrayal of the cause we'd all fought for side by side. The meeting was not permitted.

After midnight a couple of days later, a guard awakened me again.

"Dress," he said. Since I didn't have any nightclothes, I never undressed for the night; it didn't take me long to be ready to go.

"Put your hands behind your back and march," the guard said.

I walked in front of him toward the elevator. We rode up to the floor where interrogations were usually held. As we stepped out of the elevator, we turned right and stopped at the first padded door. While the guard opened the door, I glimpsed a horrible sight from the corner of my eye. On the floor was the battered, unconscious body of a lawyer friend in a pool of his own blood and urine. My heart raced.

The guard confirmed my fears. "This will happen to you if you don't cooperate," he said.

Shortly, a door opened and I was pushed in. In no time, they delivered several blows to my body and then offered me a chair. One of the secret service officers put a stack of papers in front of me and yelled, "You don't have to read it, just sign it!"

"I do not sign anything before reading it first," I said.

"Being this late in the night, just to show you my kindness toward you, I will give you ten minutes to read and sign it," the officer yelled.

He pulled out a cigarette, lit it, and gave it to me. Since I hadn't had a cigarette for a long time, it made me dizzy.

I read while I smoked. The stack of papers contained the charges against me. The main charge was organizing and participating in a revolutionary movement funded by the West against the newly formed Hungarian Communist government. The other charges were espionage and sabotage.

I refused to sign.

As I turned the pages, I found a telegram containing the following message, "Come home immediately! I am in trouble and I need your help. Bela."

It was clear to me that the telegram was sent by the secret service in my name to lure Apponyi home and catch him in my apartment.

By now, my torturers realized that they couldn't break down my spirit. They added one more charge, espionage against the Soviet forces in Hungary.

As the interrogator leaned back in his chair smoking his own cigarette, he smiled—with his mouth, not his eyes. "By the way, we are sending you to a place you'll never return from," he said.

2

Trial by Soviet Military Tribunal
(15–17 July 1948)

From the beginning, I had a sense of destiny, as though my life was assigned to me by fate and had to be fulfilled. This gave me an inner security, as though I could never prove it to myself, it proved itself to me. I did not have this certainly; it had me. Nobody could rob me of the conviction that it was enjoined upon me to do what God wanted. That gave me the strength to go on my own way. Often, I had the feeling that in all decisive matters, I was no longer among men, but was alone with God.

Carl G. Jung

The "Eleven"

Around 10 P.M., early for an interrogation, I heard a loud bang on the door. It opened and a guard burst into the cell. My heart began to race. I didn't know what an interrogation at this unusual time meant. It couldn't be anything good.

The guard looked around. He pointed at me and ordered me to dress, gather my belongings, and walk in front of him. I had nothing except the few pieces of clothing I was arrested in. He prodded me roughly with his rifle to walk briskly and we quickly reached the courtyard. A special van designed to transfer prisoners between prisons was waiting.

In the drizzly, chilly night, I was shivering in my thin clothing from apprehension and the cold. My ten friends were also brought out one by one and I was reunited with the other members of the Apponyi conspiracy case for the first time since our arrest.

Although we were under the watchful eyes of the secret service, we managed to communicate and reassured each other that we were in good mental and physical health.

In the van, we were each placed in a two-by-two foot enclosed compartment. The engine started and the van lurched forward. Of course, we didn't know our destination. After a short ride, the van stopped. Russian soldiers surrounded it and herded us onto the front lawn of what had once been an elegant villa. The villa, on Queen Vilma Street in one of Budapest's most elegant districts, belonged to a well-known Hungarian nobleman named Count Teleki. It was in shambles after the shelling, bombing, and looting by the hordes of barbaric Soviet invaders. What was left was used as the headquarters of the soviet secret police in Budapest.

The Soviets used the villa as a temporary holding place for those unfortunate—mainly Hungarian citizens—awaiting investigation and trial by the Soviet military tribunal.

Seeing the Russian soldiers, I realized I was in the hands of the Soviets and their military court would decide my future. Despair engulfed me. I feared an uncertain future full of unknown horrors.

As we got off the van, I saw my ten friends again—only the second time since my arrest on 15 March. There were fourteen people involved, according to my knowledge, in the Apponyi conspiracy case. As we waited on the lawn of the villa, I noticed that three were missing—two former air force officers and the pregnant wife of one of our friends who was separated from us and kept in a Hungarian jail in Budapest. We didn't have a chance to talk, but managed to make eye contact.

The eleven members of the group included five former air force officers, a former cadet in a military school, a lawyer, three men from a small village near the Austrian-Hungarian border, and me.

The three villagers consisted of a veterinarian; a professional officer in the Army Counter Intelligence Division; and the husband of the pregnant woman, a well-to-do man who owned a mill and a large estate, reason enough for the Communist ideology to eliminate someone.

The Russian soldiers pushed us roughly into the entrance hall of the villa and lined us up in front of a table. Several clerks were sitting around it, sorting through the documents the secret service agents had carried in. They called our names one by one and identified each of us by our papers. When they were satisfied as to our identities, they put the paperwork into a pile and the processing of the prisoners was complete. One of the Russian guards took us to the basement one by one.

That was the last time I saw my Hungarian Communist torturers.

I was awed at finding myself in such a magnificent mansion, though it was just a shell of what it had been. The hordes of Soviet soldiers were apparently unaware of the intellectual value of Western culture represented by the art collection on the walls. Tears welled up in my eyes at seeing the senseless destruction of priceless art collected over many centuries.

We were left in a semi-dark cellar that had been used to store coal and wood for the winter. It contained a cast iron furnace that was used to heat the whole house and had been hastily divided into individual cells to house prisoners. There were two pieces of lumber on the floor to serve as a bed in each cell. Water dripped from the unfinished ceiling. It was infested with rats and smelled musty.

As I looked around, my mind was wandering from one extreme to the other. I walked up and down the cell and prayed, which gave me some comfort.

In the darkness of the cell, the days went by slowly and I lost all sense of time. When they delivered my evening meal consisting of thin, unappetizing cabbage soup and a piece of water-soaked, dark brown bread, I guessed the time to be around 6 P.M. I was hungry, but unable to eat. Each time a guard walked his rounds, he yelled something. I surmised that I was violating the rules of the prison by standing up or walking during the night and lying down during the day. Soon, I learned that taps was at 8 P.M. and reveille was at 6 A.M. The nights were depressing. I couldn't sleep. If I did, rats walked over my body and woke me up.

During my stay there in complete isolation, I lost all contact with my friends and the outside world. There was nobody to talk to, nothing to read. Since the street was closed to civilians, no sounds of life from the outside world could be heard inside my cell.

There were no facilities for morning hygiene, not even water to wash our faces and hands. A ten-gallon cast iron container in the corridor served as a toilet for all the prisoners housed in the cellar. Each time somebody needed to relieve himself, he signaled the guard to open the door. There was no privacy.

Then early one morning in May, at one of my darkest moments, a guard opened the door and said something that sounded like, "Davaj, davaj." From the tone of his voice and his gesturing, I gathered that he wanted me to march in front of him. I followed his order and we went upstairs to the entrance hall where my ten friends were waiting. When the guard left us alone for a short time, we discussed and developed a strategy for the coming interrogations and preparations for trial.

The Hungarian Secret Service, during the previous two months, had learned only bits and pieces of our activities in the Apponyi conspiracy case, which wasn't enough to convict us. Since they considered us undesirable elements of Communist Hungary, they wanted us eliminated. The easiest solution was to hand us over to the Soviets and let them convict us according to their "lawless law."

We vowed not to give out any names of those involved. We placed our fate in the hands of the Almighty and asked for strength to keep our vows. The guard returned shortly and we fell silent.

A prison van pulled up to the entrance and we were herded into its windowless cubicles. They were small and had no light or ventilation. There was just room enough to stand. As soon as the van was loaded, it drove away.

The heat, the poor air quality, and the uncertainty of our destination made the trip almost unbearable. In the windowless cubicle, all sense of time and distance disappeared. Fear, cold, and hot shivers raced through my already battered body. I shifted my weight from one foot to the other as I formed scenarios in my mind ranging from slim hope to dark hopelessness. Then I shook myself back to reality.

The van finally came to a stop after what seemed like an eternity. Judging by the position of the sun, I estimated the time to be late afternoon and that the trip had taken between three and four hours.

As the door opened, we were let out in front of a beautiful old mansion enclosed by an old wrought iron fence. The view was panoramic with mountains in the background. The house was well kept and judging from its style, it must have been built during the Austro-Hungarian Empire around the turn of century. From the setting, background, and neighborhood, I guessed we were in Austria, near Vienna. Later, I learned we were in Baden, near Vienna, one of my favorite places. I had flown over that lovely area several times during World War II.

The soldier in charge handed our files to the Russian receiving panel, which immediately began processing the paperwork, identifying each prisoner by the file sent by the Hungarians.

After the receiving process, we were called one by one to the table. The NKVD (Soviet Secret Political Police) soldiers searched our belongings, including our pockets, for knives, nails, or anything else that could cause injury to others or to ourselves. Then they put each of us into a separate room to keep the members of the Apponyi group from communicating with each other.

I was escorted to the first floor to a large room with a hardwood floor, a high ceiling, and hand-carved window frames, doors, and moldings. The walls were covered with a rich fabric. It could have been a library or a drawing room for a baron, a relative of the Austrian royal family, or at least a high-ranking statesman. The room had three large windows with plywood panels nailed to the outside to block our view and keep us isolated.

The room was half full. I walked around and introduced myself to the others lying on the floor along the wall facing the entrance door. Among them were several Soviet soldiers and officers who were arrested for stealing from the locals and raping women.

I stopped at a fellow prisoner who reminded me of Quasimodo in an old movie. He was deformed, hunchbacked, and many of his teeth were missing. I had the feeling he was younger than what one would have guessed by his looks. He was short and skinny and wore a well-worn, dirty business suit and patent leather shoes without laces—the first step after the NKVD took somebody into custody was to remove belts, shoelaces, handkerchiefs, and any other loose items they might have.

He coughed frequently during my short stop to talk with him. We conversed in German and I found out he was an

Austrian Jew from Vienna, a professor at the University of Vienna who spoke German and French. He was also a well-known philosopher and the author of several books. His name was Louis Pollack.

Right away, a sense of friendship developed between us and in a short while, we became good friends. He invited me to take my place on the floor next to him. I accepted his invitation and after meeting the others in the room, I settled on the floor near him. I didn't have a blanket or anything else, so I put my jacket on the floor to mark my place.

On my other side was a Soviet officer. The others in the room were intellectuals from Western countries and ordinary Russian murderers and criminals.

Louis told me he was kidnapped on a street in the center of Vienna and this was his second month in Soviet captivity. He was charged with espionage and had already suffered several interrogations. From him, I learned the daily routine of the mansion—and a sobering prediction of what lay in my future. Reveille was at 6 A.M. Meals were served three times a day—bread and soup in the morning, soup and porridge or mashed potatoes and a small dried salty fish for lunch, and soup for supper.

When I woke up the next morning, everyone else was still sleeping. In the quiet room, I enjoyed seeing the early May sunshine filtering through the narrow gap between the window frame and the plywood panel. I heard birds chirping outside. In my imagination, I could even smell the spring flowers. The local train went by and stopped either at a station or at a road crossing. A long whistle could be heard as it continued on its journey. The spring sounds and sunshine mixed with my loss of freedom and the uncertain future depressed me.

Shortly, my fellow inmates woke up and I didn't feel so alone in my miserable situation, which made me feel better.

That day was uneventful until the afternoon when the schools dismissed the children. I could hear girls and boys playing hide-and-seek outside. It was hard for me to imagine in my bleak situation that life outside went on happily.

In the mansion, daily interrogations were routine, conducted through an interpreter. The interpreter's knowledge of the language he translated was limited. Many times when he was unable to translate, he told the prisoner, "Don't tell him that! He is emotionally unstable, easily angered, and will rough you up."

The interrogations were usually conducted during the day. Nightly sessions were rare, used only in urgent situations when a case was scheduled for trial the following day and a piece of information was still missing. The interrogators knew the value of a cigarette as a tool for extracting information.

At one of the interrogations, the NKVD officer asked me, "When did Apponyi visit you first?"

Before I could answer, he pulled out a cigarette, lit it, and handed it to me. Immediately, he asked the same question again.

"In early December," I replied

"What happened at that meeting?"

"He gave me a book to use for transmitting messages back and forth," I said."

Then the NKVD officer asked, "What happened to that book?"

"I do not know. It was on the top of the piano in my apartment the day I was picked up by the secret service police," I responded.

During one of the interrogation sessions, the NKVD officer produced the book. I recognized it right away. Apponyi had left it with me after his first visit and I put it on the piano where it had collected dust waiting to be used. At the time of my arrest, one of the secret service agents picked it up and took it with him.

Holding the book, the NKVD officer asked, "How did you code the information?"

Since the book didn't contain any real information, so nobody was in danger of being caught, I replied, "I used invisible ink. The coding was based on a mathematical formula. The first page contains the first character, then page two the second one, and so on."

The interrogator listened avidly, wanting to be sure that the interpreter understood and translated every sentence correctly. He made the interpreter repeat every word of my explanation. When he was satisfied, he nodded and continued, "How do you read the coded information?"

"I use infrared light," I said.

I didn't tell him, however, that two types of ink were used for coding. For the first type, the activating energy was heat. When heat between eighty and eight-five degrees Fahrenheit was applied, the coded letters glowed yellow. Only the letters coded by the second type of ink required infrared light to be visible. Under infrared light, the coded letters glowed blue.

To mislead an unauthorized person trying to decode the message, the first ten pages of the book contained false information and were coded with infrared-sensitive ink. The real message started on page eleven and was coded with heat-sensitive ink.

Of course, the NKVD officer grew excited thinking that he'd learned the secret and would be able to decode the information and use it in court against me. He reached into his pocket and pulled out a handful of cigarettes, lit one, put it in my mouth, and handed me the rest as a reward. When the interrogation session ended, he called for a guard and I was taken back to the holding room.

I shared the cigarettes I'd brought back in my pocket with my roommates. This made everybody happy.

I spent the remainder of that day conversing and interacting with the others. I had many interesting discussions, but I enjoyed my philosophical exchanges with Louis the most. We discussed the universe and religious subjects such as the virginity of the Virgin Mary and the Trinity.

A week later, Louis approached me and said, "Bela, I need to share with you something important."

"Go ahead," I said.

"I have an advanced case of tuberculosis. You have to be careful! That is the reason that when a cigarette goes around, I am always the last one to take it. Nobody else is aware of this."

I thanked him for the confidence and was more careful about taking anything from him from then on.

When the time came for my next interrogation, the guard took me to the room where a NKVD officer and the interpreter were anxiously waiting for me. I noticed right away the infrared light over my open book. The interrogator was extremely friendly. He offered me a chair, handed me a lit cigarette, and started immediately on that session's topic.

"I verified that this book contains coded information," he said.

Then he demonstrated his findings, looking happy like a child with his first toy automobile.

"I won't let you go until all the secret messages in this book are decoded," he said. He added, "I will send in some food for you."

He put a package of cigarettes on the table and left. Soon, the food arrived and we started decoding.

It was a slow process. I wrote down the message letter by letter on the piece of paper the NKVD officer left for me. Shortly after, the first word, "everything," was produced. Since this is a commonly used word, the translator understood it immediately and wrote it in Russian.

Two hours later, the complete message contained in the book was deciphered: "Everything is well with me. Let me know when you are coming."

I explained the meaning of the message to the interpreter and he translated and wrote it down in Russian using the Cyrillic alphabet.

It was late afternoon when the interrogator returned. He was disappointed when he saw the decoded message. It did not reveal a large espionage ring, which he had expected. He ended the interrogation for that day and summoned the guard to take me back to the holding room.

By early July, my investigation was completed and the case was ready for trial. At our next session, the NKVD officer gave me a lit cigarette and pushed a stack of paper in front of me, saying, "The translator will help you to read and understand the charges. Then sign it!"

The translator explained that I was charged with espionage, sabotage against the Soviet armed forces stationed in Hungary, and armed organization against the Communist Hungarian government.

I disagreed and refused to sign it. "Since I cannot read it," I told the NKVD interrogator through the translator, "I cannot understand it and the charges against me as translated by the interpreter are not true. I am refusing to sign it."

"Whatever your sentence is," the interrogator replied, "you will survive it. There is no more death penalty in the Soviet Union. It has been replaced by twenty-five years of hard labor."

Since I'd arrived, every weekday evening around 6 P.M. I had heard movements outside, doors opening and closing, and then several shots. Louis explained to me that the room next to ours was where the prisoners sentenced to death were kept and executions took place shortly after 6 P.M. From early July on, however, no movement or shots had been heard. The silence was a mystery to me until the interrogator explained the change in the Soviet penal system that abolished execution.

What does this mean for me? I wondered. *Is my life being spared for some special unexplainable reason? But can I survive twenty-five years . . . if that is what my sentence is going to be?*

A couple of days later at a hearing, the NKVD investigator asked, "Are you going to sign the confession document prepared for your trial? It will start tomorrow morning, 14 July 1948, at 10 A.M."

"No, I refuse to sign it. It is not my confession," I said.

"Let me write in the space allocated for a signature that you refused to sign it," he said. "The trial will start tomorrow whether you sign it or not."

After returning to the holding room, I told Louis what had happened and asked for his advice. "Louis, you are an old timer here and saw many people going through the same process I'm going through now. I need your help. Please give me some pointers and tell me what I should or shouldn't do at the trial."

"Bela," he said after a brief pause, "it makes no difference whether you admit the charges or not, sign it or not—you will be sentenced to twenty-five years. For your sake, it is important to preserve your dignity and accept gracefully your predicament."

After my conversation with Louis, I felt that I needed time to prepare myself mentally for the trial and for the twenty-five-year sentence. If that would be my fate, I would be in jail or a labor camp until 1973—an eternity. I would be an old man by the end of my sentence and wouldn't see my loved ones for many years. My mother would be seventy-five years old when my hell ended—provided she lived that long.

I lay down, closed my eyes, and began praying. "Our Father, who art in heaven, hallowed be Thy name. Thy Kingdom come, Thy will be . . ."

Soon, supper arrived. I was hungry, but unable to eat. The night was long. My mood oscillated from one extreme to the other. I was desperate and ready to commit suicide one moment, happy the next thinking that after the trial, I would be reunited with my friends, even if only briefly.

I prayed again and again and asked the Almighty to keep our group together.

Just before reveille, I fell asleep. When I woke up, I saw sunlight shining in my face and heard the birds again as I had many times before. This gave me comfort and strength to face an uncertain future.

After breakfast, the door opened and a guard pointed at me, yelling, "Davaj, davaj."

He took me to a large room made into a makeshift courtroom. Facing the entrance door was a long table covered with a red cloth and three chairs behind it. In the middle of the room were twenty chairs for the prisoners on trial. There was no other furniture in the room and no crucifix on the wall. The only decoration was a life-size portrait of Joseph Stalin.

I was the first to arrive. I took one of the chairs brought in for the defendants. Shortly after, one by one, the other ten members of the group were escorted in. When the eleven of us were inside the courtroom, the NKVD soldier in charge closed the door and posted an armed guard at the entrance and one in each corner of the room.

Suddenly, one of the guards yelled in Russian, "Stand up!" and an offensive odor filled the room from the hallway. It was so unpleasant that it stirred up my empty stomach. Looking for the source of the odor, I turned my head towards the open door.

Seconds later, three uniformed Soviet officers entered the room, bringing back memories of World War II. The Soviet soldiers that invaded Hungary had never heard of perfume or cologne. Some of them even drank it for its alcohol content and several died of methyl alcohol poisoning. The military judges entering the room, a heavyset major and two slim captains, had soaked their uniforms in perfume and cologne. Each used a different brand, creating an unpleasant mixture that bothered my stomach.

The Russians' cologne brought to mind several conveniences, routine by Western standards, which were unfamiliar to Soviet soldiers who encountered them in Hungary. The invading Russians didn't know that if you wanted hot water, you just turned on the faucet. When a major wanted to take a bath, he had his subordinates light a fire outside under a huge cast-iron kettle filled with water. When it was hot enough, the soldiers carried it, bucket by bucket, to a tub until it was filled and ready for the major to luxuriate in his bath. Indoor toilets were also unknown to the average Russian.

In occupied Hungary, they matter-of-factly confiscated anything they wanted, including food. Several incidents were making the rounds in the occupied areas and became big jokes among Hungarians. One was about a Russian soldier who rushed into a house with a good-sized, stolen fish in his hand. Unable to speak each other's language, the soldier and the occupant of the house resorted to sign language. The Russian signed that he wanted to wash and prepare his fish when he spotted the water-filled toilet bowl through the open bathroom door. He rushed in and put the fish into the toilet bowl to wash it. He noticed the small handle on the water tank and became fascinated by it. Accidentally, he pushed it down and was startled by the water rushing into the bowl, taking his beautiful fish down into the sewer. He became enraged and cursed and threatened the lady for having a machine that robbed him of his fish. From then on, we called our toilets *zabra* machines" (stealing machines).

As the Soviet officials and guards filed in and took up their designated positions, I was jolted back from my nostalgia to cruel reality.

The judges occupied the three chairs. The major, the presiding judge, took the center one and the other two sat on either side. Behind the table stood the translator. A clerk carried a box containing our files. There were two other officers present, the defense lawyer and the prosecutor. Both were assigned to our case by the Soviet military legal system. I recognized the prosecutor right away. He had been the interrogator during my hearings.

When the tribunal was assembled, the door was closed and a soldier armed with an automatic submachine gun stood guard.

Twenty-three people were in the courtroom during the trial—the three military judges, the prosecutor, the defense lawyer, one clerk, one translator, five guards, and us, the eleven defendants.

I was the first one to be tried. It was the major who, after whispered consultation with the officers beside him, started the proceedings. The opening gambit was one I now knew by heart. "Name? Age? Date of birth? Born where? Parents' names? Their nationalities? Father's occupation? Mother's maiden name?" And so on, through the long catalog lying in front of him.

I had no doubt of my answers. I had wearily repeated them during all of my encounters with NKVD, from my transfer by the Hungarian Secret Service to the Soviets at Budapest, to my arrival at Baden near Vienna. If by this repetition they hoped I would vary an occasional answer, it was poor psychology. I had answered the same questions so often that I replied the same way every time without any thought. The same old questions, the same answers . . .

The charges were read to me. The major took a long time going through the indictments. He labored over the place names, the names of alleged Hungarian revolutionaries, and dates covering a period of several months during which I was accused of having committed specific acts of espionage against the Soviet Union. As the questioning got under way, I found myself grudgingly admiring the resolute singleness of purpose of the Russian mind.

The voices droned on, "You, Bela Gogos, being a well educated, middle-class Hungarian and an officer of the anti-Soviet Hungarian Air Force, having regularly visited cities like Papa, where large numbers of Soviet military personnel were stationed, are therefore beyond any doubt a Hungarian spy and an enemy of the people of the Union of Socialist Soviet Republics." I began to daydream.

After two hours, the guards behind me were replaced, a regular occurrence throughout the trial.

As I stood answering the major's questions, which caused me no difficulty because they were the long, routine preliminaries, I was developing my strategy for the trial. I decided that it would be to my advantage not to antagonize the court. I freely admitted those facts that were undeniable. When an accusation was manifestly false, I refuted it, but asked the court's permission to explain why it was untrue. They let me talk quite a lot. The informality of the proceedings impressed me. The members of the court smoked cigarettes endlessly.

The prosecutor read the charges from the document I had refused to sign. The translator had difficulties with the legal terms and the process moved along at the speed of a snail. The presiding judge asked me, "Did you organize an armed movement against the Communist Hungarian government?"

"I was involved in a movement, but I was not the organizer," I replied.

"Was Apponyi the central point of this movement?" the other judge asked me.

"No, he was not."

The judge continued, "Who was?"

"Somebody I never met and do not know his name. He lives in Germany," I replied.

The judges discussed at length the espionage charges against the Soviet Army stationed in Hungary. They showed great interest in the coded book picked up in my apartment by the secret service at the time of my arrest.

At noon, the trial was adjourned until 2 P.M. and shortly after returning to the holding room, lunch arrived. Since I still had a queasy stomach, I couldn't eat. After lunch, I sat down beside Louis and described my experience with the perfumes. He laughed.

"I remember in April 1944 when the Soviets occupied Vienna and looted the stores, their favorite items were wrist-watches, cologne, and perfume," he said. "I personally witnessed a soldier opening the first bottle and soaking his uniform. He drank a second bottle and put several in his pockets. Then he walked out to the street where he hoped that each bottle would buy him a pretty *barisnya* (woman). He rarely succeeded."

Immediately after the Soviets occupied Vienna, they dragged away and raped women of all ages, including nuns in convents. They also looted in a kind of free-for-all. After a few weeks, the Soviet military stepped in and severely punished, often with death, any soldiers caught raping and looting. Then the soldiers tried enticing women with goods missed during the long war.

After recounting his experiences with the occupying Soviet forces in Vienna, Louis asked, "How did the trial go?"

"Due to the slowness of the translator, it dragged," I replied.

"Since your case was the first one, it will take a whole day, and the other ten will be completed in two days," Louis said. "The sentences will be announced at the end of the third day."

The trial resumed on time at 2 P.M. I was on the defendant's stand until 4 P.M., when the day's proceedings ended rather abruptly.

The next day, 16 July 1948, five more members of the group were tried. Each had just a few questions directed at them. The process moved more quickly.

On the morning of the third day, the five remaining in the case were called to the defendant's stand. By noon, their hearings were completed. At 2 P.M., when the trial resumed, the presiding judge announced, "The hearings are completed and you will shortly hear your sentences."

Then the three judges left to decide our fate.

They returned less than an hour later. The presiding judge carried a piece of paper in his hand. The senior guard, standing at the door, closed it and directed us to stand up.

The judge began reading our sentences. "Gogos—twenty-five years of prison and hard labor."

I showed no emotion.

The judge continued, "Do you have any wish to be granted?"

"I do not have any wish to be granted by you, but I am asking the Almighty to erase this evil empire of yours from the face of this earth," I said.

The translator cut me off. "I dare not translate this for your sake. They will impose an extra harsh punishment on you."

The presiding judge noticed our exchange. "What's going on? What did the defendant say?" he asked.

The translator had no choice but to translate my wish. The judge paused. He didn't respond, but asked the clerk to document my wishes.

Then the judge read the sentences of the others. "Sinko—twenty-five years of hard labor. What is your wish?"

"I would like to have my wife notified," Sinko said.

"We will consider it," the judge replied. "It will be part of your file that will follow you wherever you go."

The judge continued until all eleven sentences were read. Out of eleven, five defendants received twenty-five years of hard labor; the other six defendants got twenty years.

The Soviet penal code under which we were convicted was Paragraph 58 and Subparagraphs 6 (espionage), 8 (sabotage), and 11 (conspiracy).

When the sentences had been read, the three judges left the courtroom. The prosecutor and the defense lawyer followed them. The clerk packed the documents in a box and carried it out.

In the courtroom, only the five guards, the translator, and the eleven defendants remained. For a while, we sat in stunned silence, unable to absorb the court's decisions. Meanwhile, our emotions were rising, approaching the breaking point.

The heavy weight of three words, "never," "forever," and "eternity" wouldn't leave my mind. The twenty-five-year sentence was an eternity; I would stay in Soviet captivity forever. I recalled my hearing at the dreaded Hungarian Secret Service when the interrogator said, "I will send you to a place you will never return from." His words were ingrained deeply in my mind.

While we waited, the tension was building to the point of explosion. Suddenly, as if by mental telepathy, the eleven of us jumped up in unison, kicked the chairs aside, gathered together in the middle of the room, and embraced.

I broke the silence. "We solemnly swear that we will protect each other against anybody, including the Soviet captors. We will sacrifice our own lives to save any of our friends. God!

Help us in our dire situation and guide us through our unknown fate!"

We loudly repeated our vows to each other.

"We shall survive the Red Hell and return to our loved ones," I continued. "This happened to us not by chance, but as part of God's plan. We will humbly accept His will, whatever it may be."

Tears ran down on our cheeks. Seeing us, the guards grew nervous and surrounded us with their submachine guns at the ready. The guard in charge remained at the door to prevent anyone from entering or leaving the room.

After a brief silence, I began singing the Hungarian national anthem and the others joined in:

> "Bless the Magyar, O our God,
> Bountifully, gladly!
> Shield with Thy protecting hand
> When his foes smite madly!
> Fate, of old, has rent him sore;
> May it now bring healing!
> Bygone sins are all aton'd
> Ev'n the future sealing."

Our voices filled the room and reverberated from the walls. It could even be heard in the corridor behind the closed door. When we finished, silence filled the room.

The puzzled guards, realizing that we weren't violent, stepped back and put their guns back on their shoulders.

After a brief silence, the translator explained to the guards, "They vowed to help each other no matter what lies on the road ahead, then they sang the Hungarian national anthem."

The guards, understanding our emotional outburst, were sympathetic. We were escorted back to our rooms one by one. I was the first to go.

When I entered the room, I was still in a highly charged emotional state. I sat down beside my friend Louis.

"Is your trial over?" he asked anxiously.

"Yes."

"What is your sentence?"

"Twenty-five years of prison and hard labor," I replied.

"Under what paragraph were you convicted?" he asked.

"Paragraph 58, Subparagraphs 6, 8, and 11 for espionage, sabotage, and conspiracy."

"What was your wish?"

"I did not have any wish to be granted by the Soviets, but asked the Almighty to erase this evil empire from the face of the Earth."

Louis looked concerned. "That was not a bright idea. It will be on your trial documentation and will follow you wherever you go. You will be under constant observation. If anything should happen in the camp—a conspiracy, an escape, a riot, or any violence—you will be the first one put into solitary confinement.

"Soon, you will be taken to a room where everybody has already been tried and convicted," Louis continued. "Tomorrow or the day after, you will be transported to the central jail at Neunkirchen. It isn't far from here and was built under the regime of Hitler."

We didn't finish our conversation. The door opened and a guard entered and pointed at me, indicating that I should collect my things and march in front of him. I had just enough time to say good-bye to my dear friend Louis. I embraced him for the last time and followed the guard.

Louis' last words to me were, "Bela, God bless you! I hope you are always strong enough to face your fate and overcome the obstacles that will surely emerge, and somewhere down the road be reunited with your loved ones."

3

Post Trial,
Neunkirchen
(20 July 1948)

I know there is a God—and I see a storm coming;
if He has a place for me, I believe that I am ready.

John F. Kennedy

I was led into a large, empty room. One by one, the other members of the Apponyi group were brought in. The joy we felt at seeing each other would be difficult to describe. By late afternoon, the eleven of us were reunited for the first time since our arrest. We picked a spot on the floor along the long wall. An important consideration in picking the spot was who would snore on your right and left side. On my right was Joco and on the left a former classmate in the Air Force Academy. We placed whatever we had to sleep on on the floor. While in jail in Budapest, Joco's wife brought him a blanket. He shared it with me and for the first time since my transfer to the Soviets, I didn't have to sleep on the bare floor.

Time went by fast. Before supper, we began sharing our experiences during our imprisonment. We were arrested on 15 March and it was 17 July, four months and two days later.

Supper arrived on time, followed by taps at 8 P.M. We were talking . . . and talking . . . and talking until the guard ordered, "Stop talking and be quiet."

He came back three times. Each time, his voice was raised a couple of decibels. On his third visit, he yelled at us and indicated that he was running out of patience. That night, we could hardly sleep from the excitement and joy of being together again.

The next day, we woke up before reveille and whispered to each other. After breakfast, we huddled together on the floor and related more of what had happened to each of us since our arrests.

The brutal henchmen of the Hungarian Secret Service had beaten up each of us. The injuries they inflicted ranged from relatively small to permanent disability. Everybody except our lawyer friend, Andy, recovered fully. Both of Andy's feet and soles were permanently damaged. He could hardly walk. The Soviet captors in Baden provided some medical treatment, but not enough for him to fully recover.

Our next highest priority was to discuss the circumstances and events leading to our arrest and find out whom the traitors were. During our discussions, we confirmed with certainty that the two fellow officers who visited me in my apartment on 11 March 1948 were the traitors. Both were agent provocateurs hired by the secret service. Baki was assigned to tail me and watch my every movement. He had to report his observations to his communist superiors on a daily basis. The secret service planned to have Baki lure Apponyi to my apartment and arrest both of us there at the same time. Baki even sent a telegram to Apponyi in my name, asking him to come to Budapest because I needed his help urgently. During our interrogations, my friends and I had seen Baki on several occasions. He would sneak out of the room behind our backs as we were facing the wall waiting for our next interrogation.

My friend, Joco, identified the other traitor, Kassai, whose real name was Berger, also an officer in the Hungarian Air

Force serving in the same tactical reconnaissance squadron as Joco. Their squadron was equipped with single-seater German-built Focke-Wulf 189 planes. In these planes, the only crew is the pilot, who also performs the duties of navigator, gunner, and photographer. Berger flew several sorties on the Russian front and was an ambitious, self-promoter aspiring to rise to the next rank, earn decorations, and eventually be inducted into the Knighthood—at any cost. In 1944, near the end of World War II, returning from a sortie to the Russian front, he emerged from his plane bleeding. A couple of seconds later, he collapsed and was taken immediately by ambulance to a field hospital. That night, at the dinner table, the squadron leader announced that Russian fighters injured Berger in a dogfight. At the end of his announcement, he called him, "the latest hero of our squadron."

Berger's only wound, around his waist, was treated and he was discharged after an overnight stay. The squadron leader assigned an officer to the routine investigation of his "heroic" act and to submit his findings to him as soon as possible. He needed the report to justify his promotion.

During the investigation, the officer became suspicious when he could find only one bullet hole in the canopy directly above the pilot's head. It is hard to imagine how an enemy fighter could put a bullet into the top of an enemy plane's canopy. Further investigation revealed that the entry of the bullet was on the inside, not the outside of the canopy. How could a bullet from an enemy fighter during a dogfight enter the canopy from the inside? The officer reported this to his squadron leader, who ordered a complete medical examination of Berger's injury. It was on his left side, two inches above his waistline. There were not one, but two bullet holes in his skin. Berger could not explain the second hole in his skin and the missing second bullet hole in the canopy.

It was determined that Berger, on the way home from his uneventful sortie to the Russian front, planned how he would inflict an injury using his service revolver and claim that he was in a dogfight with a Russian fighter. Thus, he would be treated as a hero and promoted. He hoped that the self-inflicted injury would be enough to justify his promotion and induction into Knighthood. He pulled out his service revolver, pinched his skin on his left side, and from underneath, shot a bullet through his own skin. But he didn't realize that the bullet would leave two holes in his skin and only one in the canopy, leading to the discovery of his dishonest act.

The documentation containing the medical report and the investigating officer's opinions were completed. The report, however, wasn't used as originally planned. Instead, it was under consideration for use in court martial proceedings. But because the war ended on the 9 May 1945, a court martial never took place.

Both Baki and Berger were agent provocateurs. Baki had the assignment from the Hungarian Secret Service to turn Apponyi and me into the hands of the secret service police. Berger was assigned to two cities and a small village near the Hungarian-Austrian border to keep the suspected conspirators under surveillance. These places are located in Transdanubia in the western part of Hungary.

The last two pieces of the puzzle were the role of Apponyi and the answer to the question, "Why did they wait until 15 March to arrest me?" Everybody else was arrested and taken to secret service headquarters on 14 March.

Apponyi's role was to put together an anticommunist movement in western Hungary including Budapest, and to establish a line of communication with me, the central figure in Hungary, and the organizer, a former Hungarian general, who did not return to Hungary after World War II, but took up residence in Munich, Germany.

The reason I was the last suspect taken in was that the secret service hoped that Apponyi would show up in my apartment where they would arrest both of us at the same time. Since I was considered by the Hungarian Secret Service to be a potential fugitive, they dared not wait any longer and arrested me in the early hours of 15 March.

Recalling these events, exchanging our feelings and experiences since our arrests, and having each other's company was real joy. But it didn't last long.

The next morning after breakfast as we huddled together in the middle of the room and picked up our discussion where we'd left off the night before, the door opened. Standing there were two soldiers. One soldier stepped in while the other remained outside.

"Pick up your stuff and follow me!"

We did as he instructed and formed a line two abreast to follow him. The other soldier brought up the rear.

"Follow orders and do not make any foolish moves. If you disobey our orders, you will be shot," the guard in front said as he began walking.

Shortly, we were in the front yard of the mansion. It was a hot summer day, the first time in many days that we saw daylight and sunshine. The air was crystal clear and the view was panoramic with distant mountains clearly visible. Birds sat chirping on the gutters or flew over our heads. The neighborhood children had already played soccer in the backyard that day. The local train went by at its usual time. The passengers standing at windows looked delighted at the beautiful view.

Free people, taking pleasure in these ordinary, everyday activities, were almost in touching distance, yet, for us, so far away.

The villa's magnificent wrought-iron gate was closed. A soldier outside was watching locals pass by. Inside the yard was a pick up truck with its tailgate lowered and a makeshift ramp in position. We formed a single line and the soldiers tied our arms behind our backs. Since there were not enough handcuffs available, they used strips of coarse linen material cut from towels issued for the prisoners. They made a tight knot to assure that we could not undo it.

One by one, we walked up the ramp to the platform with the help of a soldier and were ordered to sit down. With our arms tied, it was difficult to sit down without assistance. The guards provided it as needed. When all eleven of us were on the truck, two soldiers took up positions behind the cab. Meanwhile, a clerk carried out a box containing our files. He read our names and when he was satisfied that everybody's file was there, he put the box into the cab. Then the driver climbed in and started the engine. The gate opened and the truck pulled away.

Our journey took us through the village. The truck stopped at road and railroad crossings. At one railroad crossing, several Austrian bystanders were waiting for the train to go by. A couple, curious about the people on the truck, came close and asked in German, "Are there any Austrians among you?"

"We are Hungarians convicted for twenty-five years prison and hard labor," I said in German.

The guards dared not chase the couple away and were unable to stop us from talking to them. Finally, the crossing-gate opened and the truck moved on. But before we pulled away, I yelled, "Louis Pollack, a professor at the University of Vienna, is in Soviet captivity in Baden! Please notify his relatives."

Before I could continue, a guard stepped over to me and hit my head with his rifle butt. I fell over and by the time I came to, we were beyond hearing distance.

We left the village and continued on a winding country road through a wooded area where tree branches formed a tunnel overhead. If we had been tourists, we would have enjoyed the beauty of the scenery.

Soon, another incident made the guards nervous. Our lawyer friend, Andy, couldn't tolerate his uncomfortable position on the bottom of the truck any longer. He fell over in excruciating pain from his injured limbs and began screaming. One of the guards went over to him and when he realized Andy was injured and in pain, untied the knot and freed his arms, then let him continue the trip in a standing position. Andy's pain and suffering had a frightening, depressing effect on the rest of us. We realized how helpless we were in the hands of the Soviet NKVD who could end our lives without justification.

Some time later, one of our friends had to relieve himself. He called the guards, but they paid no attention to him. Finally, when he could not stand it any longer, he fouled his pants. In our small community of hardship, we shared his agony and embarrassment.

Soon, we had left the wooded area. The county road ended and merged into a major highway. After a couple of miles, we passed the road sign "Neunkirchen 10 km."

I remembered Louis Pollack telling me that our next stopover would be in a jail built during Hitler's regime in Neunkirchen. From there, we would be transferred to Lvov in the Ukraine, to the central distribution center for prisoners convicted by the Soviets in Central and East Europe. From Lvov, we would be transported to our final destination—Siberia, Inta/Vorkuta above the Arctic Circle, or Lubyanka, Moscow's central prison.

A short time later, the steeple of a distant church with mountains in the background grew visible—a peaceful, picturesque scene.

Within minutes, we were in the oldest suburb of Neunkirchen with narrow winding streets. The houses, built around the turn of the century, were old, but were clean and neat. Children were playing hide and seek on the streets. Most of the residents were working on farms or in nearby factories, though some of the older men and women were sitting on stone benches in front of their houses, gossiping and watching the traffic.

Seeing us sitting on the bottom of the truck, they couldn't have realized that human beings just like them were being transported to an unknown destination in "Red Hell" and might never return. They were almost within touching distance, but an invisible wall separated us. The townspeople were free while we had bound hands and a frightening road ahead of us.

During our ride, we scanned the road continually, looking for the jail. *No, it could not be in this neighborhood,* I told myself. Finally, our truck arrived at a large, open field where it made a sharp left turn. Suddenly, we saw a tall, gray wall with barbed wire on top and several watchtowers evenly distributed along the long wall.

It made a horrifying first impression. We knew that beyond the barbed-wire walls, the life as we knew it was nonexistent and our lives would change forever.

The truck pulled onto a private road that ran parallel to the wall. After a short ride, we arrived at a gate of heavy steel. The gate had been gray, but the Soviets painted it red to symbolize the Soviet Empire, "Red Hell" for the prisoners herded inside. The red gate would remind future generations in that region of the Soviet occupation and the horrors they inflicted on Europe.

On the left side of the gate was a small booth for the NKVD soldier in charge of traffic exiting and entering the jail. For us, "exit" didn't exist. Or, if it did, it would only be to the cemetery or another Red Hell.

The three walls of the booth above waist level were made of bulletproof glass. There were two doors, one leading inside and the other one outside.

The truck stopped in front of the red gate. The driver stayed in the cab until the NKVD guard approached and asked for his identification. When he was satisfied, the guard returned to the other two soldiers and checked their IDs. Then the heavy gate opened and the driver drove the truck into a small fenced-in area with a roof over it.

A small table stood in the enclosure. The driver stepped out of the cab and carried the box containing our files to the table. The soldier in charge of receiving and transferring prisoners opened the box and checked the files.

One of the soldiers lowered the tailgate and freed our arms by undoing the knots around our wrists. When he finished, he barked, "Jump off and line up."

In no time, we were all off the truck except Andy, who was in pain and could hardly walk. Two NKVD men had to grab and carry him off the truck.

The soldier in charge of receiving prisoners picked up the first file and read the name. The person whose name was read had to step forward and answer the questions, "Your name? Date of birth? Paragraph under which you were convicted?"

Since the files were in Russian, using the Cyrillic alphabet, communication was nearly impossible. We could not even understand our names the way the soldier pronounced them. The Russian pronunciation of "Hitler" is "Gitler." The soldier, realizing he could not do his job because of the language barrier, left and returned shortly with a German-speaking translator. Every one of us spoke German.

A security check followed the initial "check-in." It was taking place in the next room where two soldiers were already waiting for us. A long table in the middle was the only furniture in the room.

As we entered, one of the soldiers yelled, "Undress and place your clothes and personal belongings on the table, then line up facing the wall with your hands behind your backs!"

As if we had not already been humiliated and degraded enough, more salt was rubbed into our wounded self-esteem and dignity. We had no choice and had to follow orders. We put our clothes, neatly separated, on the table. Standing there naked, we were embarrassed and completely deprived of our dignity. But we were powerless and we knew that from then on, our fate was in the hands of a brutal, merciless authority for months . . . years . . . an eternity.

The guards checked our clothes for nails, pins, pieces of broken glass—anything that could be used to harm others or ourselves. They dumped the contents of our pockets on the floor, removed our handkerchiefs and threw them into the pile. They cut open the cuffs of our pants and the inner linings of our jackets. Satisfied that they'd found all the hidden weapons, they threw the clothing to the floor.

Standing helplessly through this humiliating treatment, we thought we had reached the lowest point of degradation that one human being can inflict on another. It wasn't long before we were to realize how naive we were to think that was the lowest point.

The guard shouted the next order, "Walk up to me one at a time, then stop. Turn your backs towards me, spread your legs apart, and bend forward!"

He inspected our naked bodies, including our rectums, for any weapons we might have hidden there. If he felt it was necessary, he used his rubber-gloved finger to search.

Next, we had to search for our belongings through the pile of handkerchiefs and underwear, which we had worn without washing or cleaning since our transfer from the Hungarian Secret Service to the Soviet NKVD. They were soiled as a result of rare allowances for "pit stops" and had bloodstains from the frequent beatings and torture during interrogations.

In the next room, a female doctor in uniform gave us physical exams. She was concerned with our health not for humanitarian reasons, but to evaluate our capabilities as laborers. She considered us to be fit for hard labor. After we all passed the physical, including our invalid friend, Andy, the guard in charge ordered, "Dress and wait."

The way political prisoners were treated by the Soviets was such a contrast to the way General George Washington ordered Colonel Webb to treat prisoners taken in the battle of Trenton during the Revolutionary War. Washington said, "Treat the prisoners with humanity, and let them have no reason to complain. Provide everything necessary for them."

We dressed quickly, regaining some dignity by having our clothing back on. The door leading to the prison yard opened, and a guard standing outside yelled, "Step outside and wait."

We did as we were told and stepped into a small cage constructed of heavy steel bars. Another door on the opposite side of the cage led directly to the prison yard. Another guard sat in front of this inner door holding a key to the door leading to the real "Red Hell."

From there, we had a good view of the jail. It was a rectangular shape with the open prison yard enclosed by the four sides of the three-story jail. In front of the cell doors was a four-foot wide walkway used by the guards to make their rounds and check on the inmates in the cells through peepholes. The walkway was enclosed outside by a grid constructed of heavy steel bars. These bars extended from the prison yard to the roof level. Each level had a guarded entrance door. The guards changed at four-hour intervals.

As we stood in the courtyard, a guard came down from the third floor with a piece of paper in his hand.

"Gogos and Sinko, walk in front of me and follow my orders," he yelled.

We marched up to a cell on the third floor, which was diagonally opposite the stairway. The guard opened the door and prodded us into a two-inmate cell.

Two cots and a ten-gallon cast iron vessel used as a toilet were the only furnishings. The disinfectant used for the toilet had an unpleasant, penetrating odor that bothered my eyes and sinuses, but I soon got used to it. The only source of light was a twenty-five-watt bulb housed in the recess over the door that was shielded by an iron grid. There were no windows or running water in the cell.

Now that Joco and I had each other, our imprisonment became more tolerable. We had to obey strict rules; reveille was at 6 A.M., taps was at 8 P.M. During the day, we were not allowed to lie down. After taps, we were not allowed to get up or cover our heads. The guard checked the cell through the peephole at regular intervals. If he found someone lying down on a cot during the day, walking in the cell, or covering his head after taps, he banged on the door until the violation was corrected.

Every day we carried the cast iron toilet to a room equipped with a cone-shaped dump hole connected to the sewer line. Once a week, we were escorted to the prison yard for a ten-minute walk. Usually inmates in cells on the same floor were taken together. Thus, we had an opportunity to see our friends and talk until the supervising guard put a stop to it.

The first time I was escorted outside for a walk, after six days in the dimly lit room, the bright sunshine blinded me and I had to walk with half-closed eyes. Near the end of the session, my eyes got used to the light and I surveyed my surroundings.

A grid of heavy iron bars extending from the ground to roof level surrounded the prison yard. There were only two doors—one was where we had entered the jail on the first day and the other led to the stairway. The ground was covered with globs of spit, many of them bloody. I learned later that many prisoners had tuberculosis. Since there was minimal medical care, the unfortunate ones were buried in unmarked graves.

Everyone in our group except Andy was outside for our first walk. This was an indication that ten of the eleven members of the Apponyi conspiracy group were being kept together on the third floor. I was not sure of Andy's whereabouts. Since we had this opportunity to communicate with each other using sign language or other means, I learned that Andy shared a cell with another fellow from our group, but was too ill to come down and join us.

With Joco as my cellmate, the days went by relatively fast. We shared many memories of our childhood.

On the first day, we discussed a survival plan.

"No one will defend your rights, except you," I told Joco based on my POW experience. "This is how these people try to beat you under. They make you into an island and isolate you, so you break under the pressure from inside as well as from outside. You must resist even if it costs your life."

Joco agreed. We renewed our vows to each other and repeated them every night before we went to sleep.

★　★　★

To maintain discipline in our bleak life, we diligently planned daily activities. Every morning after reveille, we stood up and said a short prayer: "Almighty! Thank you for allowing us to wake up to another day in good health and to have each other. Guide us through this, our darkest, most uncertain period, and give us strength to overcome our despair. Bless each of us and our loved ones far away!"

Our daily exercise routine consisted of push-ups and sit-ups in the morning, and walking from one corner of the cell to the opposite and back for one hour every morning and one hour every afternoon. And we allocated time in the morning and afternoon for discussing entertaining and educational subjects.

One afternoon, our routine turned into a riveting session as Joco recalled one of his sorties on the Russian front.

He was flying a Me-109G, a recent addition to the squadron's fleet, and a plane he had flown only a couple of times before. He was returning to base when four deadly Russian Yak fighters intercepted him. Joco looked in his mirror and quickly to each side. "Damn!" he cursed.

The deadly Yaks were tearing after him. Joco stroked the stick forward, diving down hard. He felt his eyes bulging in their sockets and his head bounced against the canopy as negative Gs boosted him hard against his safety belt. In heavy, left spirals at full power, Joco plummeted with the Yaks hot on his tail.

The Yaks strung out behind Joco were determined that his lone Messerschmitt would not escape. Joco's negative G brake had momentarily foiled them, gaining him some distance, but he was still in a tight spot.

He began talking aloud to himself, as if he were his own guardian angel. "All right, Joco, keep your head now, and fly. Fly like you've never flown before!"

The Yaks split into two two-ship groups and sandwiched Joco neatly. They were as fast as he was.

"Hard turns, Joco. Real hard turns or you will have bullets in your stomach."

He reefed his Me-109 around hard left and the aerial soc-cer game began with Joco as the ball.

Hard right. A blast of gunfire from one of the Yaks. Hard left. A storm of tracer from the other side. Hard right. More gunfire.

"You are lucky, Joco. They're not top shooters; they open fire too soon, too far out. You are lucky again, Joco. If they knew what you know, you would be dead by now"

Hard right . . . hard left. In the blood-draining turns where the Yaks sometimes swung close to him, Joco fired his own guns.

"You know you won't hit them like that, Joco, but they will see the tracer. That may rattle them. Besides, the sound of your own guns makes you feel better."

The four relentless Soviets and a lone Hungarian streaked across the Rumanian sky, the roar of the Russian "fifties" ringing out at intervals, and Joco dodging the tracers. His adrenaline-charged body was pouring out sweat; in seconds, he could feel it running down his body under his dampening uniform and his face was steaming.

Hauling the Me-109 around in murderous turns was physically difficult. Amid the periodic hammering of the Russian guns and the groaning of his overstressed Me-109, he mumbled, "Good thing you liked gymnastics, Joco. It gave you the strength to keep your hide whole. And your coordination is saving you now."

All through the numbing turns, Joco was slowly working his way back toward base. He was gaining slightly on the Yaks, beating them by a hair at each turn and drawing away a few yards each time.

As for the Russians, they might have been losing a few yards, but they were staying glued to Joco's tail, firing often, but wildly. They couldn't quite pull enough lead on their quarry to score a hit, but they were keeping up the pressure. The kill was going to be theirs even if they had to split it four ways.

Joco swung into another grinding turn. "Keep going, Joco. Keep going. The flak near the base will take these leeches off your tail."

"Damn!" The fuel warning light on the dash glared red. The Me-109 was almost out of fuel and he was too far from base to land the fighter even if he dared.

"Make a fast bailout, Joco! Flip her over on her back quick but easy."

He released his safety belt and as he came out of the next turn, he tripped the emergency release for the canopy. The plexiglas cover whipped away in the slipstream and the wind howled and tore around the cockpit. Coming out of the next turn, Joco sucked back on the stick with all his strength, hauling it back into the pit of his belly. As the Me-109 went soaring up and over, he released the stick and shot clear of the doomed aircraft.

Sky, earth and trees, wheeling Yaks, and his own boots flashed before him as he went tumbling earthward. He pulled the D-ring and heard a rustling of silk and cord followed by the plumping sound of the opening parachute. A bone-bruising jerk shook every joint in his body as he was jarred upright in the parachute harness, swinging helplessly.

For a Hungarian fighter pilot, it was unthinkable to strafe an enemy pilot hanging in his parachute. That was murder, not war and fighting among soldiers. The chivalrous tradition may have seemed out of place in total war, but the Hungarian Air Force lived by this code to the end.

Swinging under his silk umbrella, the defenseless Joco wandered how his Russian foes would act. Would he die by midair strafing and fall to earth as a bundle of bloody rags?

The Yaks lined up on him as though for a firing pass. Joco's entrails contracted into a tight ball. The Russian fighters roared past a few yards away, there was a manly wave, and the Yaks banked around.

Joco felt happy to be alive. He felt even happier as the four Russians formed up on their leader and went streaking off to the north.

As he floated down to the good, green earth, he told himself again and again, "You are lucky, Joco. You are a lucky boy. By God, you will have a birthday party tonight."

He landed a little less than four miles from base and an army truck picked him up and took him back to his squadron.

When Joco finished his story, I was in a daze and fascinated by his words. I felt as if I had been with him in the cockpit, grasping the stick, watching the Yaks as he dodged them. "Little" Joco, my "buddy" in youthful mischievousness growing up, heroically maneuvered his way out of a life and death situation, bringing honor to the Hungarian Air Force.

Joco was a bright individual, but a poor student because of laziness and not taking time to prepare for lectures or doing the homework. His friends, even years after, remembered an amusing story that happened during a Greek lecture. The teacher asked him to read and translate a paragraph written in the Greek alphabet from Greek to Hungarian. Joco began to read, then suddenly stopped.

The teacher ran out of patience and asked him, "What is the matter with you, Joco?"

"Could you tell me the third letter in the second word in the second line? And how to pronounce it?" he asked.

The class erupted in laughter and the story amused his classmates and friends many times in the years to come.

Joco was also involved in mischief during our school years that could have turned into tragedy. Three of us—Joco, a mutual friend, and I—met regularly in the evenings once or twice a week, mostly to cook up some new adventure or just chew the fat.

One evening, we walked to the railroad station. Next to the station was an overpass for pedestrians to cross the rails. The overpass was a wooden structure, approximately forty-five feet high and one hundred and fifty feet long. On the two sides of the overpass was a four-foot tall rail constructed of a four-by-four-inch angle iron.

As we were watching the arriving and departing trains from the top, Joco had a "bright idea."

"Bela, if you walk over to the other side on the top of this rail, I will buy you a mug of beer."

I replied quickly, "If both of you do it first, I will follow you."

I didn't expect them to have the courage, but I was wrong. They were on the other side of the station within a couple of minutes. Now I had no other choice except to do it myself.

My heart raced as I climbed up the rail and I was scared to death looking at the trains and high-voltage lines under me. I was ready to give up, but told myself, "Bela, you have to do it. If you refuse, you make yourself a laughing stock and you'll be called a sissy."

The first ten steps were wobbly and slow. But overcoming the initial fright, I had enough stamina to complete the remaining distance almost at a run. The next day, when my schoolmates heard the story from Joco, I was treated as a hero. I never got the mug of beer that he promised, though.

★   ★   ★

When we finished reliving the memories of our younger days, we were jolted back to our bleak present.

In our cell, the days went by fast and we were relatively happy. Then in July, we got an unexpected, but much appreciated "treat". The day I had taken my last bath, shave, and put on clean underwear was 14 March. After months without bathing, our unshaved, dirty faces itched and our soiled underwear was foul smelling.

On 28 July, after the second walking session, we were herded downstairs to the disinfecting and bath facilities. Benches and a pass-through window filled the room we entered. We undressed and were ordered to throw our clothes through the pass-through window into a large, steam-heated disinfecting boiler. During our incarceration in dirty, unsanitary conditions, we provided a fertile ground for lice. The high temperature in the disinfecting steam boiler exterminated them.

Our next stop was the shaving room. A male barber first cut our beards and hair with crude clippers then squeezed foam on our face and gave us a good shave. It would be difficult to describe the pleasure we felt after this otherwise basic, routine activity.

From there, we marched into the shower room. A small piece of soap and a hot shower were waiting for us. The shower was delightful! In the next room, we picked up our disinfected clothing, put our soiled underwear into a container specially used for this purpose, and picked up clean underwear made of coarse linen material. Though the coarse material at first irritated my skin, I got used to it, and welcomed the feeling of having clean garments next to my skin.

We dressed and were escorted back to our cells. This day became an important one in my life . . . first shower, first shaving, and first clean underwear in many months. In the cell, we stared at each other; we were rejuvenated human beings. Life is funny. In captivity, basic necessities such as a bath, shaving, and clean underwear are valued more than fame, success, or money in the free world.

We hated the weekly searches of our cells and clothes. It degraded our pride and self-respect. We had to undress, leave the clothes on our cots, and stand facing the wall outside the cells with our hands behind our backs while the guards searched our cell and personal effects.

Even small violations were enough to send the offender to the solitary cell for a day, a week, or even longer depending on the type of the violation and the mood of the guard. Inmates in solitary cells were not allowed to lie or sit down and received food once a day in reduced portions.

The following days were uneventful, though biweekly showers and weekly walks in the prison yard broke the monotony and made us feel more like human beings again.

One morning in early September, a guard marched us to the prison yard where inmates were already lined up. With some maneuvering, we succeeded again and kept our group together. The guards tied our hands behind our backs with pieces of wire and loaded us into a special van. We were not told our destination.

When the van stopped, we scrambled off and saw that we were at a railroad station. We were stuffed into a small cattle wagon in intolerable discomfort.

The jam-packed freight wagon was as hot as a furnace and the air quickly became giddily stale. Since there was no room for sixty of us to lie or even sit at the same time, I devised a way to ease our sufferings by creating more usable space. One-third of us would lie down on the wagon floor for two hours and then stand for four. This somewhat eased our extreme discomfort. And it served as our introduction into the real "Red Hell," an indication of what awaited us there.

4

Lvov
(September 1948)

*He who would be friends with God must remain
alone or make the whole world his friend.*

                                   Mohandas K. Gandhi

The train left shortly after the prisoners were herded in and
locked in the cattle wagon. For three days, we jolted eastward.
No navigation skill was needed to figure out where we were
heading.

There were many nationalities in our freight wagon:
Austrians, Hungarians, Ukrainians, Latvians, Estonians,
Lithuanians, Germans, Poles, and Russians.

The Russians among us were ex-soldiers of the Soviet
Army, convicted for theft, killing innocent people, and raping
women in countries they invaded and occupied. As criminals,
they were sentenced to a maximum of ten years, but could be
freed in less than five. On the other hand, all non-Russian
inmates were considered political prisoners and sentenced to
twenty to twenty-five years of prison and hard labor. This was
under the Soviet Penal Code, Paragraph 58 and Subparagraphs
6, 8, and 11 (espionage, sabotage, and conspiracy against
Communist governments).

Among us was an Orthodox Jew named Simon who was born and raised in a small village on the Hungarian-Ukrainian border. Simon was captured by the Germans during World War II and deported to the concentration camp in Dachau, Germany in 1944. After the war, he settled in Vienna and lived there until he was arrested by the Russians and sentenced to twenty years for espionage. Since he was proficient in both Hungarian and Russian, he translated news he overheard from the Soviet guards.

The train's first stop was in a suburb of Budapest. Our wagon was dragged onto a siding where we spent the night. Early the next morning, I peeked through a crack in the side of the wagon and saw farmers walking past our car carrying farm products, vegetables, and fruits, unaware of human beings in the wagon. The men pulled their wares in small carts, and the women carried them in large baskets on their heads. I tried several times to make contact with one of them. A woman must have heard me call out. She stopped, put her basket down, and looked around for the source of the voice.

I was standing on Joco's shoulder to reach the small window on the side of the wagon. "We are Hungarians, convicted by the Soviets for twenty-five years and we are being shipped to the Soviet Union. Could you deliver a message to my mother in Papa?" I asked.

"Gladly," she said. "But hurry up because the guard heading in my direction must have noticed that I'm talking to someone in the wagon."

I gave her my mother's name and address and added, "The five of us are together and in good health. The Soviets sentenced us to twenty-five years and we are on our way to the Soviet Union." (There were eleven in the conspiracy group, but five of us were from my hometown, so my mother knew their families and they were in close contact during our imprisonment. The other six were from other cities.)

I was barely able to finish before the guard shooed her away. It wasn't until many years later that I found out that my mother never received my message.

A short time later, the train continued in an easterly direction. In late afternoon, we caught sight of the magnificent, majestic Carpathian Mountains in the distance. Our hearts, overflowing with sadness, were in our throats. We watched them in awed silence until we could see them no more.

After a while, someone from my group asked, "Bela, where do you think we are going?"

"We are in Transylvania and within an hour we could cross the Carpathian Mountains. From here, we either go to Fogsani, Rumania, or Lvov, Ukraine," I replied.

Based on what my friend Louis had told me, after trial, prisoners were sent to Lvov via Neunkirchen. Lvov was a central distribution center for prisoners arrested and convicted in Europe. Lvov belonged to Poland before the end of World War II, but was now in the Ukraine.

The distribution center was housed in a huge abandoned military complex built by the Poles under the Austro-Hungarian Empire at the turn of the century. We would be held there for a couple of days while the mysterious process of the Soviet bureaucracy determined our destination and fate.

We spent the night in the cattle wagon, surrounded by heavily armed Soviet soldiers, on a deserted side rail at a small railroad station. If curious passengers waiting for a train connection or local residents approached our wagon, a guard stopped them and turned them away.

We had been on the road for over thirty-six hours without food, water, and rest. Each of us was allowed to lie down for a total of twelve hours and then had to stand for twenty-four hours in the wagon, which was like a steam bath. There were a couple of handicapped inmates and my friend Andy was among them.

It was growing late and the Russians usually didn't transport prisoners at night for security reasons. So, we knew we could expect to remain on the side rail at least until the next morning.

With inhuman conditions in the wagon, the mood of the prisoners became tense to the point where a spark could ignite a full-blown uprising. I sensed the seriousness of the situation and assumed leadership with full support of the others.

I stood up with Simon at my side.

"Let's elect a committee of three and present our grievances to the person in charge of the transport," I said in Hungarian and German. Simon translated into Russian.

"If you agree, I need two individuals—one who will represent the Russians and one for the other nationalities. I will speak for the Hungarians and ask Simon to help me with the translation. I would like you to empower the committee to conduct the negotiation."

Two men stepped forward; one was Sasha, an ex-captain of the Soviet Army. The other was a young Lithuanian teacher in his thirties named Paul.

We pounded on the side of the wagon and yelled for the guard. One standing nearby walked over.

"What do you want?" he asked.

"We would like to talk to the person in charge of this transport," I said.

"You Fascists!" he yelled. "Enemy of my motherland and the Soviet people. You should be grateful that our goodhearted leader, Stalin, eliminated the death sentence from the Soviet penal system. Thank us for being alive."

Simon translated what he said into Hungarian and I repeated it in German.

The guard's reply to our request was like oil on a fire. Everyone in the wagon jumped up in unison and responded in a bedlam of shouts, each in his own language.

Meanwhile, the guard stood outside listening. He seemed to realize that he was facing a desperate group of men willing to die for their cause. The prisoners could force the door open, disarm the soldiers, and escape with the soldiers' weapons, or he could be forced to shoot everyone. He knew he had to act fast or an uprising could break out.

"Wait, I will report your demands to the sergeant and we will be back," the guard said.

"We give you ten minutes. If you are not back, we will act accordingly," I replied.

The guard returned almost immediately with the NKVD sergeant in charge. They banged on the side of the wagon.

"What is your problem?" the sergeant asked.

"We would like to talk to you about our inhumane treatment," I said. "Have the gate opened, see the conditions inside, and let's have a face-to-face meeting. Three of us will represent all the prisoners in the wagon."

Long silence followed my demand. Simon put his ear close to the gate to listen as the sergeant and a guard discussed our demands. The sergeant sent the guard away for three more armed ones in case the situation got out of control.

"Yes, we will partially open the gate and we can have a face-to-face meeting," the sergeant said. "However, I warn you not to make any foolish moves. I will have no other choice but to shoot at you and if necessary, kill you. I will listen with an open mind and will do everything in my power."

The guards removed the padlock and opened the gate partially, leaving a two-foot opening. Sasha, Paul, Simon, and I stepped to the gate. Outside, four armed soldiers stood with their submachine guns pointing at the opening. I started the communication through my translator, Simon.

"We have been in this cattle wagon for over thirty hours without water, food, and the most basic human comfort. This kind of treatment of any living creature is immoral. In civilized nations, even cows are transported under better conditions than we are. They usually put four or five heads of cattle in a wagon of this size and supply them with sufficient food and water. They can lie down and rest as they wish. The number of prisoners in a wagon of this size should not exceed twenty. Our wagon is stuffed with sixty inmates. Food, water, and rest are the basic needs of any living creature. Even prisoners are entitled to those. Please, tell us what are you going to do for us without overstepping the boundaries of your authority."

The sergeant turned to one of his soldiers. "Pick up and bring two buckets of water, four mess tins, and two ladles."

Then he turned to us. "If you need more water, we will get it for you," he said. "We have some bread in our wagon for emergency use. I will order the soldier responsible for the supplies to cut sixty portions of bread, one pound each. We are not equipped to provide hot meals."

While he talked, the two buckets of water arrived. He ordered the guard to put them down until all our grievances had been addressed.

"What can be done about the overcrowded condition in the wagon?" I continued. "Also, we would like to know how much longer we have to suffer like this. Days, weeks, or more?"

"We don't have an extra freight car available," the sergeant replied. "Even if we had one, we wouldn't have the required personnel for it. However, I can promise you that you will be at your destination no later than noon tomorrow. There you will receive hot meals and will be able to rest in less crowded conditions."

"What is our final destination?" I asked.

"Lvov," he replied.

We anxiously waited for the water to be distributed, eager to conclude our grievance presentation.

The only source of light in the closed wagon was a small window opening. When the door was closed, the interior was in semidarkness. It would have been difficult to distribute the water in a semi-dark, crowded wagon. I asked the sergeant before he walked away to have the gate left open until the water and bread had been distributed. He agreed and ordered his men to comply.

I made a quick mental calculation. Considering waste from spillage, each of us could have three ladles of water amounting to fifteen ounces. I asked Sasha and Paul to each take one bucket, two mess tins, and a ladle, and then give everyone three ladles of water each. After each man drank his share, the cup would be refilled and passed on to the next man until everybody received his share.

As the buckets were emptied, two soldiers appeared, each carrying a tray piled high with pieces of bread. I judged each piece to be approximately one pound. The bread was dark and had the consistency of mud.

After the bread was distributed, the guard brought an additional bucket of water. Now that all our stomachs were at least partially filled, we were ready to retire for the night. Only one thing was overlooked. Even a dehydrated body could not absorb all the water; some of it had to be eliminated. The traffic to the urinal was unbelievable. The wagon inside looked like a beehive.

The next morning, our wagon was hooked to a train and we continued our trek to our final destination—Lvov. As promised, we arrived before noon.

After our arrival, we went through the routine procedure: "Check-in," body search, and medical inspection. When this was finished, the prisoners were separated into groups.

We were then lined up five abreast and marched into the corridor of a huge building. The corridor was wide and large windows made it bright.

As we waited, a large group of approximately sixty female prisoners led by a female guard approached us. Their ages seemed to range between twelve and eighty, but the majority of them looked between twenty-five and thirty-five. As they reached us, one inmate stepped out of the line in front of us and lifted her skirt, exposing her naked body. Several more did the same. Some of them lifted them high enough to show their naked breasts. Then they greeted us with a bedlam of shouts and welcomed us with the sort of prison obscenities to which we weren't yet accustomed. It was the most shocking experience seeing one of them pulling her skirt up with one hand and holding a child in the other. Later, I learned that women were permitted to have their children with them in Soviet prison as another sign of the enlightenment of the communist penal "culture."

The guard was powerless and unable to make them move until the door opened and we filed into a large room. The room we entered had three big windows with a plywood panel nailed in front from outside to block the view. In the room, there were already well over a hundred prisoners.

As we entered, all eyes were on us. Some were looking for friends, relatives, and acquaintances, and others for the clothes we were wearing and packages we carried. I looked around and noticed that in the middle of the room, between two large columns, the floor was unoccupied. The eleven of us picked that spot on the floor and put down our meager belongings as a marker.

I learned later that there were many common criminals in the room, mostly Russians who surveyed the newcomers for the clothing they wore and the packages they carried. They made a mental note of their locations and during the night, when everyone was sleeping, they would quietly approach their mark. They would order him to undress, take his clothes, and throw him some dirty old rags. Whoever resisted was badly beaten. Afterwards, these criminals exchanged the clothing with the guards for tobacco and food.

As soon as we settled on the floor, I walked around and introduced myself to my fellow prisoners. Eighty percent of the prisoners spoke German, so that was how we communicated.

A refined looking man in his forties invited me to sit down and have a chat. I learned he was a Ukrainian Greek Orthodox priest taken from his church during a Sunday service. He was sentenced under Paragraph 58, Subparagraph 6 of the Soviet penal code to twenty-five years for spying. He was eager for outside news, but I was unable to offer any. He shared his experience with me and pointed out the thieves in the room that I'd have to watch out for. They were together in a corner. I learned from him that transports left daily from Lvov, mainly to a place above the Arctic Circle, Inta/Vorkuta. The average stay in Lvov was no more than three days. He was ill with high fever and the medical person had kept him from being transported out.

After our chat, I returned to my place and took a nap. Joco woke me to line up for my bread and evening meal. After eating, I lay down and immediately fell asleep. I woke to the sound of people talking and moving around me. It took me just a short while to realize the Russian criminals had already started their nightly ritual. As newcomers, tonight was our turn to be robbed. I noticed that they had already undressed one of our friends and had just begun to work on Andy.

I sprang out of the shadows as one of the bullies raised his fist to strike Andy. I smashed my fist into his face and drove blows into his belly with all my might. The man crumpled.

Simon woke up to the noise and yelled, "Friends, one of our men is in danger! Stand up and help him."

Joco immediately jumped up and I saw his elbows pumping wildly in the gloom, and then heard the breath go hissing out of the second bully. In seconds, both thieves lay unconscious on the ground, and when they came to, they staggered back to their corner. From then on, they didn't bother us again. I became the "King" and was called the "Hungarian wrestler." Whenever the thugs made their deals with the guards, they shared their goodies with me.

We had been in Lvov only three days when the guard ordered us to pick up our belongings and march in front of him to the courtyard. The eleven of us were still together. Our hands were tied behind our backs and we were loaded onto a special van waiting for us. It took us to the railroad station less than a mile away where we were herded onto a cattle wagon the same size we had traveled in from Neunkirchen to Lvov. This time, though, only forty prisoners were stuffed inside and every one of us could sit or lie down at the same time. As soon as the wagon was loaded and the gate locked, it was hooked to a train and we departed.

5

The Dreaded Lubyanka
(1948–1951)

In the secret of my heart I am in perpetual quarrel
with God that he should allow such things to go on.

Mohandas K. Gandhi

Soon, I learned our destination was Moscow's oldest and most dreaded prison, Lubyanka. Built during the reign of the Tsars, it was one of five main prisons in Moscow. Three of them—Lubyanka, Lefortovo, and Butyrka—were used only for political prisoners, though political prisoners were also held in other places of detention alongside non-political prisoners. Lefortovo was the great torture center, though torture was also practiced on a lesser scale in Lubyanka and in a special section of Butyrka.

Lubyanka had the advantage of being free of bugs. Its corridors were clean and smelled of carbolic disinfectant. It was the best known of the NKVD prisons since it lay within the headquarters of the Police Ministry and had been the scene of the some of the most famous imprisonments, interrogations, and executions. Its great wedge loomed over Dzerzhinsky Square only a few minutes walk from the Kremlin and the general tourist area.

Lubyanka was originally the headquarters of an insurance company. The Cheka, the original name of the Soviet Political Secret Service, which was later changed to NKVD, had taken over the old building, and over the years, they built over the entire block. The original building was pre-revolutionary gothic; the rest of the block was rebuilt in two bursts of activity—one in a 1930s functional style and the other in a post-war wedding cake style.

The People's Commissariat occupied the entire outer section. Inside was a courtyard and within the courtyard was the nine-story prison section, originally a hotel or boarding house run by the insurance company. Considerably adapted, it had not been rebuilt. As a result, the rooms used as cells were less unpleasant than the cells in other prisons. The windows, though largely blocked by shutters, were a good size.

Lubyanka had about 110 cells, which were all fairly small. It seems improbable that more than a few hundred prisoners were held there at a time.

Prisoners who were uncooperative during preliminary interrogations at Lubyanka were often transferred to the 160-cell Lefortovo—in particular military prisoners.

Escape from Lubyanka was nearly impossible.

Guards escorted us inside one by one. To reach the cells, we had to go through several wrought iron gates. Finally, the guards opened a cell door, pushed me inside, and locked the door behind me.

I had begun my solitary confinement. This four-foot by eight-foot cell was my home for now and who knew how long in the future.

Cell doors were equipped with peepholes for the convenience of the guards. The only items in the cell were a cot and a cast iron vessel used as a toilet.

The first few days at Lubyanka were uneventful. A new place, new rules, and new guards kept my mind busy. Meals were brought three times a day. The quality of the food was neither better nor worse than the food at previous prisons.

After a week, I discovered that I needed not only bread and porridge, but also nourishment for my mind to keep it stimulated. For survival, I made a plan every morning when I got up for how I would keep my mind occupied. For physical exercise, from reveille to bedtime, I walked from one corner of the cell to the other.

I picked up sounds of real life beyond the dingy walls—the footsteps of the guards coming to bring my meal, which I would greet with streams of profanity.

I was surviving by reliving my past, a necessary exercise of mental stimulation. I had enjoyed an interesting and active life, which I relived day by day in my cell. I strongly resented the guards' arrivals bringing me back to reality by intruding on my reveries, which were so much more pleasant than the present.

Living Off the Past . . . The Early Years

I was born in the city of Papa in the western part of Hungary on 8 February 1924. My father had immigrated to the United States in 1912 and took up residency in a suburb of New York City. In early 1914, he became homesick, purchased a ticket on a luxury liner, and returned home. Shortly after his arrival in Hungary, World War I broke out and he was drafted into the Austrian/Hungarian Army at the age of twenty-two. He spent four years on various fronts and received several medals for heroism.

After the war, the Communists governed Hungary. My father was arrested because of his anticommunist activities and was imprisoned without being tried or convicted. He was released in 1920 and took a job in my hometown, Papa, as a pharmaceutical technician at a relatively large pharmacy. My mother, who was twenty-one at the time, worked for the pharmacy owner as a household helper and babysitter. She was the second youngest of four children and was orphaned at a young age. My parents married in 1921 and had three children—my sister, Magda, my brother, Jozsef, and me, the middle child.

Papa was a medium-sized city with a population of twenty-five to thirty thousand. Most people in the town knew each other, were friendly, and were always ready to lend a pair of helping hands. The streets of Papa were paved in cobblestone. The only traffic was horse-drawn carts pulled by pairs of heavy Percherons delivering milk, beer to the pubs, and in the fall, coal for heat during the winter months. The streets were tree-lined, providing a pleasant shady walk underneath. The business center, "the Square," was in the heart of the city, with stores and small businesses, churches, and schools.

Papa boasted a promenade about 100 to 150 yards long. Mostly students used it after compulsory Sunday church services. For the children, it was an accepted social gathering place. At each end of the promenade was an ice cream parlor where boys treated their girlfriends to ice cream or delicious pastry.

After my parents married, my father accepted a supervisory position in a textile factory, part of Papa's largest industry. The factory employed most of the city's workforce and provided housing and recreational facilities such as tennis courts and an ice skating rink. The factory added a daycare center and a hall for concerts, dance programs, and plays for employees.

My hometown was also well known for its excellent schools attended by city residents and children from the countryside that commuted daily by train from as far as thirty miles away.

Upon completion of four years in public schools, I enrolled in a Catholic *gymnasium* at the age of eleven. Monks of the order of St. Benedict ran the gymnasium. The school offered an eight-year curriculum ending with a formal matriculation consisting of oral and written exams in six subjects and was a significant milestone in my life.

My high school years were important for me. The strict discipline, the rules, and the heavy class schedules formed me into the person I am now. The school had strict rules for our activities during and after school hours. Since we represented our school, our behavior outside school was expected to reflect just that. We had to wear uniforms, which included a cap with the emblem of the school on it. We were not supposed to be on the street after 8 P.M. If we wanted to go to the movies, our parents had to request it in writing in advance and it had to be approved by the school officials. School was six days a week, with six, fifty-minute lectures daily, and ten-minute breaks between the lectures. The compulsory subjects were three foreign languages: Latin for eight years, German for six years, and French for four years. We also studied mathematics, science, history, geography, religious instruction, and physical education, which were strongly emphasized with regular weekly classes. Music and art were also part of the curriculum. The only elective subject was Greek for one year.

The school was approximately one mile from home and I walked to and from school every day rain or shine. On Sundays, we attended church services. A crucifix was on the wall in every classroom. Noon prayers were a routine throughout the school.

School offered many extracurricular activities as well— sports, science, literature, music, and even model airplane building. It also organized dance classes supervised by our teachers where we were exposed to social interaction and etiquette. Our institute encouraged participation in its Boy Scout troop and offered a three-week session of summer camp.

During those years, significant changes occurred in my life. My father unexpectedly passed away at the age of forty-seven and the family was left without a breadwinner. My mother had to go to work to support three growing children. To help my mother with her expenses, I tutored several of my classmates and students from lower grades during the school year. After school, I rode my bike to their homes and returned in late afternoon or early evening. I had to stay up late many days to finish my homework and prepare for the next day's classes.

During two summer vacations, I worked as a roofer's helper for a friend's father who was in the roofing business. It didn't take me long to learn how to walk on a sloping roof with several ceramic shingles in my arms. During the last two summers of high school, another friend's father employed me on their family farm. My job was to weigh and keep an accurate record of the grain harvested. My earnings and my scholarship made it possible to continue and finish my high school education.

During those years, I spent Saturdays and Sundays at the glider port three miles from home. I usually left home early in the morning and returned late in the evening. My model airplane building and gliding experience made me decide to become an aviator.

I was a good student—at the top of my class—and my mother wanted me to become an electrical engineer. She often told me that she was willing to work hard to finance my college expenses, but I couldn't accept her offer. When the opportunity arose, I applied to the Royal Hungarian Air Force Academy and was accepted. My training started immediately after my matriculation from high school in May 1943.

Trying My Wings

The Treaty of Trianon concluded World War I for Hungary on 20 June 1920. Hungary was punished, not only by having to give away major portions of her territories to neighboring countries, but also by being forced to accept a limited army and no air force. Pilot training was reduced to a very small scale.

In the late 1930s, the sport of gliding became popular in Germany and Hungary. Numerous clubs popped up in Budapest and other cities like my birthplace, Papa. The clubs were sponsored and financed by Boy Scouts, universities, and large corporations.

In early 1940, an announcement was made at my school that had a great influence on my future. A glider club was just about to start up in Papa. A large company financed the club for its employees and its managing director told school officials that the club was willing to accept a limited number of student pilots from our school. The only prerequisite for acceptance was the school's recommendation and written parental approval.

Flying days were scheduled for Saturdays and Sundays year round. I filled out the application and since my mother refused to sign it, I signed it myself, falsifying her signature. In a few days, I was notified of my acceptance into the club, and I was elated. The first day was scheduled for the following Saturday.

The company had hired an instructor and purchased two planes, Vocsoks, designed and built in Hungary. They were primary trainers. Compared to modern fiberglass sailplanes, the performance of those gliders was very low. One of the parameters for measuring the performance of a plane is the glide ratio, the distance flown by the glider from an altitude of one unit. The glide ratio of a modern fiberglass sailplane is in the range of forty-two to fifty—our Vocsoks' was fourteen.

I could hardly wait for that Saturday to arrive. I woke up early, filled with excitement, and after a quick breakfast, rode my bike to the glider port. When I arrived, there were already several people waiting. After introducing myself, I learned that the chief instructor would arrive shortly.

Meanwhile, I wandered into the open hangar where the two beautiful "birds" were housed. From a distance, I could smell the pleasant aroma of acetone. The planes were wooden structures covered with fabric, which was coated with a lacquer thinned with acetone. Even today, after sixty years, I still can smell that aroma when I close my eyes and relive my first visit to the glider port. I walked around the two planes in awe and inspected them in great detail, but I did not dare touch them.

When the chief instructor arrived, he gathered the group together and explained rules and regulations, emphasizing the importance of discipline and safety. Then he outlined the training program and talked about the "A," "B," and "C" badges we could earn.

Everyone in the group was a student pilot with no previous gliding experience. All of us would work toward the A Badge, which required five straight glides of at least thirty seconds in duration. To launch the glider, the plane was anchored and a V-shaped bungee cord was attached to the hook located in front of the plane. With four people on each branch, the cord was stretched to a tension sufficient to launch the glider to the desired height. When the desired tension was achieved, the instructor pulled the release cord and the plane was catapulted.

The student's task was to keep the wings level and the plane gliding in a straight line. The first couple of launches were on ground level. Then the height increased, as did the student's experience. It took at least thirty-five launches before a student was ready to be launched to a height resulting in a thirty-second or longer flight. Each flight was entered into a student's flight logbook. After the requirements were met, the badge and a certificate were issued. For an A Badge, the average height was eighty-five feet.

Launches for B and C Badges were done by winch for which an old car was used. The rear end of the car was raised and a steel drum fastened to one of the rear wheels. The drum wound up a steel cable of approximately 2,000 feet long at high speed causing the sailplane to ascend to a height of 1,400 feet or higher. When the desired height was reached, the flagman standing next to the driver of the car, the winch operator, waved the flag, notifying the pilot to release the cable and start the free flight. If the pilot failed to release or the release mechanism failed, a cutting device mounted on the front of the winch car cut the cable.

The requirement for a B Badge was five flights of at least two minutes' duration each, two flights full circle to the right, two flights full circle to the left, and one flight in a figure eight, which is flown by a making a full circle to the right or left followed by a full circle in the opposite direction. Also, the landing had to be made within the range marked on the ground.

During these flights, the student-pilot learned how to establish and maintain a safe flying speed. We learned to fly by the seat of our pants since there were no instruments to rely on. When the pilot met the requirements, the flights were entered into the logbook and a certificate and a badge with two wings on it were issued.

The requirements for a C Badge were more difficult. The pilot had to maintain the release altitude—or gain altitude—for at least ten minutes. To do so, the pilot had to find a rising air mass called thermal. Since there was not much time to search for a thermal, it could take several flights for a student to fulfill the ten-minute requirement. A spot landing was also part of the C Badge requirement.

After a "nutshell" introduction to soaring, we were instructed to take a plane out to the designated take-off area. Since the plane was heavy, over 250 pounds, we used a dolly with two large wheels to move it from place to place. It took four students to transport the plane from its landing spot back to the take-off position—two on the handle to pull the dolly with the plane on it, one on the wing-tip and one on the tail. After arriving at the place designated for take-off, we positioned the plane into the wind.

Since everything was new to us, we had to learn the operation step-by-step. Our chief instructor carefully supervised every step, knowing how easy it was to damage the relatively flimsy planes.

It was the rule of the club that the first flight on every operational flight day was to be flown by an instructor before a student was allowed to fly. So, on that first day, the chief instructor stepped into the cockpit, fastened the belts, and was ready to go. From the cockpit, he gave us orders. He assigned one person to pull the release cord when the tension was sufficient to launch the plane. We needed at least four people for each branch of the bungee cord, but the instructor asked for six. At his signal, they stretched the bungee cord and when the tension was sufficient, he called out "release."

What a beautiful sight it was. Our bird jumped toward the sky to a height of 140 feet and then started to glide down. We could hear a hissing sound. Half a minute later, it landed more than half a mile away. We took the dolly, retrieved the plane, and got it ready for the first student flight. It took twenty-five minutes and four student pilots to retrieve the glider.

Now our turn to fly had arrived. The chief instructor had a list of student names in alphabetical order, which also was the sequence in which we would fly. I was the tenth out of twenty students. If everything went according to plan, I would have a chance at my first flight that day.

Around 5 P.M., the moment finally arrived to try my wings. The first "flight" was really a slide, since the Vocsok didn't leave the ground. But we still called it a flight.

I was proud when the chief instructor remarked, "Bela, you did a good job leveling the wings and sliding straight."

By nightfall, we realized that even if we had a trouble-free day, not everyone would have his turn to fly. It could take as long as nine months for an average student pilot to earn an A Badge.

As time went on, the height of our flights increased and the flight time went from zero to above thirty seconds, and we were ready to make our badge flights. It took eight months from my first flight until I received my certificate and a pin with one wing on it.

The next year, in 1941, the club received a new high-performance glider called Pilis. Its glide ratio was eighteen, a twenty-percent improvement over that of the Vocsok. Only pilots who had earned a B Badge were allowed to fly this "wonder bird." Since the club didn't have anyone with a B Badge yet, the Pilis stayed in the hangar unless our chief instructor decided to fly it himself.

By the end of 1941, almost everyone had completed the requirements for an A Badge and there were only a handful of student pilots, including myself, who had their pin with two wings on it.

During the winter of 1941-1942, we had a higher than average snowfall and flyable days were few.

In 1942, I transitioned to the Pilis. It was a significant step up. The Pilis had instruments—a speed indicator, a vertical speed indicator, an altimeter, and a compass. It took several flights to get used to them.

During the summer, I made several attempts for a C badge, but all failed. Finally, on a hot summer day, I was sitting in the cockpit waiting for a cumulus cloud to move into a favorable position. When I judged it to be in the right position, the flag-man signaled the winch operator to launch the plane. I released at 1,500 feet and after a short straight flight, I suddenly felt the Pilis going up.

I took a quick glimpse at the variometer, which indicated that I was going up at a rate of four hundred feet per minute. I started my stopwatch to make sure I would meet the ten-minute requirement. Three minutes into the flight, the altimeter indicated two thousand feet. At the ten-minute mark, I was gliding at three thousand feet and I knew I had met the C badge requirement. Since several pilots were waiting on the ground to try their luck, I began my descent and shortly touched down on the mark. My total flight time was twenty-five minutes and the barograph confirmed that I had met the ten-minute requirement for the C badge.

The rest of that year was uneventful until early November. On a foggy morning, I took a winch tow in the Pilis, a practice flight—just a take-off and precision landing—since the weather wasn't good for soaring. At the approach end of the field, there was a road with a high-voltage power line. In the final approach on the other side of the highway, I realized that I was flying low.

At this point, I had two choices—increase my speed and pull the Pilis over the power line or fly under the line and land. Flying under the line seemed the safer choice. I had almost made it when a flash of fire nearly blinded me, but I continued and landed. Safely on the ground, I found out that the Pitot tube, which is shaped like a reversed L mounted on the top of the fuselage, had caught the high-voltage power line and severed it. The only damage to the plane was some burned paint on the top of the fuselage.

Since our high school graduation was scheduled for late April 1943 and the start of the basic pilot training for early May, I did not have time to fly gliders again that year.

Gliding gave me a "feeling" for the air—the sensation and subtle pressure of the wind all around me holding me up and bearing on my glider attuned me to the air environment. I became, in the true sense, an "airman," so that the powered flight I encountered later in the air force came as nothing strange to me. Since my teenage years, climbing into an aircraft had become as familiar to me as getting on my bike.

Becoming familiar with aircraft through gliding helped me later in life. Whenever I was in an aircraft and something went wrong, I got a bad feeling—often before an instrument indication of a failure. I felt it in the seat of my pants. There can be no doubt that the earlier you get started in the flying business, the more highly developed your feeling with everything connected to aircraft.

On the other hand, even though the air force enabled me to continue my flying, I was not cut out psychologically for military life. I was young—a free spirit who sought freedom in the air. Military life became a bitter pill to be swallowed with the sweetness of flying. My aversion to the regimentation of military life tended to adversely affect my career in the air force and made life more difficult for me in Soviet prisons. Still, I was able to survive as an independent spirit, even in an environment based on conformity.

Pilot Training

In the 1930s, the Hungarian government sought total liberalization of the armaments industry and parity of equipment with the neighboring nations that were signatories to the "Little Entente" with France, i.e. Czechoslovakia, Rumania, and Yugoslavia.

In 1934, Czechoslovakia had 546 military aircraft, Yugoslavia had 470, and Rumania had 773, not to mention a navy. Hungary had only two hundred military aircraft and no navy.

The deteriorating international situation led the "Little Entente" states to sign an equal-rearmament pact with Hungary in the city of Bled on 22 August 1938. From then on, rearmament was legal. The only problem was Hungary's impoverished state. Even at the outbreak of World War II, Hungary's Air Force still struggled—with only partial success—to overcome more than a dozen years of technological backwardness.

In 1938, Hungary reorganized its air force. It opened the Royal Hungarian Miklos Horthy Military Air Force Academy in Kassa in March 1939 to boost officer training. And to accelerate the training, a new civilian basic pilot program called the Horthy Foundation was established for those entering the academy and the air force with the intention of becoming pilots. The Horthy Foundation had eight airports, each capable of training thirty student pilots between May and September. The Horthy Foundation assigned me to Vat, near Szombathely in western Hungary, approximately ninety miles from Budapest.

The Vat airport had a grass landing strip and one large hangar. There was a barracks for student pilots, two detached homes (for the superintendent and the chief mechanic and their families), a large kitchen, and a dining hall. There were seven employees of the Horthy Foundation in Vat—the superintendent (who was also the chief instructor), three instructors, and three mechanics. The hangar housed five Bucker 131s, also called Bucker Jungman.

I arrived at the Vat railroad station on a Saturday in late May 1943. Since the airport was only a short distance away, I decided to walk to the airport rather than wait for a bus. When I arrived, I saw several people standing in a group. I joined them and after introductions, they showed me the living quarters. They told me to choose a bed not yet picked by someone else. I staked my claim by placing my belongings on one.

Shortly after, the superintendent and the three instructors walked in and a question-and-answer period began. We learned about our program and the airport rules and regulations. After they left, we wandered into the hangar and inspected the airplanes. Some of the group even climbed into the pilot seat for make-believe flights.

The Bucker Jungman was a fully aerobatic biplane. Its steel tubing structure was covered with fabric. There were two versions: one hundred-horsepower and eighty-horsepower. Our planes were equipped with one hundred-horsepower engines. Besides the standard aerobatics figures such as inside loops, snap rolls, slow rolls, and spins, it was capable of performing outside loops.

By late afternoon, we had a head count of twenty-nine. One person had not arrived yet. We had dinner at 8 P.M. and retired at 10 P.M. Meanwhile, we learned that reveille was at 6 A.M., breakfast at 7 A.M., and training flights would start at 8 A.M. Sunday, the first full day, was for familiarization. Students were assigned to instructors who gave introductory flights. We also learned that our flying day did not end with the last landing. We were responsible for cleaning and refueling, and getting the planes ready for the next day.

One of the instructors explained the disciplinary action against those who violated the rules or jeopardized the safety of our flight operation. I still remember one of my punishments when the inspecting official didn't find me in bed after lights out. I had to walk the periphery of the airport three times on a hot summer day while fully dressed, with a forty-pound propeller on my shoulder.

On that first afternoon, the instructional flights began. The instructor climbed into the front seat of the plane with a student in the rear, which was the pilot seat. After the instructor applied full power, the plane took off in no time.

When it was my turn, I held the stick with my right hand. I had my left hand on the throttle and my feet on the rudder pedals. I followed the movement of the controls without exerting any resistance. The plane rose to eight hundred feet. We made a right turn and after a short straight flight, made the second right—downwind leg. One minute later, we made a right turn again for the base leg. I looked out on the right side and saw that we were lined up with the runway. We made the final turn, throttled back, and began the descent at a constant speed until the plane was a couple of feet from the ground. We applied some "back pressure" and the three wheels touched the ground simultaneously. It was a perfect three-point landing! We flew three more patterns and then the next student climbed into the pilot seat to try his wings.

During the next few weeks, we practiced takeoffs and landings. At the end of the second week, the first student soloed. One morning shortly after this, my instructor stepped from the cockpit, tied the belts, and gave me the green light to solo.

It was an exciting moment. The solo flight was my thirtieth flight. I did four perfect takeoffs and landings to full stop. During the following week, I again practiced takeoffs and landings.

To save time, landings were not to full stop, but touch-and-go, meaning after the plane landed, it didn't taxi back to takeoff position. Instead, the pilot applied full power and took off again. For every four flights, the touch-and-go landings saved fifteen to twenty minutes—as much as two to three flying hours per day, which was significant.

After I mastered the takeoffs and landings, I was ready for more serious maneuvers. My next flight was again with my instructor. Before takeoff, he told me we were going to Quadrant 1.

The air space around the airport was divided into four quadrants. Each instructor had his assigned quadrant and this way the chance of mid-air collision was minimized. During the practice flight, my instructor demonstrated spins and spin-recovery. Then we practiced banked turns of forty-five degrees and sixty degrees. Finally, he demonstrated an inside loop. After he finished, I had to repeat everything he'd just taught me. When he was satisfied with my performance, we landed. He stepped out, tied the seat belts, and gave me the go-ahead for a thirty-minute flight to practice banked turns, loops, and spins in Quadrant 1.

After a few practice flights, he climbed into the front seat again and had me demonstrate my mastery of the aerobatics he'd taught me. When he was satisfied, I did a couple of snap rolls and slow rolls. It took several tries until I could do a well-coordinated slow roll. Soon, I perfected my technique to the point that at my next practice flight, I was able to slow roll around the airport. It took approximately fifty slow rolls to return to my starting point.

During my next flight with my instructor, I learned inverted flight, "hammerhead," and outside loops. Initially, my outside loops were sloppy and occasionally I had to terminate them before completion. It took several more tries to be comfortable doing them. I still remember that on my first try, I lost more than three thousand feet and panicked when I saw the earth rushing toward me at high speed. My speed indicator was near the red line, indicating that the pilot is exceeding the safe flying speed of the aircraft. Eventually, I mastered the outside loop and was able to do "vertical 8s," which consist of an inside loop followed by an outside loop.

I completed my aerobatics training in early August. I still had two assignments—a one hundred-mile cross-country flight, and a ten thousand-feet altitude flight, which I accomplished by mid-August. From then on, all the flights were for pleasure.

After flight training was completed, there were three more events worth mentioning. On 20 August, we gave a demonstration flight in honor of Vice Admiral Horthy, the Regent of Hungary. Student pilots from every location gathered at Budapest's largest airport. We marched in front of the main stand and saluted Vice Admiral Horthy. At the same time, five airplanes flew in formation over our heads.

The second event was a flight test with an air force representative to demonstrate our flying skills during which the examiner took notes on our performance. Acceptance into the air force was based on his evaluation.

The third event was a social one. The village of Vat had its annual carnival on the last Sunday in August with music, wine, and pretty girls. The villagers graciously invited us to their celebration, which lasted until morning. Our superintendent allowed us to stay out on that night as long as we wanted.

Shortly after, our basic training was complete. I had flown eighty hours and was even more committed to a career in aviation. We all left Vat with great memories of our time spent there, ready for a new phase in our flying careers.

Air Force Academy

Vice Admiral Horthy, Regent of Hungary, had ordered the Hungarian Air Force to become an independent service effective 1 January 1939. Consequently, in the interest of officer training, the Royal Hungarian Miklos Horthy Military Air Force Academy in Kassa was instituted in 1939. The four-year curriculum was highly technical. Students who decided to study engineering after graduating from the Air Force Academy were given credits in several subjects. At the academy, all the subjects were compulsory and included military discipline, close-order drill, and arms activities for which I never developed any enthusiasm. It offered theoretical studies in aviation subjects—the history of aviation; the theory of flight; operation, design, and construction of aircraft and aircraft engines; aeronautical engineering; strength of materials; aerodynamics; and meteorology. It also offered subjects such as mathematics, physics, chemistry, photography, navigation, weaponry, history of military strategy, and code of conduct. These subjects absorbed my interest and I had no difficulty with my studies. The incentive of imminent flying training was powerful enough to push me through my studies with ease.

Flight training took place at several locations. During the first year, cadets were housed in Szombathely where they received advanced flight training. During the second and subsequent years, cadets were sent for flight training to various airfields according to their specialties. For example, fighter pilots were trained in Veszprem and bombers in Debrecen.

Our class was the fifth since the academy was established. Previous classes had been smaller, ranging from thirty to fifty cadets. We were a class of 150 cadets.

Between completion of the Horthy Foundation and the start of Air Force Academy training, we were given a weeklong break. I spent it with my mother in my hometown. We cherished those days in each other's company for the rest of our lives.

At the end of the week, I gathered my belongings. Since the academy supplied everything except toiletry items and underwear, packing didn't take long. On Sunday morning, I said a tearful good-bye to my mother and boarded the train for Szombathely where a bus waited to drive cadets to the airfield ten miles away.

At the airport, a clerk was waiting for us. He issued us uniforms and told us our class assignment. There were thirty cadets in each class. I was assigned to class A. After this, we went to our living quarters and looked for the bed with our name on it.

Before retiring for the night, we received instructions for the following day.

The next two weeks consisted of an accelerated boot camp. The days started at 6 A.M. and ended at 8 P.M. with meal breaks in between. On the last day of boot camp, we were awakened at 1 A.M. and told to dress, take our rifles, and gather in front of our building. That night, we marched fifteen miles and performed military maneuvers with an imaginary enemy in the area. We won the battle and returned to our base at 7 A.M.

After completing boot camp, we began flight training. It was a continuation of the training we'd had at Vat with Bucker Jungmans. It consisted of formation flying, aerobatics, and cross-country flights. During the next two weeks, I flew more than forty hours.

Then one morning, to our surprise, there were five Arado 96A airplanes at the takeoff area. The Bucker Jungmans were gone.

The Arado 96 had an A version and a B version. The A version had a 240-horsepower Argus engine and the B was equipped with a 480-horsepower engine. The plane had a retractable landing gear and a propeller with automatic pitch control. They were used for advanced flight and fighter training. The B version was also used for gunnery training.

The first half-day was spent familiarizing us with the plane and its peculiarities. It had a tendency to ground loop, which could be prevented by holding a straight-line direction until the plane fully stopped. The brakes had to be applied gently. During ground loops, the landing gear usually broke and we would lose a plane for weeks.

At noon, we had to pass a test to demonstrate our knowledge of the plane by climbing into the pilot seat and finding the instruments and controls blindfolded.

Flight training in the Arado began after lunch. There were three instructors and four planes. On the first flight, a demonstration, we followed the movements of the controls with our hands and feet. We were not supposed to exert any resistance to it. There was a water tower in the direction of our takeoff, which had to be cleared from the right side.

I flew with an instructor over the next week. After twelve takeoffs, I was cleared to solo.

In October, the classroom instructions began and the flight training was cut back to two half-days per week. Saturdays were just like any other day. We always had a full schedule. The classroom education ended at the end of December and was followed by mid-term exams. The results of the first semester were announced in January and the cadets were ranked. The theoretical and practical scores were combined to calculate the final grade. Our class standing was displayed on our uniform epaulettes. The cadets who earned an "excellent" mark in every subject wore two stripes with two buttons. In our year, only one cadet achieved this. In the next group, approximately twenty percent earned two stripes. Another fifty percent of the cadets were entitled to one stripe with one button. Those cadets with low marks were entitled to one stripe. Those who failed had naked epaulettes. I had two stripes.

When classroom education ended in May, a seven-day per week flying schedule began. Flight training was conducted at three airports. My class was transferred to Vat where we lived at the school of a small nearby village and commuted to the airport by bus.

Flight training continued in the Arado 96A with great emphasis on aerobatics and formation flying. Flying in close formation, if the distance between the wing tips of the two planes exceeded one foot, we received a bad evaluation for that flight.

Later in the summer of 1944, after completion of our training on the Arado 96A and B, we transitioned to a twin-engine
Focke-Wulf 58, also called a Weihe. It was used for instrument
and night-flight training. For night flight training, four student
pilots and an instructor would usually take off after 8 P.M. and
land only for refueling. The cadets rotated and changed seats in
the air. Usually, we stayed airborne until 4 A.M.

I completed this phase of my training relatively quickly and
was asked to stay on and give instruction to those cadets who
hadn't yet completed this phase of training.

In August, the cadets were divided into three groups: fighters, bombers, and reconnaissance. I was assigned to the fighter
group and transferred to Kenyeri and later to Taszar. The plan
for our training was to fly three additional types of planes:
Solyom, RE2000, and Me-109, followed by combat and gunnery training.

The biplane Solyom, used as a tactical reconnaissance aircraft, was designed and built in Hungary. An 870-horsepower
radial air-cooled engine powered it. The armament was one 7.9
mm forward firing, fixed machine gun synchronized with the
propeller.

The Solyom was not particularly successful. Nevertheless, it
served in substantial numbers in the Hungarian Air Force. Since
the Solyom had unpleasant flight traits and was not fitted with
a radio, the reconnaissance squadron eliminated them from
their unit and transferred them to the fighter-training unit to
be used as a trainer for transitioning from low- to high-power
airplanes. Due to the poor flying traits, training on the Solyom
consisted on average of only ten flights with the emphasis on
takeoffs and landings.

The RE 2000 was an Italian-designed and built fighter
plane. The Hungarian Air Force purchased the license and built
them in Hungary. The RE 2000 stayed in Russian front-line

service until the beginning of 1943. After that, they were used only as combat and gunnery trainers in fighter school. They were powered by 870 horsepower, air-cooled, radial engines. Maximum airspeed was 310 mph and stall speed was 80 mph. The armament was a forward-firing 12.7 mm machine gun.

The German-built Me-109 was the fighter pilot's dream. A typical pilot in the Hungarian Air Force had flown six or seven different types of powered aircraft by the time he was ready for the fabled Me-109. Every military pilot dreamed of flying this legendary machine. The spirited Me-109, with its powerful Daimler-Benz engine, was a superb airplane. Several versions were available for training: D, E, and F. The G version was used only for combat. Maximum speed of the E version was 342 mph. These airplanes were equipped with two 7.9 mm machine guns and two 20 mm canons mounted in the wings outside the propeller arc.

Airplanes used for combat training were equipped with photo-guns to evaluate the student-pilots' combat performance. The final step of fighter pilot training was gunnery training. Usually the student fired fifty shots at a drag-out pulled by an airplane and counted the hits. A hit of ten was excellent. The highest hit I heard of was twenty out of fifty.

The long grind through fighter pilot training was arduous and demanding. Because of lack of fuel, our class couldn't complete the training and students were forced to terminate training at various points.

★   ★   ★

In 1944, the Soviet Army occupied part of eastern Hungary and was approaching Budapest at a fast pace. A decision was made to graduate the cadets of our class on 15 November 1944 and transfer us to Zeltweg, Austria, where we would complete training and be deployed to the Russian front.

Graduation took place in the new academy building at Szentkiralyszabadja. I graduated with my class as a second lieutenant. After graduation, I spent one week with my mother and then returned to Kenyeri.

The American bombing campaign was intensifying with an emphasis on destroying the railroad system. Because of this, a serious fuel shortage developed and pilot training was the first to be cut back to conserve fuel.

The night before Christmas 1944, I took a train to Budapest to visit my girlfriend. On Christmas morning, I learned that the Russians had encircled Budapest. Transportation to and from the city was nonexistent. I learned from my girlfriend's neighbor that there were two Bucker Jungmans in Heroes Square in the center of Budapest, fueled up and ready to take off.

I rushed over and saw from the markings that the two planes belonged to the Horthy Foundation. Since nobody was there to claim responsibility for the planes, I started the engine of one with the help of two bystanders and jumped into the pilot seat. After a brief engine warm-up, the two bystanders turned the plane toward Andrassy Street and I took off. I knew the distance for takeoff was short and I had to maneuver the plane between tall buildings with wires between them.

I cleared the buildings and the wires, ascended to 4,000 feet, and headed towards Szombathely, about 120 miles west of Budapest. As I was crossing the Russian line, I was shot at, but cleared the danger zone without injury and flew to Szombathely where I landed two hours later. This was the most interesting and eventful Christmas Day of my life.

On the day after Christmas, I took a train to Kenyeri. As soon as I arrived, I was called into the office of the commanding officer. He told me I was assigned to be the officer in charge of a transport train leaving Szombathely sometime in the next two weeks, depending on how fast the cargo could be loaded. The plan was to evacuate the airport before the approaching Russian Army reached Szombathely, and to transport the machine tools from the repair shops to Zeltweg. Fifty military personnel would be on the train under my command. Two box-cars had been reserved to transport the personnel and one box-car would be used as a kitchen.

I spent the next week supervising the loading of the train. The cargo consisted of machine tools, spare parts, damaged air-planes, and some military supplies. In a week, the loading was complete and military personnel occupied the boxcars. When the locomotive arrived, the train immediately departed and I said good-bye to Szombathely.

The route was Wiener-Neustadt, Neunkirchen, Bruck am Mur, and Judenburg/Zeltweg. Our plan was to arrive in Wiener-Neustadt late at night and leave as soon as we could because of the constant bombing of railroad stations. But because of heavy railroad traffic, our train didn't arrive until noon on the following day.

At the station near Wiener-Neustadt, we were advised not to go inside because it had been bombed. No details were avail-able. The train was pushed onto an inactive track and we wait-ed for permission to leave. We were in constant contact with the railroad personnel at stations ahead of us to obtain information about the condition of the tracks along our route. We spent a whole day at a small station ten miles from Wiener-Neustadt and then continued our trip after dark.

Meanwhile, we learned that the station had suffered serious damage from bombing the previous night, but the tracks were passable. It was a relatively short trip to Wiener-Neustadt. There we witnessed the devastation firsthand. The station was in bad shape. Railroad cars were overturned and piled on top of each other with their contents spilled. There was food, chemical products, and other cargo all over the station. We were lucky that the main rail was still passable.

Our next stop was Bruck am Mur. It had a relatively small railroad station. There, we were notified that Judenburg, our final destination, was severely damaged and we wouldn't be able to unload the cargo there.

Bruck am Mur was a beautiful place surrounded by snow-covered mountains. Since we had time and there were skis on the train, a handful of people, including me, put on the skis and headed toward the top of Semmering Mountain. The view was picturesque with the station directly below us. When we finally had enough courage to ski down the virgin snow on the slope, it felt as if we would land on the station itself. The bravest went back for another run, but most of us skied down only once. By the time we returned to our train, supper was ready to be served. We spent the night there and left that scenic place behind early the next morning.

The trip from Bruck am Mur to Judenburg took only a couple of hours. Upon our arrival, I reported to my squadron leader who provided personnel to unload the train and transport the cargo to the airport. Then my squadron leader told me that we couldn't start training flights until we received fuel. At the time, it was impossible to transport fuel by rail because Allied planes were demolishing the trains transporting it. We spent the days playing cards and doing minor duties. The months of February through May were uneventful as everybody waited for the war to end.

One of my last flights was in late February. My squadron leader ordered me to fly six pilots in a twin-engine FW58-Weihe to ferry the six planes left behind when we evacuated Bosarkany. The planes were slightly damaged, but in flyable condition.

It was a snowy, cold winter day. The inclement weather made it hard to start the engines of the FW58-Weihe. Finally, the engines started and we were ready to leave when several German soldiers rushed down from the control tower and ordered me not to take off because of the poor weather conditions. But I was eager to fly and ignored their order. I applied full power and the soldiers holding the FW58-Weihe scattered in every direction. It was a comical sight.

As we arrived at Bosarkany in late afternoon, the visibility was poor with no lights anywhere. Our plane was not equipped with a radio so we couldn't communicate with airport personnel. I flew over the area several times where I guessed the airport to be located. Finally, airport personnel recognized that the plane flying over their heads belonged to the Hungarian Air Force and immediately began shooting lighting rockets. At that light level, you couldn't read a newspaper, but it was enough light to land the plane.

That night, we visited the farmers we had befriended while we were stationed at Bosarkany. They told us they were scared of the approaching Soviet Army. The soldiers, they said, raped women, killed people, took everything they could put their hands on, and left pure devastation in their wake. We stayed late into the night with our farmer friends—simple, big-hearted folks who valued our friendship immensely. Around midnight, we left to get some rest. We planned to be at the airport at 7 A.M. the next morning and ready to leave before 9 A.M.

We arrived at the airport before dawn. We were standing in front of the Weihe and I had just begun the briefing when one of our farmer friends from the village approached us in a horse-drawn cart. He had a whole pig, nice and clean, and a big barrel of wine on the cart. He put it all down next to the plane. The villagers wanted us to have the pig and the wine rather than leave them to the barbaric Soviet troops. We thanked him, loaded the pig and the wine into the plane, and said an emotional good-bye.

I continued the briefing and we all walked over to the planes, which were hidden in the woods with the fuselage between the trees and the wings camouflaged by branches. We pulled the planes out and aligned them neatly. I assigned a number to each plane from left to right. The one on the left was Number One, and the one on the other end was Number Six.

Then I tore six pieces of paper from my notebook and marked each with a number from one to six and put them into my hat. Each pilot drew one to get his plane assignment.

Then I gave my orders, "Go and preflight your planes. When you are done, come back and let me finish the briefing before you depart."

Meanwhile, I checked out the Weihe. The fuel level was more than adequate to take me back to Zeltweg and the airplane was in flyable condition. I had just completed the preflight when I saw Erwin walking toward me.

"You did a fast job, Erwin! Is everything okay?" I asked.

"No, the left wheel of my plane has a flat tire," he said.

"Let's go and see what can be done," I replied.

We walked over to his plane, an Arado 96B. I quickly assessed the situation and agreed that the plane was not flyable.

"We do not have a spare tire and even if we did, we don't have the tools and the skill to do the job and make the airplane airworthy," I said.

We pushed the plane back, camouflaged the wings, and returned to the Weihe. Meanwhile, the other pilots had completed the preflight and joined us. The other five planes, three Arado 96Bs and two 96As, had full tanks of fuel and were in flyable condition.

I continued the final briefing, "The takeoff will be in sequential order from the north end of the runway. The first to take off is Number One. The pilot of Number Two plane will help him start the engine. He will observe him taxiing to the end of the runway. As soon as he is in the air, pilot Number Two will climb into his plane and the pilot of Number Three plane will provide help and wait until he takes off, and so on, until all the planes are in the air."

In less than an hour, all five planes were on their way to Zeltweg. Only Erwin and I were still on the ground. I noticed a Me-109 in one corner of the airport. Immediately, a light bulb turned on in my head.

"Let's walk to the Me-109 and find out whether it is fly-able or not," I said to Erwin.

A preliminary inspection indicated no visible damage and a full fuel tank. It was airworthy and ready to fly.

I quickly decided, but didn't tell Erwin, that I would ferry the Me-109 to Zeltweg. We had only limited flying experience in this type of plane, but we knew it inside and out, how to takeoff, and what to watch for at landing.

I noticed that Erwin was spending more time checking the propeller than we usually did and walked over to him. He pointed to the propeller and I immediately understood his concern. There was a hole on the blade that was approximately half an inch in diameter and was about one-third of the way away from the center. We realized it was a bullet hole from the plane's last combat mission.

"Bela, what do you think?" he asked.

"Since the hole is relatively small and close to the center of the propeller, we should be able to ferry it to Zeltweg, provid-ed we run the engine at the minimum rpm (rotations per minute) to keep the plane flying."

Erwin listened and after a brief pause said, "Let's do it!"

I climbed onto the wing, picked up the parachute from the cockpit, and placed it on the wing. Erwin reached for it and put it on slowly. I sensed he was worried and might want to reconsider.

With the parachute on his back, but still unbuckled, he turned to me. "Bela, I am concerned and my advice to you is to leave the plane here. Otherwise, we are asking for trouble."

After a short silence I replied, "You ferry the Weihe and I will fly the Me-109."

He agreed.

"Erwin, the only thing I would like you to do is to help me start the engine," I said. "Stay on the ground while I take off and as soon as I'm in the air, you ferry the Weihe to Zeltweg."

As I scrambled into the cockpit, I tucked my parachute under me and hooked up my safety belt, but let it lie loosely on my lap so I could operate comfortably in the tight cockpit. I ran through the drill: fuel selector open . . . throttle one-third open . . . prime three to four times . . . water cooling closed . . . propeller to automatic . . . master ignition on both . . .

All went smoothly. Erwin cranked the inertia starter. The whirring grind rose in pitch. "Free!" Erwin's cry signified the propeller was clear. I pulled the clutch and the prop began turning. The engine caught immediately, blurting into life and filling the air with its smooth thunder.

I checked the oil pressure, fuel pressure, ammeter, and cooling system, then each of the two magnetos in turn. The rpm held solidly. During the warm-up at low rpm, the engine ran smoothly with no noticeable vibration. At a higher rpm, the vibration increased.

Then, as I moved the throttle arm forward, the vibration increased exponentially. At full power, the vibration was excessive. As I pulled the throttle back, the vibration stopped. I realized that I'd have to make a decision quickly. I needed full power only for takeoff for a brief period of time. After that, I would be able to reduce the rpm to a level where the vibration was insignificant.

I opened the canopy. "I made the go decision and I am ready to taxi," I said to Erwin.

Taxiing across the field to the takeoff point, I gave Erwin a high sign, the pilot's silent thanks for a job well done. I made a final all-around check. My bird was ready to fly. Tightening my seat belts, I gunned the Me-109 into the soft wind and she went racing across the grass, lifting easily at my touch. She soared aloft as the first fingers of sunshine stroked the high clouds.

The landing gear came up and locked in with a gentle thud. I checked the flaps and moved the trim. As soon as the plane accelerated to the minimum flying speed, I moved the throttle back and ascended to three thousand feet. As the plane stabilized, I reassessed the situation and decided to go to the next checkpoint. So far, the plane was behaving well and everything was under control. The airspeed of the plane was fifty percent over the critical speed. The distance between Bosarkany and Graz is seventy-five miles and Zeltweg from Graz is fifty miles.

Climbing away from the field, I began turning west toward Graz.

Halfway between Bosarkany and Graz, the engine was still running smoothly.

I had almost reached Graz when, without changing the position of the throttle, the vibration increased significantly. At Graz, I again assessed the condition of the engine mounting and again gave myself a go. Shortly after passing Graz, the engine and mounting deteriorated further. I made a quick mental review of my choices: make an emergency landing at the Graz airport; turn the plane over, catapult the canopy, and bail out; or continue ferrying the plane toward my destination.

I decided on the third choice, reasoning that if I made it to Zeltweg, I would save an expensive airplane for the Hungarian

Air Force. Also, my friends, fellow officers, and pilots would give me a hero's welcome.

I had barely left Graz when the vibration became more forceful. I knew it would be impossible to reach my destination and my ability to return to Graz was questionable.

Fate made the decision for me when the engine suddenly tore away from the plane with a loud bang. I heard a hissing noise as the engine disappeared and the force and sound of the wind around the plane enveloped the remainder of the plane. I realized that bailout was no longer an option and I had to prepare for a crash landing. I tightened my seat belts and waited. The controls were ineffective; the plane was falling like a leaf toward the earth. It took a relatively long time—it seemed like an eternity to me—to descend from three thousand feet to five hundred feet.

I looked out through the canopy and saw a wooded area below. It gave me some comfort and encouragement to believe that I might survive the crash by landing on top of the trees. Also, because I was near a relatively large populated area, I hoped that someone on the ground was watching and would notify a rescue team to save my life. At approximately five hundred feet of altitude, I tightened my seat belt, bent my head forward, and said, "Help me God!" Then I lost consciousness.

When I came to, I found myself in a hospital bed with nurses and doctors scurrying around me. I saw a clock on the wall. It was 10 A.M. I touched my limbs and was glad to see that both legs and arms were still attached.

I had a complete physical examination. The examining physician concluded that my case was a miracle.

"I did not find any injury or serious bruises on your body. Headache is expected after the trauma you went through, and the dull pain in your stomach caused by the stick will disappear within a day or two. I prescribed pain medication and will discharge you from the hospital. You must have a thick skull to have survived an episode like this."

It was a mystery. *Who found me? Who took me to the hospital and how? What happened to the wreckage of the plane?*

While this was happening to me, Erwin, in Zeltweg, grew progressively more distraught. He and the other pilots maintained their vigil, pacing the floor for hours after all of the plane's fuel would have been exhausted. No one among the returning pilots knew what had happened to me.

Erwin's pacing grew more rapid. His visits to the squadron leaders office for news were more frequent. Each time he returned, the others read his face—still no word.

After my discharge from the hospital, I phoned a military unit in a nearby village. I told them about my accident and requested transportation to my squadron at Zeltweg. They sent a military vehicle with a driver for me.

The trip took less than an hour. As we approached Zeltweg, my heartbeat went up. I closed my eyes and saw in front of me my fellow officers and visualized a hero's welcome. The driver stopped in front of my squadron leader's office. I got out and walked into the office. He was sitting at his desk and looked up in disbelief when he saw me standing in front of him. He jumped up, embraced me, and held me tight in a bear hug for a long time.

"What happened?" he asked.

Briefly, I described my crash landing and miraculous escape.

"I am proud of you," he said. "You have never disappointed me since I have known you. But you could have been killed because of your hasty decision and act. You are too young to die! But, due to your cool-headed decision and actions after you lost the engine, you came out of this situation unharmed."

He sent his adjutant for Erwin and the other pilots. When they saw that I was still in one piece, they burst into jubilant shouts and broad smiles. Bear hugs went around the room. The gang was together again and I received the kind of reception I had imagined.

The next morning, I took the pig to the kitchen, showed it to the cooks, and they prepared a sumptuous dinner for us. The meal was delicious—something none of us had had in a long time.

★   ★   ★

Word was in the air that the end of the war was just around the corner. I expected that would mean no more flying in the foreseeable future and an end to my flying career.

A daring idea leaped into my head. I walked over to one of our Arado 96B planes parked in front of the hangar and after a brief "preflight," put on a parachute and climbed into the cockpit. I started the engine with the help of a soldier standing nearby.

After an engine warm-up, I taxied to the end of the runway and took off. At three thousand feet, I began my aerobatics show over the field. I buzzed and shook up the commandant of the airfield with snap rolls and Cuban 8s. The climax of my air show was a maneuver straight out of an old flying movie: I roared across the field upside down at thirty feet of altitude while the spectators watched bug-eyed with a mixture of wonder and terror.

The commandant and my squadron leader were waiting when I landed. I was bawled out and sentenced to room arrest.

I could have paid a much higher price for my air show. For that, and for not following the order of the airport traffic controller at my departure for Bosarkany five days earlier, I could have been court-marshaled. But I was spared because the war came to an end.

The next few days were uneventful until 8 May 1945 when P51 Mustangs strafed the airfield and destroyed several planes. I knew the end of the war was imminent. All rumors pointed toward the Americans occupying our airfield at Zeltweg and our becoming POWs of the American Army. But the Russians didn't always follow agreements and as Zeltweg was on the dividing line between the Russian and American zones, the probability of the Russians taking us prisoner was almost equal.

Prisoner of War

Since I didn't want to fall into Russian hands, I prepared a detailed plan to escape to Italy, taking my adjutant, Julius, and Aurel, my former art history teacher, with me. Julius had been my adjutant for several months and I had known Aurel for more than two years. We had grown close and I considered them to be members of my family. As such, I felt a moral responsibility for their well being and called them my "dependents." I planned to fly to Italy in the Focke-Wulf Weihe, the plane I had flown to take six pilots to Hungary a month earlier.

I was just about ready for take off in the early morning of 8 May 1945, one day before the war ended, when a military convoy arrived and took us to my squadron leader's office.

After listening to my reason for deserting the unit, my squadron leader told me he had reliable information that the American Army would occupy Zeltweg—not the Russians. He even showed me a map with dividing lines showing the Russian and American zones. It clearly indicated that according to the agreement between the Allied Forces, the American Army would occupy Zeltweg. The squadron leader asked me to stay with the squadron.

I said that I would stay.

At 4 A.M. on 9 May 1945, I was rudely awakened by strange noises in the corridor. There was running up and down the

hallway, loud voices, and unfamiliar movement. I heard someone speaking a language I didn't recognize. I knew it could not
be English, French, or German.

Suddenly, my door opened and in the semi-darkness, I saw
two soldiers with red stars on their uniforms. I realized immediately that they were soldiers of the Soviet Army. We had
become prisoners of war of the Soviet Union—not the
American forces as we had hoped for.

Seeing the Red Army soldiers, I felt misled by my superiors and helpless. Dark pictures of what the future held for me
went through my mind. I saw myself in one of the infamous
Soviet prison camps where I might die of hunger and my loved
ones would never find out what happened to me. The best years
of my youth would be taken from me by the Soviets unless I
escaped. My mind wandered from images of a Soviet POW
camp to my loved ones whom I might not see for many years—
if ever. I even considered committing suicide.

A translator ordering us to surrender our rifles, pistols,
grenades, or explosives interrupted my thoughts. The translator
reported that if a pistol was found in anyone's possession, he
would be shot on the spot.

From then on, events unfolded at a fast pace. The Soviet
officer informed us through the translator that he would make
an announcement outside the building in ten minutes. We
waited anxiously. In front of the building, there was a hastily
assembled platform where the officer waited for us with the
translator at his side.

He announced that we were now prisoners of war of the
Soviet Union for an undetermined length of time. We would
be treated according to the Geneva Accord that dealt with the
treatment of POWs. He outlined the plan for the next few days.
We would go to a place where a train would be waiting to take
us to the Soviet Union. He gave us no further information

except that no transportation would be provided. We would have to make the journey on foot. We would leave at 6 A.M.

Everybody could take as much of their belongings as they were able to carry. Since the plan was to leave at 6 A.M., he wanted us to assemble in front of the building ten minutes before that hour.

Julius, Aurel, and I wanted to stay together. Julius had been a violin player in civilian life, an honest, dependable, and loyal man. Aurel was a well-regarded educator with a wealth of knowledge. We had met in Zeltweg two weeks earlier. While I was letting off steam during a stroll in the field at the end of the day, I had noticed a bedraggled group of men marching toward our barracks. They wore stripped-down military uniforms and I realized that they were part of a so-called "working brigade"—not fit for military service, but bound by law to serve the homeland in some capacity.

As I looked at the sea of faces, one at the very end caught my attention. He was around thirty years old. He was short, had bushy hair, sunken eyes, and was very frail—a pitiful sight. Could this man be my former art history teacher Aurel Bodo? I was stunned to realize that I knew the man. His students considered him rather strict and mean, and we had often cooked up childish pranks to annoy him.

Once, before a school dance held in our drafting room where we had to make room for the dance floor, we piled up the long benches in front of his office knowing he was inside and couldn't open the door to leave. Much later, he figured out who the pranksters were, but he didn't punish us.

These were the memories flashing through my mind as I watched this pitiful figure march by me. We caught sight of each other simultaneously and recognition flashed in his face. We both couldn't believe we were meeting again under these circumstances. That same night, I made arrangements for him to be transferred to my squadron and put him under my protective wing.

Since I now had two dependents, I would not escape unless they could come with me. But this was impossible because Aurel was in poor health and physically weak. I would accept whatever God had in store for me.

At 5:50 A.M., we assembled in front of the building. I looked around and estimated the size of the group to be over two thousand, mostly young soldiers. But there were men in their fifties as well, and several women among them, many pregnant. Some of the POWs carried a backpack and two large packages in their hands. Those were abandoned later when the going got real rough. By my estimation, there was about one Soviet guard for every fifty POWs. The guard in charge had us form a line five abreast. They used five because it made the counting easy and provided a formation that was easy to control.

At 6 A.M. sharp, the long line began to move forward. Guards were on both sides, evenly distributed. Some were on horseback covering the long line from front to back. There were also two or three horse-drawn carts to carry those who were unable to walk.

In a short time, we realized that Aurel would not be able to continue on foot and we put him on a cart. Julius and I walked behind his cart, which also carried pregnant women.

The guards constantly called us derogatory names such as "fascists" or "Fritz." They were ready to shoot anyone who stepped out of the line. In general, the conditions were inhumane. When prisoners, male or female, had to relieve themselves, they had to ask for permission. As they stepped aside, a guard stood over them until they finished, which was humiliating and degrading.

Our daily meal consisted of 250 grams of bread and one small, salted dry fish. The lack of drinking water was a serious problem. The warm weather, the salty fish, and the twelve-hour daily march dehydrated our bodies to the point of physical pain and suffering. If we were lucky, we found a natural source of water and filled our stomachs, but we didn't have canteens to fill and carry with us.

In late afternoon, we would stop. We spread out on the ground whatever we had—a coat or a blanket—and slept until morning. Then we continued our trek. The nights were chilly. Without sufficient cover, we were uncomfortable.

On the second day, we crossed the river Mur on a bridge near Graz. On a busy highway, we continued marching east. We knew that we were just a couple of miles north of Graz, heading toward the Hungarian border, probably to Szombathely. If that was our final destination, our journey would be over in less than two days. We were lucky that it didn't rain during our trek. Since there was no shelter, rain could have made our miserable situation even worse.

On the second day, in the Alps just before we reached Graz, we walked through a battlefield. Nature's greenery was sprouting amid the many dead bodies that had been there for several days. They were starting to decompose, filling the air with the foul smell of death. Even today, that sad scene and the smell come back to haunt me when I relive those days.

By the end of the second day, we had covered approximately fifty miles.

When we awakened on the third day, shivering, hungry, and thirsty, we were near the limit of what a human being can endure. But the third day was several times more difficult than the previous two. The horse-drawn carts were full of the sick and weak whose bodies had given out and were unable to walk with the group. We did not make our planned distance that day.

Waking up on the fourth day with the knowledge that our final destination was within reach gave us enough stamina to continue our journey to the end. When the guards saw our suffering, they told us as encouragement that our final destination was Szombathely. So the ragged, pitiful army marched painfully on.

In early afternoon on the fourth day, we arrived at Szombathely. The scene before us gave us no comfort. There was a "camp," which consisted of only a barbed wire fence, a gate, four observation towers, and many guards. There was no shelter inside the fence.

When we arrived, the guards opened the gate and herded us in like cattle at a slaughterhouse. At that point, our only hope was that our stay there would be short. Meanwhile, Aurel was nearing the end. He could hardly get up and had lost his desire to live.

After spending a day and two nights out in the open, four uniformed Soviet officials appeared in the camp. They placed a table next to the gate, spread out their papers, and started processing the POWs.

The first step was a medical examination. For that we had to undress. The medical examiner, a female Russian soldier, sorted the POWs into two categories based on the amount of fat on their buttocks. Julius and I were in category one. Aurel was included in category two, but after some maneuvering, we succeeded in moving him into our group.

The second step of processing took place at the table. Three POWs were processed simultaneously. This was the first time that anyone asked our name, date of birth, rank, and the military unit we belonged to. They told us that we were in the first group and would be transported to an undisclosed location in the Soviet Union.

"You will love being there. You will receive good treatment and officers will not have to work. After a couple of months, you will be sent home, but you can apply for Russian residency, and if they grant it, you can stay," the NKVD commandant of the POW camp told us. What a glorious prospect!

After processing, everybody felt relieved and looked forward to the "pleasant" experience in the Soviet Union, although the generous offer to remain in Russia did not appeal to us in the slightest.

Several trucks arrived the next day and parked in front of the entrance gate. An officer read a long list of names. Those whose names were called boarded the truck. The trucks, filled with POWs, headed to the railroad station only five miles away. Julius, Aurel, and I stayed together. At the rail station, the POWs were put onto cattle cars—boxcars that were fitted with a wooden structure midway at each end to make two levels and increase the transport capability from twenty-four to forty-eight. The middle of the boxcar was left empty and used as a toilet. The toilet was a simple contraption—a cone shaped structure made out of sheet metal mounted over a hole in the floor.

We were loaded into the first car. Julius, Aurel, and I took the first three places on the bottom. In no time, all the POWs were on board and the train was ready to leave before noon. Since European railroad cars had a different wheelbase than Russian ones, we realized that we would have to change trains at the border.

The train took us over the Carpathian Mountains to Focsani, Rumania. The trip to Focsani took twenty-four hours. The heat in the boxcar was unbearable and hunger and thirst made us suffer so much that we felt that we couldn't tolerate it any longer.

By now, Aurel was ill with dysentery. He was constantly in need of the toilet, and he had a high fever. Finally, we arrived at Focsani and were housed in burnt-out military barracks. Aurel was unable to walk, and we had to carry him to his place in the barracks. Everyone was suffering from thirst and hunger. No food was served for almost two days.

When we finally received our meal— soup, bread and salted, dry fish—I tried to feed Aurel. He couldn't eat. He had lost his strength to the point where he was unable to speak. As his head rested on my lap, I looked down on his face—the face that I remembered so well from my school days. He was a respected teacher, intelligent, knowledgeable, and always strict, but fair. Now, it was a face ravaged by dysentery, hollowed by lack of nourishment, the eyes empty of expression.

I desperately wanted to convey my feelings for him, some encouragement, but he was beyond reach. Suddenly, the noble head fell back as his soul and spirit left his wasted body. I couldn't move my eyes from his face for the longest time and it became etched in my mind forever.

Then, Julius and I tenderly carried him to the gate where the guard directed us to a pile of corpses and told us to place Aurel there. Gently, we lowered his wasted body on top of the pile. Bending my head, I said a short, silent prayer, gently touched his face, and sent him on his final journey. I hoped he would be going to a better place.

Two days later, the Russian wide-track train arrived and that same day, we were transferred onto it. It left immediately. Nobody knew the destination. Even knowing the direction, which was east, didn't give us a clue.

This trip by train was just as inhumane as our previous one. Heat, smell, hunger, and thirst characterized our journey. Three days later, we arrived at Saratov, a large industrial city on the river Volga.

The POWs were transported to the camp on trucks. We were lined up five abreast in front of the entrance gate. A guard held papers while the others counted us and compared their count with the official loading document. After a brief wait, the officer on duty came out from the entrance booth, reviewed the papers, recounted us, and when he was satisfied, he took the list and the POWs were called out by name. Whoever was called had to enter the fenced-in yard and line up five abreast. There were more than one thousand arriving POWs.

Upon entering the camp, I did a quick survey of my surroundings. There were twenty barracks, each with a capacity of two hundred POWs. The total capacity of the camp was over four thousand. There was a large building complex in the center that contained a dining hall, a kitchen, and a bakery.

The daily capacity of the bakery was over six thousand pounds of bread. At full capacity, the camp required nearly five thousand pounds of bread. As we found out later, the bread was a POW's most important source of nutrition. A working POW who fulfilled the normal quota received over four hundred grams of bread. Those who exceeded their norm received a larger portion. For example, a POW who exceeded the norm by five percent was entitled to six hundred grams. On the other hand, a non-working or under-performing POW received a little over two hundred grams.

There was a small building nearby that was used as a hospital. The number of beds in the hospital ranged from eighty to one hundred. Most of the time, the hospital was half full. The senior staff was a *feltcher* whose medical training was less than that of a medical doctor, but more than that of a nurse. He examined those who had a medical problem and dispensed medication. Only the very ill were admitted to the hospital and only for a short time.

The other building nearby housed the POW commandant, the *narjadchik*, and a clerk. The commandant was responsible for managing the internal affairs of the camp. In the morning, he organized groups according to their work projects. The commandant was also the communication link between the NKVD commanding officer and the POWs. The narjadchik made contracts with civilian officials for various projects and verified that the number of POWs assigned to the projects met the stipulation in the agreement.

One important structure was the sanitation building, close to the hospital in the center of the camp. This complex contained several rooms. There was a room on the right side where the POWs undressed. It had a window into the high-temperature disinfecting furnace. Since lice infestation was a serious problem, the POWs' clothing was disinfected there once a month. This room opened into a large bathroom containing twenty benches. On each bench, there were four wooden containers, each with a capacity to hold ten gallons of water. Usually, an attendant filled the containers with a hose two or three times during a bath. Prisoners received a small piece of soap when they entered the bathroom.

From there, the POWs stepped into a small corridor where they picked up their disinfected clothes from the floor. Everybody had to search for his own. This process was not very sanitary. The last room in that complex was a barbershop where the POWs were shaved.

The last structure, a roof without sidewalls, was an outdoor latrine. It consisted of an open pit and a piece of lumber for a seat. There was no back support. POWs learned very fast to be careful when they used the latrine or they could easily end up at the bottom of the pit. This happened on several occasions.

A barbed-wire fence enclosed the camp. A guard tower, manned twenty-four hours a day, filled each corner. The duty officer, who was responsible for controlling the incoming and outgoing traffic, guarded the entrance booth.

When all the POWs were inside, the officer read out the barracks assignments and we were dismissed. Everyone went to his assigned barracks.

There were two levels of bunks inside. Julius and I occupied two places side by side on the lower level. We had hardly settled in when an official came in to tell us that our first meal would be served in the dining hall in a few minutes. We walked over, lined up, and received our late dinner, which consisted of soup, porridge, and a dried, salty fish. Since we hadn't received bread that day, our daily bread portion was distributed with dinner. Being hungry, the POWs made the food disappear in no time.

After dinner, we went back to our barracks. Shortly after, the commandant came in and assigned the newly arrived POWs to brigades and named one person as a brigadier. The size of an average brigade was fifteen.

When the administrative phase of our processing was completed, we were free to walk around and meet the POWs who had arrived earlier. We learned from them that the camp was a distribution center. From there, new arrivals were usually sent to various locations according to work requirements. In most cases, the work places were at distant locations and the POWs were moved to smaller camps. The employers were factories, *kolkhoz* (community-operated farms) construction, and road building companies that submitted labor-force requirements to the distribution center. A subcontracting organization provided living quarters, guarded by military personnel, and meals.

Most of the POWs already in the camp were Germans who had fallen into the hands of the Soviet Army a couple of years earlier. Some were in their third or fourth year as POWs. They gave us useful information and we learned that the worst possible work assignment was construction of the Moscow-Saratov gas line.

They also told us about living conditions in POW camps. Since the end of the war, there had been some improvement in the treatment of POWs. Before, civilians would throw stones at the POWs and call them "fascists." The daily meal was so minimal that many POWs died—most of them just couldn't take it any longer and gave up.

The next day was sanitation day. Everyone had to go through the bath complex where their clothes were disinfected and they had a bath and a shave. Imagine the satisfaction we got from our first bath and shave in a month.

Our comfort and satisfaction didn't last long. The next day, my brigade was called out. We were loaded onto a truck and turned over to a guard who counted us and signed a piece of paper acknowledging that he was taking over guarding the indicated number of POWs. We traveled on a bumpy dirt road for approximately fifty miles and stopped in front of a smaller camp that had the capacity for three to four hundred prisoners.

There were twenty tents inside the fence, each capable of providing shelter for twenty POWs. They were made out of burlap and waterproofed with bitumen. In theory, it was a sound solution to waterproof the tents in this manner. But in cold weather, the bitumen became brittle and cracked. Therefore, when it rained outside, it also rained inside. They spread hay on the ground to serve as our mattresses. It was okay in good weather, but on rainy days, it soaked up the water and the POWs had to spend the night on sodden hay.

The only other buildings were an open latrine, a small booth at the entrance gate, and four guard towers, one at each corner of the camp. There was no kitchen, sanitation building, or hospital. If someone became ill, he had to be transported back to the main camp.

The next morning, a civilian supervisor appeared and told us our job was to dig a six-foot deep and three-foot wide trench for the Moscow-Saratov gas line. Also, the supervisor told us our daily norm. It was high and impossible to meet every day. Four of us formed a team: Julius; Arpad, a physical education teacher; Steve, a lieutenant in the Hungarian Army; and I.

On the first day, we fulfilled our norm, but never again. We lost weight rapidly and became physically unfit. Later, they reduced our norm, but we were still unable to meet it.

Our daily drinking water was delivered in a large tank every day at 11 A.M. It was usually enough, but if not, we had to wait until the next delivery. We worked on the gas-line project until September when we were transferred to the main camp for the winter to wait for our next work assignment.

In September, we were sent to a kolkhoz for the potato harvest. Our first activity as we arrived in the morning was to gather firewood and start a fire. The fire served two purposes—first, to warm our hands in the chilly fall weather, and second, to bake potatoes that supplemented our daily food ration.

We worked from early morning until noon when we stopped for a forty-five-minute break. During our break, the kolkhoz served lunch. Lunch usually consisted of soup, porridge, or a potato and a small piece of meat. After the break, we returned to harvesting. At 5 P.M., our workday ended. We would put the fire out and stuff our pockets with the hot potatoes that warmed our hands on our march back to the camp. There we shared our "bounty" with friends who didn't have access to extra food to supplement the meager daily ration. After a short time at the kolkhoz, our physical condition rapidly improved. Our work there lasted until late October.

During our work assignment at the kolkhoz, we had a guard, Mohamed, who was a descendant of a Tatar family. The ancestral settlement of his family had been in the vicinity of the river Volga near Saratov for many centuries.

During Stalin's reign, the family was deported to Siberia. He believed in God and deep in his soul was anticommunist.

Mohamed was the friendliest guard and sympathized with the POWs. He would come to me often in the morning and say, "*Lotchik* (pilot), I am going to see my girlfriend in the kolkhoz. I am leaving my rifle here. Please keep an eye on the group until I come back." He would put his rifle down and leave. His trust in me was touching. He always brought food for us when he returned.

Our next assignment was in a furniture factory. We worked as laborers under the supervision of Russian civilians with whom we developed a friendly relationship. Their pay depended on their output, and we were instrumental in it. To compensate us for this, they regularly brought us food, vodka, and other goodies. On their paydays, they gave us money. We usually asked them to bring us food instead of money. This job lasted until May when we were returned to the gas-line work assignment.

One day, a rumor went around that we would be repatriated. But we soon learned the chilling truth that the rumor wasn't true.

Christmas of 1945 was a sad one. It reminded us of our loved ones back home whom we had not seen or heard from for almost a year. As the Russian front in Hungary was moving through my hometown, I didn't know whether my family was alive or if any of them had died during the house-to-house fighting.

The year of 1946 went by fast. Good friends and camaraderie helped us survive. The summer of 1946 was a carbon copy of that of 1945. The constant hunger, thirst, unsanitary conditions, the high norm, and isolation made our lives miserable.

But when our morale was at the lowest, help was always there in some form. Even though we were far away from our loved ones, there was a higher power looking out for us.

In October 1946, we were handed postcards and told that we would be allowed to send two cards to relatives. We were allowed to write only, "We are in good health and being treated well." Replies arrived just before Christmas of 1946 and I found out that my loved ones were alive and in good health.

Christmas of 1946 was just as sad as the previous year. A Catholic priest in our barracks delivered the Christmas Eve service for us. The barracks was filled and the sound of "Stille Nacht" could be heard far away. That Christmas Eve gave us the strength for the coming months. It was one of the most touching and memorable Christmases of my life.

During the spring of 1947, my brigade was sent to the railroad station to unload railroad cars. We liked the job because a good portion of the cargo consisted of food items such as sugar, fish, dried fruit, potatoes, and corn. During the unloading process, we found ways to damage the containers and fill our pockets with whatever we unloaded.

One day at the station, a fellow POW came to me with a dish in his hands, filled with a liquid that smelled like vodka. He had found a tank car filled with the vodka-like liquid, filled his dish, and come to share it with me.

I must have passed out after sampling the "vodka." When I came to, I was lying in a hospital bed. I could hardly breathe and my vision was almost gone. I found out that my fellow POW died two days after we consumed the liquid we thought was vodka. It turned out to be methyl alcohol, which ties down the oxygen content of the blood and can cause blindness or even death from oxygen starvation. It took me a long time to fully recover.

About this time, rumors spread again that the POWs would be repatriated. We wished it to be true, but dared not believe it. Was our freedom finally beckoning? That spring, we worked on various projects such as the furniture factory, a community farm, and some other odd jobs.

One day, the camp commandant came in with a list in his hand. He read the list and told us that those whose names were read should go immediately to the dining hall where they would get further instructions. Since our team of four—Julius, Arpad, Steve, and I—were on the list, we walked over together. At a table, an officer, with the help of a clerk, checked our identities. When they were satisfied, they ordered us to pick up our new clothes, which included a pair of shoes.

A couple of days later, we were put on a train headed west. We dared not believe that we were really on our way home to our beautiful country.

This time, we traveled in great "comfort" since only twenty-four POWs were loaded into each boxcar. During the journey, the doors were left open. In Focsani, we changed trains and we were handed over to the Hungarian authorities. Elation overwhelmed us when, two days later, we were in Budapest again . . . in our beloved, beautiful, romantic capitol city through which the majestic blue Danube flows. Our hearts filled with joy and memories of our youthful, carefree times there. We were quickly issued our ID cards and soon, I was on my way to my hometown, Papa. I arrived there on 21 July 1947.

Short Period of Freedom

As the train pulled into the station in Papa, I was still in a daze. I thought, *Am I really free? Home? Going to see my family and friends?* Looking out the window, searching for any familiar face, I wondered who would be the first person I would recognize after two and a half years in POW camps.

The train stopped and I got off. Since I didn't have any luggage to carry, it was easy for me to lightheartedly hop off the train. I walked around the platform two or three times, but there was nobody there I knew. I started to walk home. My mother's apartment was only a ten-minute walk from the railroad station. I stopped several times to collect myself before I got there. When I gathered enough courage, I knocked on the door and waited. My heartbeat and blood pressure went up.

The door opened and there was my mother looking at me in awe and disbelief. We stood facing each other, speechless, with tears in our eyes. The last time I had seen her, she had brown hair. Now it was pure white.

After a short while, she let the first words out. "Bela, is it really you? Are you still alive?" Then we embraced for a long time. I kissed her hands and cheeks and we walked into her apartment as I clutched her hands.

Inside, happy and excited, she didn't know what to shower me with—food or drinks—but was spontaneous and generous with her embraces and kisses. She held me for a long time and wouldn't let me go. Finally, pulling herself together, she brought in food from the kitchen. It was a rather meager offering as food wasn't plentiful, but her heart was in it and that's what really mattered.

We sat down and talked for a long time. She didn't have a phone, but was eager to shout out to the whole town, to family and friends, that her son was home again. So we set out on foot and knocked on doors, stopped friends and neighbors on the street, and passed on the wonderful news.

Later, my sister and brother came home and there was another tearful reunion. They joined us in catching up on the previous two years. My mother's neighbor also came over with a bottle of wine. We stayed up past midnight exchanging stories. I was happy to see everyone well and healthy, and they were delighted at having me back home. They had buried me several times in the past two years, but the hope that I might still be alive kept them looking forward to the moment that had just become reality.

That night, I had a good night's rest in a real bed. What a wonderful feeling—clean sheets, pillows, and a comfortable bed! No early morning reveille. But I did get up fairly early the next morning. I shaved, took a bath—unknown luxuries in the POW camps, but normal daily routines outside—then joined my siblings and my mother for breakfast.

When we were finished with this enjoyable interlude, I had to shake myself back to reality and attend to a list of urgent matters—arranged in priority order. I needed a physical examination, dental work, new clothes, and to plans for my future. It was a difficult task because my total assets were only the clothes that I traveled in from Russia. I had to rely on my family for anything I needed or wanted.

I also realized that in order to succeed, I needed a college education. My dream was to study electrical engineering at the technical university in Budapest.

On the train on my way home, I had heard from other passengers that it was difficult to be accepted into the engineering program. You had to pass an entrance exam with high scores, and the entrance exams were already in progress.

I took a train to Budapest to find out the details. On the following day, I rushed to the university and learned that there were only a couple of days remaining to take the entrance exam.

Upon hearing about my hardships while a POW, the school officials gave me special treatment. They scheduled my exam for the next day. This meant that I had to take it without preparation. I went for it. Then I spent the next week in suspense. Finally, the letter of acceptance was in my hands. They even gave credits for subjects I had taken at the Air Force Academy. What a glorious moment! I could look into the future with hope. I felt sure that I would be able to reach for and achieve my goals.

The first item on my agenda was to find a room where I could stay during the school year. My Aunt Jolan invited me to live with her family until my financial situation allowed me to rent my own place. Her generosity touched me deeply. Her apartment was small and crowded already with her two children and a helper. Still, without hesitation, she took me in. With tears in my eyes, I hugged and thanked her. Then, I returned to Papa.

At home, my dear old dentist friend took care of my teeth, which were in poor shape. This was his present to me, free of charge. My mother, with money she had saved, bought me a suit, shirts, and shoes and gave me the money that was left over. She was overjoyed to be able to do this for me, and I felt that I had to compensate her for all that she had showered on me. She had even put aside money for daily expenses and education while I studied in Budapest.

For the next two weeks, I worked unloading cargo at the railroad station. The pay was good and I put away every penny I earned. Those precious days flew by too swiftly, though, and it was time for me to say good-bye to my family and friends. I left for Budapest at the beginning of September and settled in with Aunt Jolan and her family, looking forward to classes that started the second week of September. It seemed that normalcy had returned in my life. At the university, I met several of my classmates from the Air Force Academy; life appeared to be like old times.

Good-bye My Action Filled Past . . .
Welcome to the Unknown . . .

As I languished in my cell in Lubyanka, it required a great deal of inner strength to budget the memories of my past so that they would last. With care, I got through my first year without running out of this mental nourishment.

Physical exercise helped as well. I calculated that just in the first year, I walked more than four thousand miles from one corner of my cell to the other. The walking and recollections of my past were enough to maintain proper balance and preserve my physical health and sanity, despite a meager diet.

Usually, I planned out my day early in the morning while lying on my cot. I would recall a mathematical or physical science problem from my school days and work on it until I found the solution.

Dreaming of the future, I would continue my engineering education after returning home from "Red Hell." This would lead to a Ph.D. in electrical engineering. As a hobby, I would pursue soaring and flying.

Aside from recalling my past, I delved often into history, books, and movies, imagining battles, warriors, and forbidden loves far from my cell and the pain I suffered there. I knew I had to guard carefully against allowing my fantasies to become all-consuming, leaving me permanently in a place in my mind from where I would be unable to return.

During my first year, I learned to value paper and pencil— simple items I had taken for granted. One morning when I woke up, a calculus problem involving differential equations came to mind, one that I had wrestled with at a colloquium in December 1947. It was difficult to work out the solution without paper and pencil, so I resolved to somehow obtain them. I didn't realize just how big a task that would be.

I made obtaining a pencil and paper my top priority. Finally, the opportunity arose to implement my plan. There was a German-speaking guard who was friendly, especially when he found out that I was a pilot during World War II. One morning when I carried out the toilet vessel, he engaged me in a friendly conversation.

His manner indicated that he could be my means of obtaining paper and pencil. But would he be willing to help me? This could put him in a dangerous situation with his superiors if they found out. But for me, having paper and pencil could mean my very survival, so I had to overcome my hesitation and ask. To my great relief, he promised to bring the items as long as I didn't tell anyone. And the following morning, I became the happy owner of two sheets of paper and a pencil. What joy! Those simple tools made it possible to keep my mind busy for weeks. They were my salvation.

The end of my second year in solitary confinement was approaching. Only the ten-minute walks, baths, and shaves provided breaks in the monotony and despair. During the walks, I saw my friends, which brightened my otherwise grim existence. We would exchange information when an understanding guard looked the other way. Still, this was a very meager consolation.

At the end of the second year, I could no longer tolerate the solitary confinement. The days were monotonous. Today was the same as yesterday and tomorrow and the days following would be the same. I lost track of time. Only the days when we walked, took a bath, and shaved at regularly scheduled intervals gave a fixed point in our mental calendars. I became desperate. The past couldn't sustain my interest any longer. It seemed empty. Turning to the future and dreaming about freedom was futile. I had lost faith in the future and didn't believe I would ever be a free man again. Twenty-five years in prison and labor camp meant an eternity for me. My sentence would be completed in 1973—another twenty-three years away. I knew I should be concentrating on maintaining my physical and mental health, but that desire was fading.

One day, the friendly guard reminded me that it was Christmas. The majority of Russians celebrated Orthodox Christmas two weeks after Roman Catholics. This guard was a believer and for him, Christmas was an important day. He didn't dare go to church, but on 7 January, he celebrated Christmas behind closed doors.

Christmas Eve and Christmas Day were sad. They only reminded me of my stark present. My belief that I would ever be free again was growing fainter.

Then, in search of new mental nourishment and salvation, I turned to the Almighty who created the universe and controls and directs our lives. There comes a time in every man's life when he learns to pray. For me, that moment came shortly after New Year's Day 1951.

Upon awakening one morning, the mental pain had become so excruciating that I just gave up. After breakfast, I began my daily walk, but my mind was empty. I didn't want to go on living, but didn't know how to end my unbearable situation. I was desperate.

Suddenly, I found myself praying, saying the same prayer I'd said every day at noon in high school for eight years. Back then, praying hadn't had any meaning to me—it was only a collection of routine words, and nothing penetrated in my mind. Now, so many years later, those same words of prayer suddenly became meaningful and gave me comfort.

It was noon when my peaceful meditation was interrupted by the guard distributing our meals. That afternoon, I resumed my walk. My desperate mental condition eased with every step.

For the next six months, I found new stimulation for my mind—first by praying, then by meditating and analyzing the vast universe. By doing this, I calculated that the age of the universe is fourteen billion years. And a human life—whether one day or a hundred years—compared to the universe, is insignificant. On a grand scale that extends from zero on the left to fourteen billion on the right, our life span is near zero. In practical terms, it means that if I died today or one hundred years from today, it would make no difference. This thought gave me only temporary comfort and consolation.

Then I spent considerable time on concepts such as "eternity." I knew from my calculus that in terms of mathematics, it approaches infinity. But what did it mean in practical terms? If the beginning of the universe was fourteen billion years ago, then there must be a "point zero" when the measuring of time began. The question arose: what existed before "zero time?" This and similar thoughts were enough to keep my mind busy for only a short time. Then my spirits started sinking again.

I must have reached the deepest point of the darkest pit. Several times during my walk, I stopped, knelt down, and prayed. But it was only a temporary help and after a short while, desperation returned with a vengeance. Veins throbbed on the side of my head and I expected them to burst any moment.

I knew something had to happen or I would lose my mind. The time had arrived to make a plan and implement it to end this unbearable condition. The only question was how?

After making and reviewing a list of means available, I found the answer—suicide. I made a detailed plan to hang myself. I would need a piece of rope strong enough to hold my body. I would also need time. It would have to be long enough between the guards' routine checks through the peephole. According to my earlier observations, this would be a twenty- to twenty-five-minute span. Making these detailed plans gave me a strange sensation of release from the intense pressure on my body and mind.

Every two weeks when we took a bath, we were handed towels made of a coarse material. At the next bath, sometime in

mid 1951, I decided that it would be easy to pull out two
strings from the coarse towel at every bath. Nobody would
notice and I would have collected enough strings over twenty-
six weeks to make a rope of fifty-two strings, strong enough to
hold my body. The end of twenty-six weeks would be the end
of December, and I would have my rope.

I again observed the pattern the guards used to check on
inmates in their cells. It seemed that the longest time between
two observations was right after breakfast was handed into the
cells. To estimate the time between the guard's checks through
the peephole, I counted how many times I paced back and
forth in the cell. After several days' observation, I concluded that
my estimate was correct; the longest time available was right
after my morning meal.

Meanwhile, I had my rope ready and it was strong enough
to hold my body. When I finished working on the rope that day,
I carefully hid it in the mattress. There was little chance of the
guards finding it there during a search of the cell.

The only thing left was to execute the plan. On the chosen
day, I prayed on my cot and asked the Almighty to give me
enough strength to go through with it. Reveille was at the usual
time. I took the rope from the hiding place and began to proceed according to my plan.

Pressure was building in my head. The veins on both sides
were ready to burst. It felt like a race between committing suicide and losing my mind, and I realized that I had very little
time left to follow through with my plan.

The morning meal arrived on time. I took it, but didn't
eat. The "count-down" had started. There were only twenty-
five minutes left. The first step was to fasten the rope to the
steel rod in front of the cutout for the light. In order to reach
the rod, I needed something to stand on. The toilet vessel was
perfect for this.

The instant I tied the rope to the rod, the door opened and a guard stood there. He told me to gather my belongings and led me out of the cell into the corridor. I couldn't fully understand then, or for some time, what was happening. I wondered, *Am I dreaming? Are these long and lonely months over? Am I really seeing my ten friends lined up in the corridor?* This was an unbelievable last second intervention by the highest Authority and for a special reason in the future, my life was given back to me.

I struggled to speak to my friends, but no sound came from my mouth. During the three years in solitary confinement in Lubyanka, I had had no one to talk to and my vocal cords deteriorated to the point that I lost my voice and had to relearn speaking.

My parents.

My siblings.

Primary trainer – "Vocsok," 1941. Author, second from left.

Winter flying in "Vocsok," 1941. Author is in the cockpit.

"Zogling" with Joco in the cockpit in 1939.

"Pilis the Wonderbird" in museum in Hungary.

"Pilis" in aerotow, 1942.

Primary training, Vat, 1943.

Our trainer, Bucker Jungman, Vat, 1943.

The author at the Air Force Academy, 1943.

The plane used for escape on December 25, 1944.

The place of takeoff at Budapest.

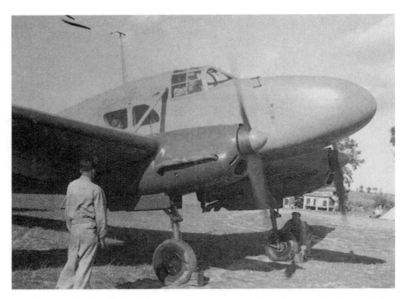

Focke-Wulf 58. In this plane the author flew six pilots to Szombathely to ferry the planes left behind to Austria in April, 1944.

Arado 96 with the author climbing into cockpit to perform the memorable airshow on May 8, 1944, one year before WWII ended.

Author before the "red hell" . . .

. . . and afterward, in November 1956.

Author with Joco in the Gulag, 1953.

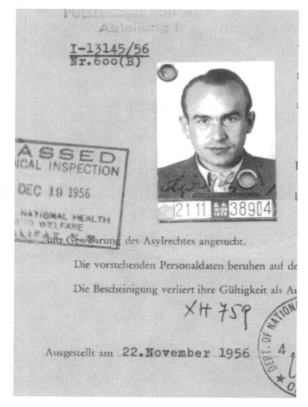

Austrian passport issued at the time of escape in November, 1956.

The author then . . .

. . . and sixty-one years later.

6

Life and Death in the Gulag
(1951–1955)

Courage is of two kinds: first, physical courage, or courage in the presence of danger to the person; and next, moral courage, or courage before responsibility, whether it be before the judgment seat of external authority, or of the inner power, the conscience.

Karl von Clausewitz

Evolution of the Gulag

In the first month after the October Revolution of 1917, Lenin was already demanding "the most draconian measures to tighten up discipline." In December, he suggested the following assortment of punishments: "Confiscation of property . . . confinement in prison, dispatch to the front, and forced labor for all that disobey the existing law." Thus, the idea of *gulag* (forced labor) had been advanced as early as the first month after the October Revolution.

According to estimates, internal repression cost the Soviet Union from the October Revolution up to 1959 a total of sixty-six million lives.

However, the trouble was that the first Soviet government was a coalition. A portion of the Peoples Commissariats had to be allotted to the left's Socialist Revolutionaries including the People's Commissariat of Justice, which fell under its auspices. Guided by a *bourgeois* concept of freedom, this People's

Commissariat of Justice brought the penal system to the verge of collapse. Sentences were too light and made hardly any use of the "progressive principle" of forced labor.

In February 1918, Lenin, the chairman of the Council of People's Commissars, demanded that the number of places of imprisonment be increased and the repression of criminals be intensified. He ordered that the sentence for bribery be not less than ten years in prison and ten years of forced labor—a total of twenty years.

The use of forced labor turned out to be very long-lived—even fifty years later, it was still popular.

The Central Penal Department of the People's Commissariat of Justice, which was created in May 1918, immediately began sending prisoners to work ("begin to organize productive labor"). But the legislation had been proclaimed only on 23 July 1918—in "Temporary Instructions on deprivation of freedom."

"Those deprived of freedom, who are capable of labor, must be recruited for physical work on a compulsory basis." It can be argued that the gulag was born from this particular instruction nine months after the October Revolution. The Corrective Labor Code defines three types of camps:

- Factory and agricultural colonies where "people deprived of freedom" were trained and disciplined.
- Camps for mass work that included those in "distant regions" for "class dangerous elements" requiring "a more severe regime."
- Punitive camps for the strict isolation of those "previously detained in other colonies and showing persistent insubordination."

The first category was mainly for very minor offenses against factory discipline and petty thievery. The second category was used for everyone sentenced under Article 58 or by the Special Board, which was established by law in 1934.

Court procedures were at best formalities, but at least the Supreme Court required the presence of an accused at trial. But comparatively few cases were dealt with by court. Rather, it was the Special Board that heard most cases. Special Board sentences were originally limited to five years, but this was abolished or ignored shortly after its establishment and sentences increased to eight or ten years.

While a man who served out his term imposed by a court was released, someone sentenced by the board was simply re-sentenced to further incarceration when his sentence ended. The formalities were completed in Moscow and a local representative of the NKVD announced a new sentence to the accused in camp.

The labor camp was one of the pillars of Stalin's entire system. Concealment of its nature from the West was one of his most extraordinary triumphs.

A detailed list of camp groups covering thirty-five clusters was drawn up as early as 1937. (A cluster usually included about 200 camps of roughly 1,200 inmates each). At Stalin's death, the number of detained prisoners was at its peak, well over twenty-eight million.

The members of the "Apponyi group" composed of "class dangerous elements" were sent to the Northeast above the Arctic Circle, to Inta/Vorkuta—class two camps.

*   *   *

Another sad but important period of my life had ended and the next one, the gulag years, was beginning.

I collected my belongings, which consisted of what little was left of my clothes, and half of Joco's blanket. Secretly, I had my two-inch long pencil and one sheet of paper. And I had my rope, which I used as a belt to tie together the front loops of my trousers.

The guard escorted me to the main hall where my ten friends and many other male and female prisoners were gathered. No talking was allowed. The prisoners sat on their bundles if they had any. If not, they stood uneasily or sat on the floor. We, the eleven of us, grouped together and communicated with our eyes. I learned that every one of us was in relatively good health and happy to have each other after three years. No one knew what was going to happen. No one, by so much as a facial expression or a glance, wanted to start the smallest speculation as to where we were going.

The guards searched our belongings and lined us up against the far wall. The line grew as other prisoners were brought in. About forty men and women were there, silent and waiting. We were taken by bus to the prison camp outside Moscow. As we descended from the bus inside the prison area, it was obvious that some of the prisoners had virtually lost the ability to walk without specific directions being given to them.

I saw once again that death was the least fate to fear under Soviet captivity.

Just inside the compound, we were told to spread our belongings on long wooden benches for another search. This time, a few of the better blankets and shirts disappeared. The NKVD weren't the only ones conducting the searches. Prisoners wearing red armbands officiously scattered our belongings. These were ordinary criminals whom the NKVD trusted and to whom they assigned certain duties.

After the search, we were herded into barracks Number 16, our first experience of prison barracks—as compared to prison cells. The building, of rough planking, was about 220 feet long and perfectly bare inside. Light came through a few windows. Along the whitewashed walls, six-foot wide wooden shelves ran. These were our beds. One shelf went along the wall at a height of about three feet, another about three feet above that. Wooden ladders fastened at intervals gave access to the upper tier. There was space for approximately 150 men on the shelves. Our group, after the women were separated, numbered about thirty. Everyone took a "'luxuriously" large space on the lower benches.

Two coal-burning stoves warmed the barracks. Dividing the barracks down the center was a partitioned area with concrete flooring; this area contained a long trough for washing clothes and space for serving food. Number 16 was a quarantine barracks and our stay there lasted only ten days.

On the eleventh day, the eleven of us were assigned to barracks Number 15, which was jammed. There was space for us only on the top shelf, and as we slept, we touched the prisoner on either side of us. When one turned, the other two had to turn as well.

Our only consolation was that the eleven of us were together. It made the first days actually pass rather enjoyably. My ten friends and I had hours to talk to each other and exchange stories of our prison experiences.

Sexual practices, both normal and abnormal, were crude and animalistic in the barracks. Homosexuality was rife throughout the camp and among both sexes, particularly the young people. One day, as an experiment, an entire barracks building was turned over to an indoctrination course in communism. The young men, whom the Russians hoped to influence, demonstrated that they had no interest in any "ism" but "homosexualism." They were brutal in their performance, unmanageable as a group, and immune to instruction.

Sexual activity was centered, for the most, part in barracks Number 10. This was used as a storehouse and a sewing room for repairing flour sacks. Ten girls were assigned to barracks

Number 10 as seamstresses to repair the flour sacks, which were vital to the prison economy.

Two guards were on constant duty to keep the male prisoners away and supervise the sewing. All of the girls were whores, and the price of sexual favors in barracks Number 10 was measured in terms of food since money had little meaning. Indeed, one of the girls was called "Third of a Loaf," the price of her sexual favors.

After a fortnight in this camp, I was herded out and shoved among a group of stunned and fearful prisoners clutching their bundled belongings. They were waiting like zombies for the next push into an always-unknown terror. Prisoners were separated into bunches of twenty and herded into brick corrals in the prison yard.

This time, we didn't go directly to another prison, but to a railroad. There, in a line of regular freight cars, were prison cars meant for us. These rolling jails, called *Stalopinskis* after a former minister of state security, were disguised as mail cars. They were designed and built for no other purpose than to transport prisoners. The Stalopinski prison car was laid out very efficiently. It represented one of the few real Soviet contributions to design. As a rule, Russia's main industrial patterns were copied from those of other nations.

Down the length of the railroad car, along one side, ran a narrow corridor through which the prisoners were herded and guards would later make their rounds to check on the prisoners. There were wire cages on the side of the corridor extending to the far side of the wall, eight cages to a car. In each cage, there were three horizontal wooden shelves, each about six or seven feet wide, like large tables extending from the wall of the car to the wire of the cage.

On each shelf, five prisoners were laid out like sausages on a tray. That made 15 prisoners per cage, 120 prisoners per car.

A regular railroad car, with the prisoners standing, could only house seventy to eighty prisoners packed like sardines. Squeezing in fifty extra prisoners per car is a genuine, undisputed accomplishment of Soviet communism.

We were ordered onto the shelves with our feet toward the wall of the car, heads against the wire of the cages. Some lay on their backs, some on their stomachs, depending on how they squirmed when ordered onto the shelf. My position was stomach down, chin against the rough board of the shelf, eyes staring straight ahead through the wire into the corridor.

There was no way to change position, to arch one's back, to do anything. We were let out to the bathroom twice a day. At other times, day or night, prisoners who couldn't hold themselves would whimperingly foul their pants and often also the prisoners next to them. Even in that community of hardship, it was difficult for some prisoners not to hate the unfortunate ones this happened to.

We stayed on those shelves for four weeks as the Stalopinskis rolled on toward the northeast.

Our first stop was Novgorod where the guards opened the gates of the cages and herded us out, blinking and dazed, into the sunshine. No one spoke or speculated—we were long past that. We waited, not moving until prodded and the way was pointed out. Only our eyes moved restlessly and furtively as we searchingly hunted, not for more sights, but for some clue as to what would happen next—any clue that might prepare us for a sudden blow or a new prison or even sudden death.

The guards herded us into the streets of the town. Livestock, mostly hogs and goats, ran across the muddy roads. Few people in the town seemed to consider us unique enough to favor us with more than casual glances. Our clothes, we noticed, didn't even set us apart from the townspeople. They were in rags just like the prisoners.

After crossing the entire town, we saw an ominous-looking brick building. It was the prison.

Our prison quarters consisted of a simple, hall-like room into which all the Stalopinski "passengers" were directed. The whitewashed walls were a floor-to-ceiling patchwork of names scratched in, penciled in, and, in a few cases, written in blood. Before the doors were slammed on us, a guard shouted that anyone caught writing on the walls would be punished.

In the morning, it was a relief to hear that all prisoners were to get a bath and—astounding news—a shave. As the long line began to move into the bath and shaving room, however, our joy was dampened. The bathing part consisted of a row of pans. The prisoners shed their clothes and squatted or stooped over the pans, splashing the water where they thought they needed it most. At irregular intervals, the filthy water was changed.

The shaving was unnerving. A female barber had been assigned the chore. The prisoners were told not to dress as they moved to her area of the bath and barbering room. Head hair she trimmed in seconds down to the scalp. Then she removed body hair, as expressionlessly as she clipped our heads. Later, from other prisoners, I learned that her work was neither an unstudied vulgarity nor an accident. Soviet prison authorities had long known that for many men, the ordeal of being exposed to a woman under such degrading circumstances was crushing to morale—should there be any random spark of it left.

When the bathing and barbering were finished, the prisoners got dressed, lined up in marching order, and headed back to the cells.

The Stalopinski in which we had come to Novgorod had departed and we had to wait for a new one. Thus, a day of rest was granted. We were marched to the tracks the next day. During those times in the Soviet Union, every regular train had one or two Stalopinskis attached as a matter of course. As we waited there, no one even bothered to stare at us, much less at the Stalopinskis when they rolled up in the line of cars. We were thrown onto the shelves in the Stalopinski, even as the regular travelers climbed into their passenger cars and sat on the benches.

Suddenly, I noticed something that had escaped me when we first arrived at the station—perhaps because we hadn't come as part of a passenger train like this one—beggars, literally scores of them, were swarming around the train crying for food or rubles.

There were criminals among us. These were older criminals called *blatnois* to distinguish them from political prisoners such as us. Until now, we had been the only kind of prisoners I had known.

The blatnois felt no particular opposition to the system that had imprisoned them. They would have been in jail sooner or later under any system. The fact that they had merely robbed, raped, beaten, or murdered was an extremely important difference in these surroundings. They were not "degenerate" agents of the fascists or capitalists. They were not saboteurs, spies, counter-revolutionaries, or any of the terrible things that we were. They were not, in short, dangerous in any way to the Soviet system as such. They were indeed often helpful.

The NKVD guards showed an obvious respect for the blatnois. The blatnois could be trusted. They could even be called on to assist guards. The blatnois wouldn't try to escape because they had all the comforts and securities in prison that they had tried to achieve on the outside by stealing.

In many instances, a secret of their success was the power they were given to run the prison from the inside. As far as the political prisoners were concerned, the blatnois were the bosses. The guards would turn away while the blatnois beat prisoners. Later, I was to see the guards turn a blind eye even from murderers. The blatnois stole from other prisoners with impunity. They could force entire shifts of prisoners to work for them and the guards protected them in their crimes.

Even in the Stalopinski, the blatnois had special privileges. Although they had to lie on the shelves like the rest of us, they were not packed five to a shelf.

There was also a woman prisoner in our group. We didn't see her because she traveled with the guards. Sometimes above the clatter of the train, or during toilet stops, we could hear her as the guards in shifts entertained her.

During the trip, whenever we stopped on the siding to let another train pass on the single line track, several guards would walk outside the cars, banging on each board with mallets to make sure none was loose. The hammering was maddening. When the bumping and banging stopped, it seemed a great relief. For a time, the prisoners would talk, shuffle their feet, or strain their eyes at cracks in the car wall to see the bleak land-scape. After a few minutes, if the train still hadn't started—and stops of several hours were most common—the silence would start, as we would have nothing else to say.

The wind would sigh through the car. It was in the silence of those stops that we realized the most desolate thing that a human can know—no one cared about us and no one could do anything about our plight. It was as though the Soviets had made time stand still and paralyzed history itself. It was then, I suppose, that most of us realized how utterly lost we were. We had only rumors about our destination and fear as to our future.

During the weeks of travel, the utter monotony was broken occasionally when one of us would see, through a crack, a prison compound. Some were crowded with men, others with women, some showed no sign of life.

As we rolled onward, day after day, the hours of light became fewer and the dense forest faded away. Pine trees had become shrubs; birch trees were thin and spotted. Bushes and grass were sparser.

We finally arrived at a forest—of poles and barbed wire. It covered part of a plateau, which was open only toward the north and northwest, being otherwise surrounded in the distance by the snow-covered peaks and slopes of the Ural Mountains. We had penetrated far into the north, to Inta at the Arctic Circle.

When the roll call at the Inta railroad siding was finished, the Russian guard barked something like, "Shagiom marsh!" It sounded like "get going" in any language. We crossed the tracks and walked two abreast toward a small group of buildings, which I later learned was the *peresylka*, the transit camp for new arrivals. The NKVD guards with machine guns and two police dogs took up the rear.

Inside the peresylka, I was given an examination that lasted less than a minute by a female doctor and pronounced fit for heavy-duty work. I was issued the slave outfit common to all of Russia, a blue cotton-padded jacket (*bushlat*), cotton-padded pants, and a cotton hat (*shapka*) that had flaps for the ears. Across the head and the back of my bushlat, my "slave name," A584, (*Pyatsot-vocemdesyet-chitiry*) was sewn on. There was little chance to forget who or where I was. From the coded number, the NKVD official could tell at a glance that I was a political prisoner.

Two weeks later, I was herded onto a bus heading toward an unknown destination, along with a group that was composed mainly of Russians and Ukrainians. The Russians had been arrested for "treason" or "agitation" or were former Red Army men who had been captured by the Germans in World War II—an unpardonable offense punishable by twenty-five years of hard labor. Most Ukrainians were from the nationalist Bandera Army that had fought the Reds for independence.

We were taken through the town of Inta itself, which was comparatively "modern" with street lamps, cobblestone roads, and planked wooden sidewalks, and a bronze statue of Stalin— the most important landmark.

In the darkening streets, we could see a few hundred slaves like ourselves. Their numbers were still visible on their clothes in the evening lights, as, with picks and axes, they worked repairing streets and breaking ground for new apartment buildings for NKVD officials.

From the town, we rode north about twenty miles into a far northern region of the Inta compound. Our destination was Camp 1, with four thousand men in two of the many coal mines of Inta.

With 120 other men, I was assigned to a low, ugly barracks, Number 25, about a mile and half from Mine 2, where I was to work as a slave for many years to come. By now, only three of our original group remained together. The other eight were sent to different camps to work in other mines. I didn't hear from them for many years, and I didn't know whether they were dead or alive. Joco, Bert, and I stayed together in the same camp. Joco and I worked in Mine 2 and Bert worked in Mine 1. Occasionally, the three of us could get together to talk.

Our barracks was a low, crudely built building. Posts had been jammed into the frozen ground, and boards nailed along them, inside and out, to create walls. The space between the walls was filled with ashes for insulation. The walls were then covered with mud and straw to fill the holes. When completed, the whole thing was whitewashed.

It was late in the year and the six weeks of summer was over. There were only two seasons that far north—summer and winter. A sheet of snow already covered the ground. Prisoners were working outside the barracks, packing the snow into large blocks and propping them up against the side of the barracks as protection against the real cold ahead. Within a short time, the temperature would drop from forty degrees Fahrenheit to negative fifty degrees Fahrenheit (below zero).

I looked at the "bunk" to which I had been assigned. It was a segment of a two-foot wide hard wooden shelf, one of the two shelves, upper and lower, that ran the full length of both sides of the barracks. Joco, Bert, and I got an upper shelf. A wooden ladder in front enabled us to climb up to it. No bedding was provided for the hard wooden slab. When everyone had taken their places, there was only enough room to sleep on my side pressed against the man next to me. But I was lucky. Some men were sleeping on the floor and were just as crowded as I was.

The barracks was dark, with only two small windows on either side and two naked light bulbs hanging from the ceiling. One source of heat was provided by a mud stove at either end, stoked by a slave whose health, ruined by the work and the cold, rendered him useless in the mine. The 100 to 120 prisoners who jammed the building generated additional heat. At the far end was the drying room, a stinking hole where prisoners back from the mine hung up their dirty clothes to dry.

It was a human jungle, smelly and overcrowded. Everyone, including the guards, spat large globs openly on the floor. The Russians cursed in one continuous flow. Slaves, guards, red officials—especially the hard female prisoners—relied on cursing more than on a regular vocabulary.

When the prisoners, after a long day's work, climbed onto their shelf for the night, the hungry bedbugs assaulted them, crawling onto them from the walls or falling off the ceiling. At first, we waged war with them strenuously, crushing them on our bodies and on the walls, and almost suffocating from their stink. After several hours, we weakened and let them drink our blood without protest.

We lived under these conditions for three months when we finally decided to refuse to work unless we got a bedbug-free barracks. The next day, we were moved to another barracks and our infested one was sealed and filled with the gas of burning sulfur. When we returned two days later, most of the bedbugs were exterminated and our nights became more tolerable.

There was no toilet in the barracks. A crude outhouse with a hole in the snow was our toilet facility. It was about 150 yards from the barracks. During my first days there, I ran like a deer through the deep snow in negative twenty degrees Fahrenheit weather, then raced back, holding my unbuttoned pants to make it without freezing.

A few days after I arrived, I became familiar with the security setup. From what I saw, we were precious "cargo" indeed. Inside the camp, the NKVD guards were unarmed for fear of being overpowered and having their guns taken away. But the camp was surrounded by a twelve-foot-high barbed wire fence punctuated with tall towers manned by guards with machine-guns. A telephone and an electric alarm system connected the towers. A few yards inside the outer fence was a lower fence that was three feet high. The area between the fences was designated a prohibited zone and lit up all through the night and dark days with powerful arc lights. The guards had orders to shoot on sight anyone seen there. The police dogs, conscientious NKVD allies, could scout the entire camp by means of a guide wire strung close to the outer fence.

Inta was escape-proof. It might have been possible to get past the fences under the cover of a snowstorm, but the tundra, the snow, and the cold would defeat everyone. The local Komi nomads got ten thousand rubles for every slave they brought back. It was more money than they had ever seen.

The NKVD commandant and his political officer ran the camp. The population of the camp was about four thousand prisoners. They threw prisoners into the *bor*, a camp prison within a prison, merely on the word of NKVD informers, *stukachey*.

Under the commandant and political officer were the prison officials, the narjadchik, in charge of an entire work shift; the *desetnicks* in charge of one type of work (i.e. coal mining); and the *brigadiers*, overlords of anywhere from five to twenty men.

Unofficially, however, Inta had a different type of master. Our camp was ruled with a steel fist by about 250 blatnois, the Russian criminals who kept the political prisoners in abject fear. There were about eight of them in my barracks, living on a shelf at the far end that would normally hold more than twenty prisoners. They spent their time sleeping, stealing whatever they admired, sharpening the knives they made, playing home-made *balalaikas*, and dancing the *plashska*, a fast dance.

No brigadier, including my boss, a former Red Army Commissar and *politruk* serving a twenty-year sentence for being captured by the Nazis, would dare ask a blatnois to work. If one of the blatnois as much as lifted a shovel, his comrades would murder him instantly.

The blatnois were unemotional, professional criminals, mostly in their twenties, serving comparatively short sentences for theft and murder. They had begun life as vagrant children traveling in small bands throughout the Soviet Union, robbing as they went. They had been raised under the Communists, but knew nothing about politics and cared less. Their *starshi* (chief), a cold-eyed, twenty-three-year-old Muscovite, controlled his men with iron discipline, which was the blatnois' strength over the politicals.

Shortly after I arrived, a Latvian was beaten up badly. He had refused to give his new bushlat to a blatnois in exchange for an old one. One blatnois did the actual fighting while two helpers stood by. The Latvian made a move toward the blatnois, but as he did, one of the thief's helpers tripped him. He fell on his face to a chorus of laughter. When he got up to fight again, the blatnois standing behind him pushed him off balance. As he staggered, he was hit ferociously in the face until it was a pudgy mass of crimson. The Latvian's frightened slave friends drifted away from the brutal beating without lifting a finger.

Beatings were routine. A few days later, I had dropped into a nearby barracks and was talking with a friend when a Ukrainian walked from man to man, fear etched in his eyes. He was whispering an announcement.

"What did he say?" I asked.

"The blatnois are playing cards," he answered with trepidation.

"What is so important about their playing cards?" I asked.

He looked at me patiently as if I was a child. "Come, you will see."

We walked toward the far end of the barracks. Five blatnois were seated on stools below the naked electric bulb. Between them was a table improvised from a large board. I stood at a safe distance, but close enough to see they were playing cards intensely; their eyes were focused on the dealer's hands.

"What are the stakes?" I asked.

"They are very high," the Ukrainian answered solemnly. "Murder. The low scorer has to kill the man marked for death by the blatnois. It happens every week."

A cautious few of us had gathered near the playing table, but when the blatnois kicked over the board as a sign that the game was over, the small crowd quickly disappeared. I went back to my friend's shelf and watched the drama unfold.

The loser, a young, blond haired blatnois of about eighteen, pulled a knife out of his belt and calmly approached the lower shelf of the bunk about halfway between me and the place where they had been playing.

He had a padded jacket in one hand and the knife in the other. Sleeping on the shelf was a well-fed prisoner, one of the cooks in the kitchen. The blatnois walked silently, without causing a creak in the old flooring, then leaped at the cook. In one swift, professional movement, he threw the bushlat over the cook's head, held him down with a vise-like grip around the neck, then jabbed the long blade up to the hilt a dozen times into the victim's chest and stomach.

The cook screeched through the bushlat. Dripping blood from his chest, he pushed the blatnois off him. He got off the shelf and started to run down the barracks aisle toward the door. He got fifteen feet, but then collapsed and died in a pool of his own blood.

The cook had paid the ultimate penalty for defying the blatnois. As a cook, he was an important part of the blatnois' schemes. When a new prisoner arrived, the blatnois often made a deal—they would buy the woolen suit he was arrested in and pay for it with a month's extra ration, a second plate of soup at both meals. The blatnois chief would take the prisoner down to the cook, introduce him and explain, "This man is to get extra soup every day for thirty days."

The cook had refused to go along with the scheme.

The blatnois killer was given the usual two-month sentence in the camp prison, not a day of it in the cold cell, a special torture cage reserved for political prisoners.

Many similar incidents made me wonder, *Are we human beings?* The blatnois committed murder without batting an eyelash or any remorse, and the other prisoners could only watch, feeling helpless and filled with guilt.

Shortly after this, early one afternoon, I noticed a large group of men, mostly Estonian, Lithuanian, and Latvian, walking toward the barracks next to ours. They all carried a plank of wood, a steel rod, or something that could be used to fight with. They entered the barracks where several blatnois were playing cards. When the blatnois saw the big group, they jumped up to leave, but all the entrances were blocked, so they tried the only escape routes left—the windows. The first to jump through a window was badly cut, but the way he carried the window frame around his neck looked comical. He died from loss of blood. The other blatnois ran into the commandant's building seeking protection from the NKVD guards. The next day, all the blatnois were transferred to another camp, which lifted our morale and mood.

My life in Inta was the closest thing possible to a living death. It was a grueling combination of slow and continuous starvation, exhausting work, killing cold, and abject monotony that destroyed many a healthier and stronger man than me.

There was no time wasted in Inta. I went to work producing coal for the Soviets the day I got there. I was assigned to Mine 2, which contained anthracite, a high quality coal embedded in slate at a forty-five-degree angle. The width of the coal varied between two and a half and four feet.

The plan was to extract the coal in phases. Phase 1 production extended from the surface to three thousand feet, which was called the base level. On the base level, a tunnel seven feet wide and six feet high was built where the coal was collected and transported to the elevator. The coal slid by gravity to the tunnel. In the tunnel, a chute was installed. Opening and closing the chute controlled the filling of the wagons.

The brigadier, in charge of digging the tunnel deep inside the mine, oversaw the operation of lengthening the tunnel, which had been dug into hard shale and had to be extended as coal production proceeded. The first step of the operation was to drill holes for explosives using a four-foot long drill with a cowhide bit on the end. It required twenty holes to blast a three-foot extension.

Since the political prisoners couldn't be trusted with explosives, the mine hired civilians to fill the holes with explosives, place an electrical fuse inside each hole, connect the fuses with wires, and, as a final step, do the blasting. As soon as the area was cleared of dust and gases, which took approximately ten to fifteen minutes, rails were laid, wagons rolled in, and the slate was loaded into them. The filled wagons were transported to the surface by elevators.

A successful blasting usually yielded 150 cubic feet of slate. The hardest, most demanding job was to load the slate onto wagons, push them out, and bring in empty ones. Since I was the new one in the brigade, my assignment was to load the slate into the wagons. Some of the others chosen for this job complained that they couldn't handle such heavy work.

When we returned to our barracks one evening, one disgruntled prisoner yelled, "Son of a bitch" at our brigadier, Koslov, a former Red Army political officer. Koslov turned and looked disdainfully at the prisoner, then pointed to another prisoner, a mine slave half-propped up on his bunk. Mine slaves had the most difficult job, working twelve hours a day in the two-and-a-half-foot high tunnels, crawling on their stomachs and knees like rodents, to chip out the coal. The miners usually lost weight rapidly and ended up in the infirmary or dead. Koslov wanted the complainer to realize that if he wasn't happy in his current job, he could be transferred to a mining brigade—and in no time look just like this miner. This one had an animal-like expression on his face, his hair had turned mostly white, and his eyes were sunk deep into his cadaverous face. All his bones showed under a thin covering of skin.

I turned away, sick.

For the next two years, though, my looks were not much better than those of the mine slaves'. I didn't expect to live through the winter of 1952-1953.

My day began about 4:45 A.M. when a guard came through yelling, "Vsten" (get up). Breakfast was served at 5:30 A.M. When I first stepped out of the barracks each morning, the air was so cold and thin that it took my breath away for several seconds. There were two meals a day, in the morning and in the evening. Each morning I received a one-pound loaf of sticky, black bread. This was the basic ration for the day—if the norm was fulfilled. If not, the bread ration was reduced in proportion to how much the norm was missed. The bread was baked less than an hour and soaked with sixty percent water. It was about one-third the size of an American one-pound rye loaf. It was too wet to eat as it was, so I usually toasted mine over the barracks' stove as the others did.

Breakfast consisted of a scoop of *kasha* (grayish grits) and a small bowl of watery soup with a few cabbage leaves on the bottom. There was nothing to drink except water. Supper, about twelve hours later, was the same kasha and thin soup plus a thimbleful of sunflower oil to pour over the kasha, a one and-one-quarter square inch piece of fish, and a roll the size of a small egg. Every ten days, instead of the fish, we got two ounces of tough reindeer meat. Once, on May Day, we had pork.

My whole day's food ration totaled less than nine hundred calories. A Russian doctor told me that was less than the ration of an office worker with a desk job. I was continually starving, my stomach in a knot, crying for more. It is a feeling you never get used to.

I had heard about the Inta winter. "It gets bad here in the winter!" my old-timer friends told me. "The cold gets in your bones so bad you don't want to live any longer. It gets down to thirty, fifty, even seventy degrees below zero." I never quite believed it until I experienced it.

I worked in the mine the first year. After the morning meal, we lined up in excruciating negative thirty-five-degree Fahrenheit cold, hopping from one foot to the other to keep from freezing while the plodding NKVD men called the roll.

The mine was a mile and a half away from camp. Two hundred of us, covered by ten guards and two police dogs, made the trip twice a day through a forty-foot wide corridor connecting the mines with the camp. The corridor had the same barbed wire on either side, and the same brilliantly lit prohibited zone as the perimeter of the camp. About twenty guard towers were alternately spaced on both sides of the corridor. A guard, armed with a machine gun, manned each tower and was relieved every two hours.

Winter came quickly in Inta. By November or December, the mile-and-a-half trip to and from work took us over an hour each way as we trudged through snow up to our hips. Every week, the thermometer dipped another five degrees. Within a short time, going to work under armed guards became like a polar expedition—almost unbearable.

I encountered an ugly storm not long after I arrived there. It snowed all night and by morning, the twelve-foot high barbed wire fence on the corridor was only a foot above the snow in some spots. I had never seen anything like it in my life. We ran to the mine through the snow. The pace was killing, but it was the only way to generate warmth. The snow blew up in front of my face in great swirls. At times, there was no visibility. The wind howled mercilessly. I pulled my bushlat over my head and staggered with my arm covering my face.

"Don't break out of line or you will be shot," one of the NKVD guards yelled.

I could have stepped right over the buried barbed wire fence several times along the corridor, but there was nowhere to go except deeper into the snowstorm.

Suddenly, the slave next to me tapped me on the shoulder and pointed to my chin. It had turned white, the first frightening sign of frostbite. I pulled my hand from under my bushlat and started to rush the circulation back, the only hope of stopping frostbite. It took ten minutes to get my chin red again. I stopped just in time, as the back of my exposed hand had begun to turn white.

Others were not as lucky. Hundreds of Inta slaves walked around with missing toes and fingers that had been amputated after frostbite to stop the gangrene from spreading.

I didn't notice the poor physical condition of the prisoners until I injured myself and had to go to the dispensary. There I saw how skinny the prisoners were. They had gone to the dispensary for relief from the pain of their pelvic bones actually protruding through their skin. All they got was a new bandage, no extra food and no time off from work.

We worked twelve hours a day and got a day of rest every ten days. On that snowy day when the temperature was fifty-eight degrees below zero and I narrowly escaped frostbite on my chin, there was another roll call. Volodja, a student from Stalingrad, was missing, lost somewhere in the snow corridor. The next day when the storm subsided, his frozen body was found buried face down in the snow. The cold had frozen a life-like expression on his face.

Since my job was three thousand feet below the surface, it was a blessing when we arrived at the mine. For twelve hours, I didn't have to suffer from cold and snow.

Mechanically, the Soviet mines were very poorly equipped. This was in part because of Russia's backwardness, but also because of other factors, which the chief engineer explained to me. While Russia had both on paper and in "show mines" the most modern machinery, it wasn't possible to put these to widespread use because modern machines, which could be operated by one person, would have replaced hundreds of slaves. This "one person" would be able—if he was an anticommunist (evil minded—according to the Soviet dictionary)—to slow down or stop the work of the equivalent of hundreds of slaves as represented by the output of the machine. But if you have the slaves to do the work, little harm results if one or two out of hundreds are evil-minded. Why take the risk of using machines?

The mine elevator was a machine that couldn't be replaced by slave power. So they used the best one available—an American one made in Iowa in the 1930s. Almost all the electrical machinery there was made in America or Germany.

I felt more and more like a primitive slave, my starving body loading and pushing the wagons in an age of mechanization. I didn't know the language and I worked all day without a real friend at my side. I was sure that even slaves in other times and places had had it better than this.

In the first year at Inta, 1952, I had just enough stamina to make it back to the camp at the end of the shift each day. After supper in the *stolovaya* (mess hall), I would collapse on my hard shelf in my filthy snow-and-sweat-soaked work clothes. My face was dirty, but there was no facility or means to wash off the dust, and sweat collected on my face during the twelve-hour shift in the mine. My face was deep red from the cold, and for several hours after coming indoors, I felt as if a log fire were six inches from my nose. I could hardly lift my stiff legs. My shoulder was blue from the slate wagon and the palms of my hands turned to elephant skin, each palm a large callus, insensitive to cold, heat, or pain.

After a month of this backbreaking and futile labor, I could feel myself cracking. Constant hard labor, lack of food, and the feeling of being lost to the world slowly corroded my will. Chills of self-doubt began flowing through me for the first time, made all the more desperate by the status I held among my friends. I was their leader.

The starvation, harsh climate, and work had eaten away my body fat and left me with a skin covering that hung over my bones. My weight dropped below one hundred pounds. My bones pushed against the skin. It turned a deeper brown than the rest of my yellowing, but still not bleeding, body. My rear end just disappeared, the skin hanging in big folds like a toy accordion.

The lack of oxygen in the Inta air complicated my problems. I longed for sleep, but even sleeping all through my days off couldn't shake the exhaustion.

God, I am near the end of my rope, I thought to myself desperately one night. *If the Soviets push me just a little further, I will break.*

The other prisoners were even more wretched looking than I was, although the Russians among us took life in the gulag fatalistically. *What can we do? The regime and I were never friends. The NKVD won, so here we are.*

They were ill and decrepit far beyond their age. Most suffered from abnormally high blood pressure or heart disease. I had only a slightly elevated blood pressure, but my wrists and ankles swelled regularly into puffy masses of skin. Everyone had a cadaverous appearance, a fact that hit me hard every ten days when we were taken to the camp *banya* (bath). We got a hot bath and a shave and our slaves' marks were restored, heads shaved down to the scalp. With our clothes off and the filth washed away, pelvic bones stood out clearly. Only the Baltic and

Ukrainian prisoners, who received food packages from home, looked somewhat better.

Our teeth and gums rotted from lack of vitamins. The only dental care was extraction. Most prisoners had missing teeth, especially the lower ones. I lost a few, and those I had left were discolored, decayed, and loose. Dental problems followed a pattern: The gum around a tooth would start to swell. The fluid inside the flesh gradually pressed against the tooth until it loosened and fell out—generally while eating. Some prisoners frantically tried to stop the inevitable process by puncturing the swelling gum with a needle and draining the fluid.

The heavy labor was almost impossible to avoid. Refusing to work meant time in the cold cell where prisoners were stripped down to their underwear if they had any, and chained to the wall in an unheated, stonewalled room. Their thighs were straddled over a concrete block that rubbed the fierce cold into the sensitive skin on the inside of the thighs.

One of my fellow prisoners told me, "After one night in the cell, you will do anything they want. All I wanted was to get into a warm room."

No one stood directly over us while we worked, but we had our communist "norm," a work requirement more diabolic than any ancient slave master's. My norm was to load and transport all the slate that came out after the blasting. If I didn't do my job in time, the other members of the brigade had to wait for me, which meant the productivity of the brigade fell below the requirement established by the norm. Those of us who didn't fulfill their norm were put on punishment rations of less then that of the normal diet, which started a vicious cycle. Those on punishment rations became weaker and even less able to fulfill their norm. The brigadiers, who were always anxious to get the best workers, moved these poor starving souls from job to job until their weakened bodies just gave out.

Those who were fortunate had a sympathetic feltcher who declared them fit for only lighter work.

There was one form of release from the gulag that not even an NKVD guard could take away—death.

Corpses, rotting from scurvy, were tossed out in the open air where they piled up at the main entrance in front of the booth used by the NKVD soldier who controlled traffic through the camp's main gate.

Mostly it was not a surgeon, but a convoy guard who verified that the prisoner was really dead and not pretending. The guard would run a bayonet through the corpse and smashed the skull with a big mallet. And right there they tied to the big toe of the corpse's right foot a tag containing his identification number.

At one time, the Russians used to bury the dead prisoners in their underwear. Then came the regulation to bury them naked so as not to waste any underwear on them. It could still be used for the living.

I reached a state where my will alone kept my body alive. I knew that as soon as I lost my will, my body would die.

Some prisoners who couldn't take the grind dreamed of elaborate escape plans, but these always failed. Until 1952, escapees were shot immediately if caught. After that, they were thrown into the cold cell, but not before the NKVD guards had beaten them until they were half dead.

The only way to beat the Communist system, and many prisoners used it, was to disable yourself so badly that you could only be a floor sweeper or the *sushilshik*, the stoker of the barracks' stove.

Early one afternoon, when my friend Gaspar and I were assigned to a brigade whose duties were to split wood for the kitchen, Gaspar suddenly called my attention to a fellow prisoner from Caucasus who had been arrested during World War

II for resisting the Communist genocide in his nation. He was holding in his left hand the hatchet he used to chop wood. All eyes were on him as he placed his right hand palm down on the chopping block. Then, with his left hand, he swung the hatchet down in a resounding blow. It struck the hand just above the wrist severing it cleanly from his arm. As he lifted the stump, the blood welled out, covering his face and clothes. The force of the blow had thrown his severed hand onto the ground.

We immediately notified the NKVD guard and he was taken away. He spent two months in the camp jail, but he never again did a day's heavy work for the Soviets.

★　　★　　★

I lived in this mad world for years with little to occupy my mind. Playing cards and singing were strictly forbidden. No more than five men were allowed to congregate at one time. The sound of Russian blared out of the barracks' loudspeakers.

Time passed in weeks, and weeks turned into months. I wondered whether my relatives knew where I was. I received no mail or packages, and I was not allowed to write to my mother, brother, or sister.

Mostly I thought about food—strangely enough, not about exotic dishes or steak or ice cream, but plain milk and fruit. I saw shining white glasses of milk and clean pears and apples in my dreams, but I never saw them in reality for almost nine years.

Sitting on the bunk, I would watch as some of the others opened packages—for them the difference between life and death. The Russian packages from rural areas were good evidence of the widespread poverty, generally just a bag of onions, some tea leaves, and dried vegetables. Only rarely was a small piece of bacon included. The Latvians, Lithuanians, and Estonians, whose countries' former prosperity had not yet been completely destroyed by Red rule, got packages full of candies, sugar, bacon, lard, and sausages. Each package was quickly divided among the prisoners' hungry friends, who tried to make the wonderful gifts last a day or two.

My stomach envied those who got packages or who had friends that got them. I had neither. Then I heard there was a chance to pick up bits of leftover food at the kitchen after the evening meal. One night, before the evening roll call when we were locked in for the night, I went to the stolovaya and approached one of the well-fed cooks. I begged in rehearsed Russian, pointing at the discarded fish heads and a small pile of kasha scrapings from the prison officials' plates. The cook looked me over to see if I was a friend, a friend of a friend, or a man with substantial *blat* (bribe money). When he decided he didn't know me from Adam, he kicked me out of the kitchen with a menacing wave of his food chopper. I went back to the barracks a little hungrier, lonelier, and more disgruntled than usual.

"Bela, everything in Inta depends on whom you know," Volodjka, a Ukrainian in my barracks, told me. "You need friends in the kitchen for a little extra food, and a contact in the hospital will never hurt you. If you are part of a tight-knit group, not even the blatnois will bother you. With enough blat, the brigadiers and narjadchik will give you the right job," he said. "There are few Russians who cannot be bribed."

He was right. Learning the Russian language was my first project to survive. My teacher was a barracks mate, Ivan, a former student at Moscow University, one of the many disgruntled Soviet intellectuals in camp. Without realizing it, I had already picked up a few words and was making excellent progress in no time.

"Soon you will speak better than many of the Ukrainians," Ivan said.

I worked at it every spare minute, and in a short time, I could speak halting, grammatically incorrect Russian.

The new language helped me out of my cocoon, and my circle of friends grew rapidly. Four prisoners, Vaska, Ivan, Grishka, and Sasha, became my closest friends. Vaska, a twenty-five-year-old Ukrainian peasant, worked the main elevator, which transported the coal from the mine to the surface. A fervent Ukrainian nationalist, Vaska had fought with the Ukrainian Bander Army during World War II against both the Nazis and Communists.

Ivan, a thirty-year old Ukrainian, had some secondary education—somewhat rare in the rural areas.

Grishka was a forty-year-old Russian from Latvia. He was a strong man with a golden heart. He had only a rudimentary education, less than four years in public school.

"Bela," Grishka once said to me, "if I could save your life at the cost of mine, I would do it without hesitation."

He had been charged and convicted of espionage (Paragraph 58, Subparagraph 6), sabotage (Paragraph 58, Subparagraph 8), and agitation (Paragraph 58, Subparagraph 11), and sentenced to ten years of hard labor.

Sasha had been a colonel in the Soviet Air Force and was a hero twice over during World War II. He was arrested and convicted because Beria had his eyes on Sasha's wife and reasoned that if Sasha were sent to the gulag, he'd have free access to her.

Sasha spent more time in the cold cell than in the barracks. "I will never work," he told the guards. "I am a hero of the Soviet Union. I was the most decorated fighter pilot—with the highest number of kills in aerial combat—and I would rather suffer in the cold cell than build the Soviet society where thirty percent of the people are victims of the Communist system. When I was in Moscow, I did not know the existence of this huge gulag system."

Since both of us had served in the air force, I in the Hungarian and Sasha in the Soviet, we became close friends. He was also a big help to me in learning Russian. He arranged to get Russian textbooks from relatives to help me learn grammar and master the Cyrillic script, which was foreign to me.

My new friends made my life a little more bearable. I shared in the meager food packages they received from home. At times, a friend in the kitchen found a little extra cabbage soup or fat to help protect my shrunken body against the cold. When I was sent to the hospital to build up my strength, my friends brought me bread saved from their own rations and other favors for which I shall always be grateful.

Learning Russian dispelled some of my fears, which also helped. The language sounds so harsh to a Westerner that I had always thought everyone was screaming at me. Later, I realized it was just the Russian way of speaking. Actually, the Russians were masters of bluff. But when you stood up to them aggressively, they invariably backed down.

Through my newly acquired friends and my new command of the language, I came to know more than one hundred slaves in my barracks and others throughout the camp. Inta contained many notables of the Communist world. There was a man who was a colleague of Trotsky and had been in dozens of slave camps during the previous nineteen years. He was initially sentenced to eight years and when it was over, was sentenced in absentia to another eight. This was his third term in the gulag.

Not everyone in Inta was an ex-Red. Inta was a veritable League of Nations, a polyglot army of slaves from every walk of life and many countries. There were hundreds from the Baltics—Lithuanians, Latvians, and Estonians—whose nations had been occupied by Hitler's army and then, in 1940, gobbled up by the Russians and made into Soviet Republics.

There were slaves from Iraq, Iran, Mongolia, China, and the Czech Republic. There were several Russian and Ukrainian Jews, victims of Stalin's anti-Semitic purges of 1949–1953.

And of course there were Hungarian slaves in our camp: Kanyo, an electrical engineer; Joco, my closest friend; Bert, a cadet in the Hungarian Military Academy; Steve Szalai, a university student in electrical engineering; Pista Bacsek, a supervisor in a Budapest textile factory; Les Toth, a clerk; and I.

A number of my fellow prisoners were clergymen, Catholic priests from Lithuania, Protestant ministers from Latvia and Germany, and Russian Orthodox priests. Religion was one of the most serious crimes in Inta. Possession of the Bible meant at least a month in jail.

But, despite all controls, religion flourished. Many groups held clandestine services at makeshift altars in the belly of the mine.

Prisoners had been funneled into Inta from camps in Vorkuta, Tadzik and Irkutsk in Soviet Asia, and Omsk in Siberia. Some of the Ukrainians in our camp literally fell over every newcomer, questioning them about what prison camp they came from and how many prisoners were there. Through adding and cross checking, a fair approximation of the number of people interned in Russia could be established. The total population of the Inta/Vorkuta complex was between four hundred thousand and five hundred thousand working in mines, brick factories, power plants, railroad lines, on streets, city and village construction, in food transportation, as prison help, and at hospitals. According to records, we were able to piece together that, throughout the entire Soviet Union in mid-1954, a total of twenty-five to twenty-eight million people were held in slave labor camps, concentration camps, secret camps for foreigners, POW camps, repatriation camps, NKVD prisons, juvenile labor camps, and juvenile detention homes. An additional twelve million not in custody were interned in restricted areas.

Sex was openly for sale in Inta to those who could afford it. For the 4,500 men in Camp 1, there were 10 women, all "free people." They worked the mine ventilators on the surface, switching them on and off as needed. Their lives were not much better than ours. Many of them were former female prisoners who now lived in exile in little settlements near the camp. They earned four hundred rubles a month, which wasn't enough to live on. For extra money, they turned to prostitution. The standard fee was twenty-five rubles. Only two of the women were attractive; the rest were typical Russians—built like tanks. Some of them were tattooed like blatnois and they all cursed with a vengeance that put us to shame, but didn't seem to hurt their business.

During the first year, when we had no money, the prostitutes were a luxury of the prison officials, blatnois, and free people only. Our order of desires was food, then clean, decent clothing. After these two were satisfied, the next were sex, books, music, and other mental activities. Sex and mental activities were ranked equally.

Mine 2 was a precarious, primitive hole with little modern equipment and no thought given to safety. There were cave-ins almost every week in which one or more slaves were injured or killed. The ceilings of the mine tunnels often collapsed because the wooden posts that shored up the ceilings were spaced too far apart. Department managers saved the wood that was provided for shoring and sold it to the Komi nomads, pocketing the cash. Another scheme was to show a saving of so many feet of wood on their monthly reports to receive a government bonus.

Working in the mine for over a year, I observed the primitive, or rather, the lack of mine automation. For example, there was no traffic-signal system underground, and collisions and other accidents that slowed down the coal production were frequent.

In my free time, I designed a simple underground traffic-signal system that could be implemented easily using readily available parts. I submitted a complete set of drawings to the mine's chief engineer, Vachagin, who had been deported from Stalingrad to Inta for "agitation," and sentenced to ten years of deportation, but no jail or forced labor. He liked my proposal and made me responsible for its implementation.

Three months later, Mine 2 had an underground traffic signal system that reduced traffic accidents to almost zero. The improvement in traffic became known among mine officials, and everyone talked about the Hungarian lotchik who designed the system.

From then on, my life changed completely. Within a couple of days, I was transferred to a new job created especially for me. I was promoted to an engineer and reported directly to the chief engineer. And I was granted a free pass to Mines 1 and 2, meaning I was allowed to go to either mine at any time— though I still needed a guard to escort me from the camp to the mines and back.

It was the nicest thing that had happened to me in six years. I started working in my newly created position the next day. I had a small office in the lamp shop responsible for charging and maintaining the miners' lights. The lights were composed of an alkaline battery fastened to a miner's belt and a light head connected by a cable to the battery, which they wore on their hats. The charging stations, the machine shops, and the warehouse were under my supervision.

In the new job, I had to submit a monthly progress report to the chief engineer, who forwarded it to the chief executive officer of Mines 1 and 2. The first report took a considerable amount of time, but the time spent on it was a good investment.

"Bela," Vachagin said to me, "I have not seen such a nice, error-free, well-composed report since I started in this position."

This new job was a university education for me in Soviet life. There were fifty free people in Mines 1 and 2—forty workers and ten communist executives: the president, the chief engineer, department managers, and chief mechanics.

My being a Hungarian lotchik genuinely intrigued them. At first, they tried hard to keep our relationship stiff and formal; I was only slave A584. But the temptation to discuss Hungary and other European countries was too much for them. In a month, we were all good friends, sitting in my office talking through much of the cold nights. Often, when they bought some delicacy—a piece of real cheese—they would share it with me. It was wonderful.

I found that the average free worker, other than the executives, was completely dissatisfied not only with Inta, but also with the Soviet Union. The ones I met were not sophisticated enough politically to discuss communism or capitalism, but they knew that they just did not make enough money. They lived in one of the four villages or thirty *posiyoloks*, dreary little settlements with a store and a row of one-story barracks-like buildings in the shadow of the coal mines. Each family had one room and shared a communal kitchen and bathroom with several other families.

"I make eight hundred rubles a month. I have figured it takes at least 1,500 rubles to exist at all," one of the mechanics told me. "My wife works at Inta for six hundred rubles, but it is still not enough."

The "long ruble" these people were seeking at Inta was long, but not long enough to last from payday to payday. Yet, had they been working in any other area—except a few capital cities and propaganda mines—their ruble would have been worth exactly half what it was in Inta.

For the average "free worker" in Inta, clothes were prohibitively priced. At that time, the ruble was worth twenty-five cents at the official rate, but it was actually about one-fourth that in purchasing power.

I learned from the free workers that the situation was much the same all over the Soviet Union, except for executives, *stakhanovites* (overproducers), and highly skilled workers. It was a nation of families living in one-room apartments, existing on substandard salaries. The singular exception was found in the large cities like Leningrad and Moscow, where workers could get as much as double pay, although they also lived one family to a room.

There was a tremendous disparity in pay in the workers' paradise. Bulbenkov, the director of our mine group, was paid thirty-five thousand rubles per month—fifty times more than that of the average worker. He and his wife paraded in heavy fur coats, caps, and a horse-drawn buggy, a great luxury in Inta. Bulbenkov called himself a "true communist."

"Bela, tell me, how rich are your Hungarian workers?" one of the department managers asked me, laughing, but with skepticism.

Each time I described economic conditions in Hungary during the pre-communist years, I could see their eyes open like awed school children.

"Well, you may have prosperity there, but it is only a bubble that will burst," one of the seven department managers told me. "When we get prosperity in the Soviet Union, it will be forever. Perhaps it is not so good here now, but *budit, budit,* (it will be, it will be)."

The communists openly admitted to me that there was little freedom in the Soviet Union. The freedom they missed most was to quit a job and take another one.

The people of the Soviet Union knew that the government played fast and loose with the truth. Coal production in Mine One was six hundred tons a day, yet the published norm, which we always fulfilled on paper, was one thousand tons. Lying about production figures in every phase of the Soviet economy went all the way to the top, and nobody took the figures seriously.

Life in my new job was better than I had known since my arrival at Inta. In fact, conditions improved a little for everyone. In 1952, the NKVD decided on a bold plan. They started to pay the slaves a small salary. Starvation, low morale, and self-disablement hurt coal production badly and the Kremlin hoped a few rubles of incentive might help.

My pay as an engineer was approximately six hundred rubles a month, out of which the camp took three hundred rubles for room and board, and another fee for camp administration. I was paying for my own imprisonment. Of the remaining three hundred rubles, I paid one hundred rubles a month in income taxes to the Soviet government. The rest, about two hundred rubles, was mine to spend.

The few extra rubles gave the slave camp some superficial aspects of civilization. We were able to purchase in the camp canteen tea, margarine, sugar, and marmalade for a snack after the slightly reduced evening meal. On free days, we could go to the "restaurant" to buy extra cabbage soup, kasha, or fish. But the extra money didn't go very far.

Many men used much of their salaries for prostitutes, others for pure alcohol (at one hundred rubles a pint), which, when added to tea, was a powerful antidote for Inta's monotony.

Even the most dull-witted coal miners, who crouched in their two-and-a half-foot tunnels day in and day out, seemed to emerge out of their living death a little.

The Soviet incentive plan worked on larger scale as well. Coal production rose twenty percent—though it would back-fire dramatically in another, more vital way.

As half-starved animals, we had no strength or courage to protest. But with fuller bellies, we looked objectively at our plight for the first time. We were fed up with the inhuman working and living conditions, the impossible cold, the perse-cution by blatnois, the NKVD stukachey, the long winter nights, the monotony, and the helplessness.

Many of the free people and guards were as fed up with Arctic isolation as the prisoners. There was bitter conflict between the "Red Boards," the Red Army men who were responsible for guarding the area outside the barbed wires, and the "Blue Boards," the NKVD who handled camp policy and administration.

"The NKVD men get six times our pay, and many of them are living in the town with their wives," a Red Army soldier once told me. "They have dancing, movies, vodka, and women. We live here in barracks that are not much better than yours. This winter, ten boys standing guard on the tundra have already committed suicide."

The Red Army soldiers looked at the NKVD guards as glo-rified policemen and jailers. Basically, the Army enlisted men were sympathetic with the mine slaves.

Our own discontent was not organized; we had formed groups strictly along national lines, but were not united. The Baltic people had the strongest organization and the Russians the weakest.

There was no central slave organization to coordinate such a mad dream as rebellion. Each camp was separated from the others by a twelve-foot fence and hundreds of yards of tundra. Our only contact among camps was through transferred prisoners. There was obviously no communication system for a full-scale uprising against General Derevyenko and the Kremlin.

There were, however, isolated bits of sabotage. In Mines 1 and 2, a few spirited ex-communist Soviet students stole dynamite sticks from the coal-blasting department a few at a time. When they had enough, they blew up the power stations and blasted one of the mine shafts.

Meanwhile, Inta's *intelligentsia* sat around dreaming of a rebellion or a mass strike against the Kremlin.

But an average Russian just couldn't understand such a concept. "They are mad dreamers. I have lived under the communists for thirty-five years, and I have never seen anyone oppose them," one *moujik* (peasant) told me. "What have we to rebel with? Our bare hands?"

The moujik made sense. Yet, within a few months' time, three closely related incidents were to set the stage for a dramatic, violent uprising. It all started in Vorkuta, where one hundred thousand slaves started a violent rebellion against the Soviets. This became one of the most significant events of modern times.

It was Stalin who was our mortal enemy, not Derevyenko, Beria, or even the killing cold, and we painstakingly studied his most recent pictures in Pravda. "He doesn't look too well to me," one slave commented hopefully. "See how old and tired his eyes are!"

Then, on 1 March 1953, came the news we had waited so long to hear: Stalin had been stricken by a stroke. On the morning of 6 March 1953, his death was announced over the loudspeaker in Mines 1 and 2.

Stalin's death sent a wave of frenzied expectation through-out Inta and Vorkuta. Maybe Malenkov, the new premier, would close all the slave camps and free us.

On 14 April 1953, Beria's birthday, we heard rumors of a general amnesty. Later that day, Beria announced an amnesty for all prisoners serving five-year sentences or less. In all, five thousand men were released from Inta and Vorkuta, mostly blatnois and workers arrested for chronic absenteeism.

In early May, I was transferred to Vorkuta to Mine 16.

7

Strike at Vorkuta
(21 July 1953)

I have been many times driven to my knees by the over-whelming conviction that I had nowhere else to go. My own wisdom, and that of all about me, seemed insufficient for that day.

Abraham Lincoln

The free workers spoke almost lovingly about Georgi Malenkov, the new Soviet premier. In a short time, the amount of consumer goods in the store had almost doubled. Prices had also dropped.

But in our camp and in Mines 1 and 2, April and May 1953 were bitterly disappointing as slave life went on unchanged. Inta and Vorkuta rumbled with discontent and sabotage became more frequent. It was clear that we were ready for trouble of some kind and only a spark was needed to set it off.

The first spark came in June. Early in the month, over Radio Moscow, we heard of the arrest for treason of our jailer, NKVD Chief Beria, head of the People's Commissariat of Internal Affairs. (He was executed on 23 September).

The second spark occurred on 18 June when the East Germans started a rebellion against the Communist regime. Months later, some two hundred heroes from that rebellion, boys from East Berlin ages sixteen to twenty-two, arrived at Vorkuta to start their fifteen- to twenty-five-year terms as slave laborers.

The next month, in July 1953, we became cocky slaves. We discussed the chance of striking for our freedom—though no one seemed to know what to do. Many men, especially the Russians, were unable to make a decision.

Fortunately, it was made for us. Mines 17 and 18 in Vorkuta went on strike. Derevyenko himself went into the barracks and asked the slaves to go back to work. His request was met with laughter.

At 5 A.M. the next day, the workers of Mine 17 in Vorkuta failed to report for *rasvod* (morning roll call), following secret instructions from an elected leader not to report to work. They demanded to be taken back to the barracks instead of the mine. The guards tried to be firm, but without specific instructions from Derevyenko to shoot, they knew there was nothing they could do.

Reports of the strike in Mine 17 at Vorkuta spread like wildfire throughout the Vorkuta region. Throughout the day, rumors kept coming through the free workers. There was more talk than work that day.

The strike spread to other mines.

One of the men asked me that night, "Bela, do you think it is true, or is it just more *parasha* (rumor)?"

"It is true," I said. "Sasha told me today. He is a good communist and wants to prove that he and they are well informed."

The next day, 22 July, the skeptics were convinced. Mine 7 had joined the strike. For a while, full coal cars came through, but later that day, the Mine 7 coal cars were three-quarters empty.

Written with chalk across the inside of each car in big, bold Russian letters was: "To hell with your coal. We want freedom."

There were handwritten leaflets addressed to us pasted all over the cars. "Comrades from Mines 12, 14, and 16, don't let us down! You know we are striking."

The other mines immediately formed their own strike committees, made up mostly of Russian intellectuals, some still Marxist, but all violently anti-Soviet.

In the second week in July, fifty prison boxcars filled with slaves arrived in Vorkuta, guarded by a tender car bristling with machine guns. They came from the Karaganda slave camp in the Kazakhstan Republic, sent north because of the acute labor shortage in Vorkuta, where twenty percent of our slaves were physically crippled. As an inducement, the Karagandas had been promised higher wages and resettlement with excellent housing in Vorkuta as free exiles.

But of course, the Soviet government had lied. The Karagandas were split among the camps and settled as regular prisoners. About two hundred who were brought into Mine 16 were aware of the strikes going on elsewhere and refused to work unless the government promises were carried out.

One of the promises was that they would be issued mining clothes, which slaves didn't have. When the Karagandas refused to work in their regular clothes, the brigadier went to the storeroom with them to see what they could find. But there was no order for the Karagandas to receive the clothing, so they stood about protesting.

Meanwhile, posters with strikers' demands were being put up throughout the camp. The strike date had been set for 25 July. But it was 24 July and the strike was already under way.

The strikers' slogan was, "Not an ounce of coal for the Plan."

A list of demands was drawn up:

- Removal of the barbed wires.
- Barracks to be kept unlocked at nights.
- Release for all charged with violations in connection with the war.

- Release of all political prisoners who had served ten years or more in Russian prisons.
- Thorough check of the trial transcript of all political prisoners and release of innocents.

Meanwhile, the commandant of the camp arrested thirty of the Karagandas who had refused to work that morning. Immediately, the strike committee and some two thousand other prisoners stormed toward the prison and stood before the gate yelling, "Free the Karagandas."

The commandant came out and tried to calm the prisoners. "There is no cause for trouble, men. I promise that the Karagandas will be released before 6 P.M. tonight."

It was 3:15 P.M. when several *chornie viorns* (police wagons) drove up along with several police cars and four truckloads of troops. They obviously had come to take the Karagandas to the central prison. About one hundred Red Army and NKVD troops piled out of the trucks and blocked the camp gates.

The slaves cursed violently in unison and shoulder-to-shoulder rushed to bar the troops' way into the camp. The guards had to retreat.

Since the bor was off-limits, it was possible for the NKVD to cut through the fence and reach the bor from the rear.

Suddenly, the thirty Karaganda slaves, who had overcome their three drunken guards, dashed out of the prison into the yard. The prisoners sent up a tremendous yell of jubilation. A second later, the NKVD political lieutenant yelled, "Open fire!" All fifty Red Army men and a few of the NKVD disobeyed the political officer and didn't fire. Next to the lieutenant, a Red Army soldier stood with his machine gun pointed stubbornly at the ground.

Then the NKVD lieutenant put away his own pistol, grabbed the soldier's weapon, and started firing, which lasted only twenty seconds. When it was over, two were dead and others were taken away to die.

Seeing the dead prisoners, the strike committee walked to the front gate and addressed the NKVD officials. "The strike committee is officially relieving you of command of all camps! From this moment on, we prisoners will be in complete charge. No officers or guards will be allowed within the gate without the permission of the committee."

It worked. With courage, the coal strike had been transformed into an uprising. The Vorkuta slave rebellion of 1953 had begun.

The prisoners immediately formed an independent "Slave Republic." A member of the strike committee was put in charge of each barracks. A young Russian graduate of a Soviet technical school was put in command of mines. All the food in the stolovaya, the dining hall, the canteen, and the restaurant was commandeered and new higher rations were set for all. Prisoners in the bor were released and the committee appointed its own police, though it was hardly necessary. Perfect discipline was maintained.

Not one of the 4,500 slave laborers was working in the mines. A few free workers were permitted to man the pits—to work the ventilators, keep the hallways clear of methane gas, and pump out the excess water—but not one lump of coal was allowed to be removed.

Sympathetic free workers maintained contact with the other camps. In this way, the strike demands of each camp were almost exactly the same. The strikers unanimously agreed to deal only with a representative of the Politburo in Moscow or with a member of the Central Communist Party Committee.

The Kremlin in Moscow was paralyzed by its own internal power struggle and afraid to issue definite orders on how to handle the slave rebellion—other than with "extreme caution."

The strikers knew that Malenkov's nervous, unstable new regime needed the coal badly and could not afford to have the uprising spread.

Simultaneously, similar uprisings were taking place all through the twenty-million-slave gulag region. In one of the camps in Karaganda, tanks and machine guns had cut down two hundred slaves in a similar uprising. Free people brought us the news that the uprising, which had started in Vorkuta, sparked uprisings elsewhere—in the Ural ore mines, in the coal mines outside Moscow, and on the enormous collective farms of the Ukraine.

Later on the afternoon of the first day of the strike, three hundred soldiers were deployed around our camp in newly dug trenches. I could see machine guns and mortars being put in place. At 6:30 P.M., the political officer requested permission to enter the camp. He came through the gates unarmed and unescorted and read a concession statement from General Derevyenko.

The officer read:

> As of 23 July 1953, all prisoners will receive up to three hundred rubles per month in compensation.
>
> The bars are to be removed from the windows of the barracks.
>
> The barracks will no longer be locked for the night.
>
> Evening roll call will be eliminated.
>
> With the permission of the commanding officer, prisoners may receive visitors from home once a year.
>
> Slave numbers will no longer be required on prisoners' clothing.
>
> An attempt will be made to provide better housing, food, and clothing.
>
> Soviet citizens can mail letters once a month instead of twice a year.

The next three days were pure bliss. Nature had joined forces with us and granted us cloudless, sunny days. I was sitting with a friend by the fence when a Red Army soldier who was patrolling stopped in front of me.

"What's going on?" he asked through the gate. "Have you gained anything?"

We told him about Derevyenko's concessions and our good life these last three days.

"Good," he said. "We are on your side. I don't care if you strike until doomsday. No Red Army man will ever fire on you."

On 27 July 1953, Derevyenko himself came to speak to us, accompanied by Dichtin, the minister of internal affairs for the Komi Republic. They, too, were unarmed and unescorted. Of course, there were three hundred troops with mortars and machine guns directly outside the fence.

They continued the kid-glove treatment that had thus far characterized the official attitude towards the uprising. Derevyenko walked from one group to another talking in a fatherly manner.

"You now have most of your demands. What more do you want?"

"We are waiting for the Kremlin to make a final decision on our demands," a member of the strike committee declared.

Just before he left the camp, Derevyenko announced that the deputy minister of internal affairs for the entire Soviet Union was flying up from Moscow to talk to us. This news was received as another strike victory, but I believe many of us, deep in our hearts, were worried. The deputy minister had the reputation for both shrewdness and cruelty.

The next day, 28 July, another beautiful day, we buried our two dead. The burial was in the open football field where

4,500 of us, wearing black mourning ribbons, filed by to pay our final respects.

At noon on 29 July, a slave striker ran into my barracks. "Get up! Masslenikov, the general from Moscow, is coming down the road!" he announced loudly.

I got off my shelf and ran down to the gate just in time to see a long black car driving into the camp between two lines of one hundred heavily armed guards.

Masslenikov emerged from the limousine. The driver made a U-turn and parked between the lines of NKVD troops with its nose pointing toward the open gate. Outside, there were at least one hundred troops patrolling.

An entourage of thirty officers, mostly colonels, followed Masslenikov to the football field where we had put chairs and a long table for them in advance. They had come to hear our demands and we were ready for them. The strike committee had chosen twenty speakers to present our viewpoint. A mass of 4,500 slaves was assembled on the football field facing the Kremlin officers.

What followed was the most stirring scene I have witnessed in my life. First, the strike leader presented our demands. Then, from the ranks, one man at a time stepped out to speak. The speeches were moving, intelligent, and biting.

A former professor of history at the University of Leningrad traced the history of slavery from pre-pharaonic times through the slave trade on the Gold Coast. "But never in the history of man," he said, "has working slavery been so extensive and so cruelly exploited as here in the Soviet Union, the liberator of the working class!"

The next speaker was a former Red Army officer.

"I was raised under Communism and wanted no other way," he began. "During the war, I was decorated many times. I suffered seventeen bullet wounds and returned to fight again.

The eighteenth time I was wounded, I fell unconscious on the field. When I came to, I was a German POW. I escaped and spent the rest of the war fighting the Nazis with a band of Soviet partisans. In 1946, when our government learned that I had once been a German POW, I was sentenced to twenty years at Inta. Now, I have come to the conclusion that communism breeds only slavery."

A Pole spoke for the foreigners. Two former high-ranking Soviet bureaucrats spoke about the abuse of Marxist doctrines and its perversion in the Soviet Union.

Masslenikov was noticeably pale and shocked. He listened for over an hour, not speaking except to interrupt occasionally. "Remember, you are insulting the great Soviet Union."

When the speeches were over, he got up and left for the next camp without a word.

Masslenikov completed his rounds of the striking camps the next day without making a dent in the strikers' unity. The uneasy truce continued.

On 1 August at 9 A.M., Masslenikov again drove up to the camp gate. He asked for our strike leader. His battalion was deployed on the tundra in battle formation.

"The ultimatum is work or death," Masslenikov said.

Our strike committee leader pondered for a few seconds. "Give us twenty-four hours to think it over," he said. As events unfolded, our strike committee leader's mastery of diplomacy saved many lives.

Masslenikov looked at him distrustfully. "Agreed."

From our camp, Masslenikov and his troops moved up the road to the next mine.

We were cut off from events and waited in abeyance for more than an hour. At 11 A.M., we heard bursts of gunfire. The sounds of the shots filled the empty tundra for two full minutes.

A few minutes later, there was a call for all camp doctors to rush to that mine.

Later, we were told enough to reconstruct the scene. Masslenikov had driven up to the camp gates, backed by his 1,200 troops surrounding the fences. Arms locked, 2,500 slaves were packed in front of the gates.

"Go back to your barracks!" Masslenikov called over the loudspeaker. "Follow the example of the other mines. They are already working in the pits."

The crowd responded with insults and pushed close to the fence. At Masslenikov's hand signal, a squad of troops opened the gate and advanced into the camp. But as the prisoners walked toward them defiantly, the soldiers turned and ran.

A few minutes later, two giant fire hoses were pushed through the side fences. Four bulky Ukrainian prisoners rushed over and jammed the nozzles shut. When the pumps were turned on, the water trickled harmlessly onto the tundra.

"I warned you, go back to your barracks," Masslenikov ordered again.

When no one moved, the NKVD chief tried persuasion. "All those who want to return to work, come outside the gate."

Every prisoner's eye swung in a circle around him and glared as fifty men walked out. Masslenikov looked disgustedly at the small group and yelled, "Get back in."

Then he called out on the loudspeaker a third time. "End this rebellion now! Go back to your barracks! Get yourselves ready to work! This is the last warning I will give you."

As the prisoners stood by the gate, heavy machine guns were set up twenty yards from the fence and the NKVD soldiers opened fire. The staccato of the machine guns punctuated the screams of the wounded for two full minutes until no one was left standing. Blood covered everyone. More than 500 were seriously wounded and 110 were killed instantly.

Masslenikov ordered the gates opened and barked orders to the living to come out onto the tundra. He said those who still refused to work would be killed on the spot. The survivors wailed as they stepped over the bodies of their fallen comrades and walked toward the gate.

The next day, when we heard what had happened, we returned to work.

Masslenikov had broken the back of the rebellion with a bloodbath.

In the following weeks, the NKVD made up for its indecision during the strike. Every few hours another man was dragged away and sent to a central bor set up for the strike leaders. In all, seven thousand slaves were arrested. Three NKVD officers and two guards were also arrested and charged with helping to inspire the rebellion. Of the seven thousand seized, three hundred were executed without trial, another one thousand men were transferred to the Far East, and the rest were given additional three-to five-year sentences.

By Western standards, I guess the slave rebellion was a failure. We had struck for freedom and were still gulag slaves. But that is an oversimplification. The mere fact that a rebellion did take place in the Soviet Union made it an instantaneous, glorious success. Its effect on the communist world was electrifying. We—one hundred thousand slaves—in those ten days, showed the Kremlin that its internal solidarity was a sham.

If nothing else, the story of this first organized resistance to the Soviet mammoth in thirty-five years, the strike of slave workers in the "workers' paradise" had traveled through the Russian grapevine and gave hope to twenty million gulag slaves.

Vorkuta never again quieted down. A triumphant spirit, buoyed by the wage increase we had received, was the strikers' legacy.

At this point, however, I had lost all hope for an early release. During the strike, for no logical reason, I somehow expected a chain of events that would end up with me a free man back in Hungary. But that dream was now subdued and there were still nineteen years left of my sentence.

I had never even been allowed to send a postcard to my mother in Hungary. Only a selected few prisoners had the privilege of sending cards to their relatives through the International Red Cross, but I was never one of them. However, I was given one remnant and glimmer of hope—a postcard that I finally managed to send in the name of another prisoner.

Immediately after the strike, I was transferred back to Inta at the request of the director and chief engineer of Mine 2.

8

Rising From the Bottom
(1953)

*I have felt His hand upon me in great trials and submitted to His guid-
ance, and I trust that as He shall further open the way, I will be ready to walk
therein, relying on His help and trusting in His goodness and wisdom.*

Abraham Lincoln

I accepted the fact that I would spend another nineteen
years in slave camps. From that moment on, whatever I did was
with the purpose of making my life simply bearable, and
obtaining enough food to quench my hunger.

My wish list wasn't long. I wanted more cabbage soup,
kasha, maybe a bigger piece of salted fish, and a larger piece of
bread than our daily portions.

The next item on my list was to be able to take a shower
and exchange the sweat-soaked, coal-dust covered work clothes
for clean ones after each long shift in the belly of the earth.

Another wish was food for my mind. Initially, a book or
nice music would have satisfied my mental hunger. Though I
loved concerts and plays, I knew those were a dream that would
have been impossible to realize.

The last wish on my list was to have someone who would
care for me and share my happiness and sorrow and with whom
I could discuss my problems.

Around the time of the strike in July 1953, my living conditions slowly began to improve. The first significant change came with the new job. Initially, the new job alone didn't fill my empty stomach, but it opened the way toward satisfying excruciating hunger. Also, this new job allowed me to exercise my mind and to satisfy my desire for creativity.

At this time, one of my friends, Steve Bacsek, became the camp's maintenance man. His responsibilities included keeping the kitchen, bakery, hospitals, stolovaya, and the offices of Soviet camp officials clean and sanitary. The buildings in the camp were wooden structures. Interior walls were covered with whitewashed stucco, which was easily damaged and a favorite place for spiders, bedbugs, and other insects. Repairing and whitewashing the wall exterminated the bugs.

The kitchen and bakery took at least four days of his time every week and he always needed help. He usually picked helpers from among his friends who would get extra food while working in the kitchen, bakery, or stolovaya.

Shortly after he took his new job, the camp officials were told to expect a visit by a general from Moscow. During such visits, the officials would walk into the kitchen, bakery, and stolovaya and check for cleanliness and sanitary conditions. Before the general's visit, the camp officials walked through those places, pre-inspected them, and made a list of items needing repair. This time, they picked the bakery. Around 8 P.M., Steve walked into our barracks looking for helpers. I eagerly offered my help and set the time to start working at 9 P.M.

The stucco walls of the bakery were in poor condition. The first step was to remove the loose pieces of stucco from the walls. When we finished, we had a big pile of debris in the middle of the room that had to be carried out before we could continue the repair job.

I went outside to find a wheelbarrow. When I returned, I noticed several shelves filled with freshly baked bread and a plan entered my mind. I couldn't pass up an opportunity to take a couple of loaves to my barracks and feed my hungry friends.

I quickly grabbed two loaves and put them on the bottom of the wheelbarrow, covered them up with the stucco pieces removed from the wall, loaded the wheelbarrow, and was on my way to the dumping site. There, I dug out the two loaves from under the rubble, dumped out the debris, and rushed to the barracks. I woke up Joco and gave him the two loaves. He woke up our friends, cut the bread, and by the time I left, I saw four happy faces sending the fresh bread into their empty stomachs. It didn't matter that the bread was covered with dust from the plaster—hunger prevailed over dirt. It wasn't until a year later that I related the story to Steve.

"How did you manage to do that without my noticing it?" he asked.

One day, the director of Mine 2 called me into his office for technical advice. During the winter, the coal piled up in the yard and was hauled away in May and June when the weather improved. There was no way for him to know how much coal had been produced since the last inventory. Since everyone in the Soviet Union was lying about economic production, the dispatchers reported more coal than was actually produced. So the amount of coal on paper never agreed with the actual amount stored in the yard.

To obtain an accurate figure, the amount of coal hauled away would have to be added to the amount remaining on the ground. This inventory was taken only once a year, during the summer. At the time, the director had to account for the missing coal. If he couldn't, he could be thrown in jail. He had a choice—either admit to the missing amount or lie and make the amount hauled away plus what was on the ground equal to production claimed on paper. This was a dangerous game, because the difference over the years could have been significant. Usually it was.

The director, who knew about my engineering background, asked me for a practical solution that could be implemented with relative ease using resources readily available to him. He was also interested in how much time it would require to plan and build the prototype device. He gave me two weeks to come up with a proposal. This gave me a very welcome reprieve from the harsh daily routine of the work in the belly of the earth. I could sit comfortably at a desk in a warm office where nobody could interrupt me while I worked on a design. A week later, I had the initial plan completed.

The coal was brought up to the surface by an elevator. I knew from my engineering background that the current in the wire feeding the electric motor that lifted the elevator was proportional to the load of the elevator. My first task was to determine how much operating range I had. It was defined as the difference of the currents between a fully loaded and an empty elevator.

The second step was to make a list of what I would need for the project, and the availability of those parts. At this point, I knew the solution. A current transformer had to be installed in the circuit feeding the motor running the elevator. The output of this transformer had to be connected to an electromagnetic circuit to record the current.

To record the amount of coal as a function of time, I bent the end of the hand that scribed a graph on the recording media fastened to a cylinder rotating at a constant speed. For this, I needed a constant-speed motor to drive the recording medium, a thin copper film covered by soot.

The hand of the Ampere meter would draw a graph on the copper film. This represented the amount of coal brought to the surface as a function of time. It was a simple design and easy to implement.

The next task was to gather the required components for my "coal recorder." The only item available was an old Ampere meter. There was no transformer or small, constant-speed, electric motor. I estimated it would take three months to build the transformer and motor. I needed another three months to assemble the parts, calibrate the device, write an operation manual, and train a service technician.

Two weeks later, I presented my proposal to the director and the chief engineer. They liked the concept, gave approval for implementation, and made the resources under their control available to me. This included the machine shop, the lamp shop, and the stock room.

The chief engineer instructed the narjadchik to give me the highest performance rating. Thus, I received the largest piece of bread and some extra food.

Returning to the office at the end of day, I would often find a piece of bread and occasionally cheese or meat on my desk. I knew it was the chief engineer who left the food for me.

Initially, implementation went smoothly and quickly. Then I reached the point when I needed the paper drive, composed of a small, constant-speed electric motor, and a reduction mechanism to reduce the speed of the motor from two thousand rotations per minute to one rotation every forty-eight hours. To build such a device from available resources stretched my capabilities.

One morning, the chief engineer walked in and inquired about my progress. I told him my concern about building the drive mechanism. After a short pause, he asked me whether a barograph would do the job. In his previous assignment as chief engineer at a meteorological station that was completely refurbished during his tenure, the old instruments were scrapped. He had salvaged a barograph used to measure and record atmospheric pressure. In this device, the paper chart was fastened to the surface of a five-inch diameter drum. The rotation of the drum could be set to either twenty-four or forty-eight hours by a mechanical switch. The drive mechanism was spring-driven and had to be re-wound weekly or biweekly, depending on the setting of the switch.

The next day, I had the barograph in my possession. The only task remaining was to assemble the components.

At the end of the fifth month, the prototype was in working order and was sitting on my desk during the evaluation period. For the prototype, copper foil covered with soot was used as the recording medium. The writing mechanism was a needle fastened to the end of the hand that drew the graph, indicating the amount of coal brought to the surface as a function of time. The use of a chart scribed on copper foil was a tedious and cumbersome process, which required materials and technique I didn't have.

During the evaluation period, my first modification was to design and fabricate an inking mechanism that would draw the graph on a paper chart. I did this and it worked well. However, cleaning and filling the pen required constant care. At the end of the evaluation period, when it worked satisfactorily, I mounted the instrument into a wooden box built in the machine shop. It had a glass front and a lock to keep unauthorized persons away from the recording mechanism.

At the end of six months, the instrument was ready to be installed in the director's office. Initially, it required a significant amount of care. Regular servicing of the device was my responsibility. I changed the tape, cleaned and filled the writing mechanism, and kept an accurate record of daily production.

I became an instant hero in the eyes of the chief engineer and the director of the mine. For me, it meant survival. I had more than fulfilled my norm on paper—it was two hundred percent—and my daily bread ration more than doubled.

The news about the new instrument spread quickly among the dispatchers. Initially, they were surprised when the director readjusted the amount of coal claimed to an uninflated level. They quickly realized that the only one who could raise their paper-production fulfillment of the norm from 90 percent to 120 percent or higher was the Hungarian lotchik.

The desperate dispatchers began telling me that their families needed the extra money they had earned from inflated production levels just to survive. Without the additional income, they wouldn't be able to feed their children and buy clothes and shoes for them. I boosted the level of their production on paper. In compensation, they brought me food and at pay time, gave me money.

The money came at the most needed time. Bert, one of my friends, became seriously ill with tuberculosis. No medication was available in the camp. The Latvian feltcher told me that he could get the newly discovered Streptomycin in sufficient amounts to cure Bert. He also assured me that he would keep Bert in the infirmary as long as necessary. The money I received from the dispatchers was coming in regularly and was just enough to pay for the medicine. Bert started to gain weight and six months later, the lab test indicated no sign of tuberculosis. When he left the infirmary, we bought a job for him that didn't require much physical effort to earn the maximum bread portion possible.

Meanwhile, the coal recorder did its job recording daily production. The system was installed in the director's office in January 1955. I knew that I had three or four months before they would discover the shortage.

Should they discover that I had manipulated the instrument, they would have sentenced me to jail according to the

Soviet penal code and could have thrown me in jail or a labor camp with Soviet criminals.

The free workers knew that they could contact me if they needed something that wasn't available in local stores. For example, they could get motorbikes in the village, but no spare parts, so it was impossible to find a replacement battery to keep their motorbikes running.

Battery-operated vehicles were used underground to move the wagons. Spare batteries for these vehicles were stored in the stockroom. When someone came to me to repair his battery, I reused only the case and replaced the old lead plates with those cut from the spare batteries. The money and food I received for this and other services went into a community pool used for extra food, clothes, and other needs.

The winter at Inta/Vorkuta was long and cold. The days were short. During four months, from November through February, the sun never came up and darkness engulfed our world. Mine 2 was approximately three miles from the village. The roads to the mine were unlit and in poor condition. The civilian workers had to walk in complete darkness. No flashlights were available in the village stores and if someone could purchase one through relatives in big cities, no replacement batteries were available.

One day, the director of the mine came to the lamp shop and asked me to fabricate a hand-held lamp for him. I delivered it the next day and he was pleased with it. Soon, all of the civilian workers found out the source of the director's hand lamp. Over the next few days, orders came in for huge quantities of lamps that I was unable to fill. The mine employees who bought hand-held lamps compensated me generously. They paid in money or brought food, vodka, and clothing. We serviced the portable lights, changed bulbs, and charged the batteries for a modest fee.

Table lamps were luxury items. They were available only in large cities in a relatively limited selection. I realized this would be a popular and desirable item to fabricate and sell. I designed a simple model using readily available resources. My friends in the machine shop fabricated the bronze base and stand. I polished and lacquered them.

The lampshade required inventiveness, artistic inclination, and tools that were not readily available to me. The frame for the shade was constructed from wire. The pieces were tied together using silver solder on the early shades and brass on the later ones. For soldering, I fabricated a small Bunsen burner with a fine tip using gasoline under pressure as fuel. At the right setting, it was capable of melting both silver and brass.

Building the prototype was a tedious and time-consuming process. Several different techniques had to be developed and refined before quantities could be produced.

The shade was covered with thick paper sewn to the frame with woolen yarn. The last step was to paint decorative figures in multi-color using watercolor. One of my friends made a sketch of a dancing couple. For each color, a separate stencil had to be cut. The paint was sprinkled on the shade with a toothbrush. A light coating of oil was brushed on after the paint had dried. The final step was to assemble the lamp.

I put the prototype on my desk where everybody who walked by could see it. The lamp, even by Western standards, was a beautiful piece.

I received orders in great quantities for this lamp and would have been busy for a long time producing them. Customers were willing to pay any price.

Several women were working in the mine office located next to mine. One pretty Russian girl in the office, who used to call the non-Russian political prisoners derogatory names such as Fritz, Nazi, or Capitalist, changed her tone fast after seeing the lamp. She wanted one badly. She knew that I had money and food, but no cozy, discrete relationship with a woman.

"Make me a lamp like this and I'll visit you any night. I'll please you and fulfill your desires," she proposed.

Her offer was a strong temptation, but because of her constant taunting in a hateful, derogatory manner, I wouldn't even consider her "gracious" offer.

While my friend Bert stayed in the infirmary, I met every day with Ozie, the Latvian feltcher. We enjoyed each other's company and had long discussions about science, engineering, and physics. Since his education was similar to mine, it was easy to pick a topic and spend the whole evening discussing it, arguing and reasoning. One of my favorite subjects was Latin. We collected phrases. What a refreshing diversion this was for both of us.

One evening, Helmy, an Armenian friend of his, joined us. He was a dental technician in civilian life. He told us that he was in the process of setting up a dental lab somewhere in the mine. It was a dangerous undertaking because the NKVD visited the workplace daily. Helmy was an honest, hardworking, anticommunist. He asked me to help him carry out his plan. I needed a couple of days to evaluate the pros and cons before I could make a commitment to help him.

"I will help you set up a small laboratory in a corner of the lamp shop under my technical supervision," I said to him a week later.

The deal was that Joco, Helmy, and I would fabricate crowns and bridges and install them for prisoners who had the means to pay for them. Helmy volunteered to prepare the teeth, do the dental work, make the impression, and pass it over to us to fabricate the crowns and the bridges.

Meanwhile, I looked for stainless steel material suitable for crowns. I needed a stainless steel plate ten- to twenty-thousands of an inch thick. One day, I noticed a welder in one of the shops using a stainless-steel welding rod. After talking to him, he offered his assistance. In two days, he delivered a stainless steel plate made to our specifications.

Our first job was an individual crown. Helmy made the impression. Joco fabricated the mold, and, using a lead hammer, shaped the plate into a crown. At that time, he was working underground as a pump operator and had time to work on the teeth between switching the pump on and off.

Joco stored his tools in a handmade cotton bag that he left hidden behind some supporting timber after his shift ended.

Initially, Joco and Helmy fabricated single crowns. When they had acquired experience and mastered the technique, they accepted orders for multi-unit bridges. The units were tied together using silver solder. For this, the Bunsen burner, fabricated earlier for lampshades, came in handy.

Final polishing was done in the lamp shop, using a fine grit polishing paste on a disk developed for polishing the brass pieces of the table lamp. Our little dental laboratory was functioning fabulously.

Then there came a sudden turn of events.

One day, Joco came to me at the end of his shift telling me that a NKVD soldier came over to him while he was working on a crown, took everything he had—his tools, finished and half-finished crowns and bridges, and walked away. We were stunned. Our moonlighting had come to an end.

The next day, Joco was taken into the office of the commandant.

"Are you a dentist?" he asked Joco.

"I am not a dentist, but I finished dental school," Joco replied. "I couldn't receive my diploma because I was arrested on the same day my last final examination was scheduled."

Grinning, the director opened his mouth, and showed his teeth, which were in bad shape.

"Could you fix my teeth?" he asked.

"Sure, I could," Joco said. "But our tools were taken away last night by one of your guards."

The commandant pulled out the drawer of his desk and handed over the bag containing the tools and half-finished parts. Joco's jaw dropped and he let out a sigh of relief.

The commandant wanted Joco to start on his teeth immediately.

"I have to think it over before I can say yes," Joco said. "I'll let you know tomorrow."

He wanted to jump with sheer joy, but he restrained himself. He didn't want the commandant to feel that he was doing us a favor, and let him sweat for a while.

Joco discussed the commandant's request with Helmy and me. Of course we were elated and knew that the three of us didn't have to worry about our moonlighting. We agreed that we would do it, though there was really never any doubt about our decision. No one could or would pass up such an opportunity.

The next day, Joco went to the commandant's office to let him know we would fix his teeth and it would take six months from start to finish. It would mean that for at least six months no NKVD guard would bother us. In essence, it was a temporary license to openly sell our dental services to prisoners who could pay for them.

Six months later, we finished the commandant's dental work. From then on, we were free to continue our dental practice without worrying about the guards interfering.

Meanwhile, we continued our nightly meetings with Ozie and others. One night, Ozie had a very pleasant surprise for me. He had just received a package from Latvia. In it was *The Aeneid* by Virgil in original Latin. He had asked someone back home to buy and send it to him for me. I was delighted and for the next couple of months, I had something to keep my mind occupied.

The severe weather conditions in the Arctic North caused many people, prisoners and free workers, to suffer from rheumatism. There was no medicine or other means available to ease the pain. Ozie asked me if I could design and build a massaging device. Since I knew how one worked, I agreed.

The next day, I spent my whole shift working on the design. The device was made of a high-voltage transformer, a mechanical vibrator, and a potentiometer to control the amount of current flowing to the two electrodes connected to the device. The instrument was mounted in a nicely finished wooden case and delivered to Ozie. He was pleased and began to use it immediately. In return, he offered me a daily portion of food—bread, breakfast, and dinner. Since I didn't need it, I asked him to give it to Bert, who needed the extra food.

I received orders for two more devices. One came from Vachagin, our chief engineer. The other was from a dispatcher. I didn't accept any compensation from Vachagin, but I charged the dispatcher a fair price.

The winter of 1954 was approaching at a fast pace. I filled my free evenings devouring and interpreting *The Aeneid*. Initially, the reading went slowly. But as I gained experience, I could read several pages a night. If I had trouble with the translation or with a word or expression, I could ask Ozie or a Catholic priest who was a friend of mine.

Shortly after I finished reading *The Aeneid*, Vachagin brought me two books by Theodore Dreiser, *An American*

Tragedy and *Sister Carrie.* Both books were in Russian. By then, I had a good knowledge of the language and reading and comprehension were growing easier and even more enjoyable.

One day, a mine executive gave me a book on calculus and one on modern physics, both textbooks used in engineering courses at universities in Russia.

Around Christmas, the director of the mine surprised me with the *Kreutzer Sonata* by Leo Tolstoy.

Later that winter, Ozie shared with me his secret desire to build an X-ray machine for the infirmary. He handed me a book on X-ray machine technology written in German and asked for my help. I made a list of parts needed to build a simple machine: an X-ray tube, a projection screen, a transformer, switches, and an electronic timer. The required range for the timer was from one microsecond (one millionth of a second) to several seconds.

Ozie and I divided the task of obtaining the parts. He told me that he could get an X-ray tube and a projection screen from Latvia provided that the camp management approved it. The NKVD commandant did approve it with the condition that the parts would be shipped directly to him and he would give them to us as needed.

I agreed to design and fabricate the transformer and get the other easily available parts. But obtaining a timer was a problem, as it is an electronic device that uses vacuum tubes. The NKVD didn't trust the prisoners with electronic parts like tubes that could be used to build a radio transmitter. Having it in the camp would be a major violation punishable with several years of prison. A violator could be charged with espionage and in some cases sentenced to death. The timer remained an open issue.

Christmas of 1954 was a painful day. I missed my family very much. It was the seventh Christmas without them. What used to be a joyful celebration in the circle of family, friends, and bright flickering candles was now a somber, gloomy occasion.

But we were determined to observe it with as much dignity as possible. What was in our hearts would make this most solemn celebration come to pass. On Christmas Eve, Joco, Bert, and I got together in the barracks. We had saved some sugar and bread for the occasion. I had a piece of cheese that I'd gotten from Vachagin and a bottle of vodka.

The celebration was moving. We said a short prayer, remembering our loved ones five thousand miles away, and the sound of "Silent Night" softly filled our barracks. When the words died away, we retired for the night and in our dreams, we joined our loved ones far away in Hungary.

On Christmas Day, Vachagin called me into his office with a mischievous look in his eyes and solemnly handed me a package. "Open it after I leave and have a merry Christmas."

Then he handed me a key and told me to lock the door and not let anybody in.

"I will come back at the end of the shift before you have to leave for the camp," Vachagin said.

His gift was so unexpected. I was filled with emotion as I opened the package. There were cookies, ham, cheese, and other goodies—even a bottle of good, Russian vodka—things I hadn't seen throughout my years in Soviet prisons and camps. The kindness and generosity of this big stern looking, hunk of a man overwhelmed me.

Kindness often comes from the most unexpected source. I will remember Christmas of 1954 as long as I live.

9

Indoctrination Before Repatriation
(1955)

A special delegation from the Kremlin itself came to see us. I jumped when I saw that General Masslenikoff, the butcher of Vorkuta, headed it. Four colonels accompanied him. They carried and placed on the table a big bundle of papers. The general walked to the table and made the announcement "You will leave for Hungary tomorrow . . .

One day in early March 1955, I had just returned from the mine when the *nevalney* (barracks master) rushed in excitedly.

"Lotchik, the camp director is looking for you. You and the other Hungarians have orders to proceed to Moscow," he said.

I looked up at him and laughed. But a few minutes later, Joco and Bert arrived with the same news.

I rushed nervously to the administration building and stood in front of the NKVD chief.

"You are to leave for Moscow at 7 A.M. tomorrow morning," he said.

"To Moscow?" I asked.

"As far as I know, you are going home," the commandant said.

After Stalin died in 1953, the new Soviet president decided to repatriate all the foreigners who were convicted between 1945 and 1953. The first group had been sent home in 1953. The rest of us waited for our turn.

Still, I was incredulous at the news. I heard the commandant correctly, but the words didn't sink in. I wouldn't let them.
Why should I be released? There was no general amnesty. I had
lost touch with the outside world. Inta and its regulations were
the only reality I understood.

But I prayed for his words to be true.

Very few prisoners of Arctic camps ever lived to see freedom. Few were transported back to Moscow. A few had left in
November or December of 1954, but no one ever heard
whether they were finally released or were being held in other
camps.

Now that it was my turn to leave, I wondered what my fate
would be.

I was given a form with fourteen items on it that had to
be signed by various departments such as the kitchen, bath,
stockroom, library, office, infirmary, and even the political
branches. It was simple, essentially asking whether I owed anything to those departments, and was a mere formality without
any real meaning. The forms were designed for Moscow's
rulers to show the outside world that prisoners were treated
humanely.

Having heard the news of my release, many men of many
nationalities came to ask if I would send word to their loved
ones when I got home.

I would have liked to talk to other prisoners to gain more
insight into the true conditions in the Soviet Union, especially
in the gulag. I intended to describe what political prisoners
were exposed to and the Soviet people had to endure in their
own country upon my return to the free world.

I knew some prisoners in the camps who have been
deported from their hometowns because they knew too much
about things the Soviets wanted kept secret. They had lived
close to the place where the first Soviet atomic tests were made.

The Kremlin leadership didn't want the free world to know that unfinished bombs and laboratories had blown up. But foreign instruments had recorded the explosion, and the Soviets had felt obliged to announce it as a successful test. But were all the tests successful?

I never had a chance to say good-bye to the chief engineer, the mine director, the dispatchers, and other mine officials.

Overwhelmed by anticipation, I didn't get much sleep that night. But the sleepless hours flew by and before I knew it, hundreds of my fellow prisoners were there to wave farewell as I was escorted to the railroad by an unarmed guard. At the Inta station, I walked right up to the parked Stalopinski and waited for the NKVD officer walking behind me to order me to board.

He laughed. "No, no, Lotchik! That's not for you any more. Get into one of the passenger cars."

The three of us, Joco, Bert, and I, without handcuffs, but accompanied by two NKVD officers, traveled in a Pullman car of a passenger train from Inta to Moscow.

The NKVD officers explained that they didn't speak Hungarian, so our conversation with them had to be in Russian. Mastering the language all those years in the gulag came in handy.

There was no dining car, so we ate cold meals. As we stopped at stations along the way, children and old women ran alongside the train selling hot potatoes, eggs, and ladles of milk. Chains of beggars filed through the cars, old and young, sick and blind, complaining that they had no work and no home. The officers kept them moving along. It was obvious that in front of us "foreigners," the beggars were a source of embarrassment.

The officers did not feign embarrassment or seem to object, however, when girls and women traveling on the train undressed at night down to their underclothing before lying down to sleep. A very few had colorful pajamas that they not only wore sleeping, but when they left the train to shop along the platform. Even when we arrived in Moscow, some went into the streets in their pajamas.

It took four days to reach Moscow, which was a big change for us. A dozen NKVD officials waited at the station to receive us. We were escorted to a bus that I recognized from the outside to be a prison car. This took us to Boutyrki, the Soviet Union's most elaborate prison. It was equipped with the latest torture technology and its personnel were well trained to extract anything they wanted from prisoners.

After our few personal belongings, such as a hand carved chess set, an engraved cup, a piece of nice clothing, were taken from us, we were shown to our room. This was a large, three-bed cell with fresh sheets—a comfort we hadn't know during our prison years when we slept on bare floors or bunks—and even a clean toilet vessel.

The next day, two colonels visited us. They asked us how we were. Speaking for the three of us, I asked them what would happen next.

"You are not going back to a labor camp," one of the colonels said.

"Where would you like to go if you were set free?" another one asked.

"To Hungary!" we replied in unison.

Shortly after the visit, we were called down to the reception room where we were issued new pants, jackets, and shoes.

Two weeks passed and we became impatient. Finally, wearing our prison clothes and with our new outfits in small suitcases, we were taken to a camp at Potma/Javas, some three hundred miles to the southeast in the Soviet Mordvinian Republic. Camp Potma/Javas had held many Tsarist prisoners at one time.

We were marched to an old, relatively small camp. Our suitcases were taken into security, we were checked in, and, to our surprise, told to report for work at 8 A.M. the next morning.

The barracks at Potma/Javas were identical to those in Inta. We picked sleeping places on the lower shelf. Within minutes, other Hungarian prisoners who had arrived a couple days earlier crowded the room. I was reunited with members of the Apponyi conspiracy case who had been sent to different camps seven years earlier, not knowing the fates of the others.

Dozens of questions were put to us—"Where are you from? What camp? When were you arrested? Destination?"

The question as to our next destination interested us the most. "Where can I go from here?" I wondered.

Potma/Javas, they explained, was the repatriation camp. Sooner or later, we would be going home. No one works here, they said, except for doing camp upkeep. This was different from what we had been told upon entering. Was someone fooling us?

The next morning, we did not report to work. A guard soon came and hauled us off to the camp commander. He dressed us down for not obeying orders. I explained to him, on behalf of the three of us, that we had been told in Moscow that we were not going to another slave camp. If they wanted us to work, they would have to send us back to a work camp.

The camp commander's face turned red with anger. "Where did you learn Russian?" he asked.

"I learned it in your camps," I said.

He shook his head. "You speak better than a Russian lawyer," he grumbled.

He then dismissed us with orders to see the narjadchik to pick a work project that we liked and report to work the next morning.

I noticed that the watchtowers were empty at this camp. There were only a few guards, and they were unarmed. The camp was quite pleasant and surrounded by trees. It was the first time we had seen trees in seven years. Inta and Vorkuta were above the Arctic Circle, surrounded by tundra, where the permanent frost line was about two feet below ground level.

We had arrived in early spring when nature was awakening from its long hibernation and the trees were just starting to bud. The birds came out of their hiding places and delivered the most pleasant concert every morning. It sounded like a welcoming song for those who had just returned to life from death.

At first, new groups of prisoners arrived daily. But after two weeks, no more prisoners came. The total head count of the camp was 700, made up of 550 Hungarians, 100 Germans, and 50 Poles and other nationalities. The prisoners formed social groups and occupied barracks according to their nationalities.

During our stay in Potma/Javas, lifelong friendships developed between people with similar interests and backgrounds.

Among us were Bela Kovacs, the former secretary of the Small Holders Party and minister of agriculture; Placid Olafson, a Catholic monk of the Order of St. Benedictine; Gaspar Szep, a veterinary student with whom I formed a lifelong friendship; Steve Bacsek, the painter at Inta; and Les Shuppan, an electrician from a small city in Hungary. I had first met Les at Baden by Wien. Then we were together in Lvov. From there, he was sent to Kolima where he worked for years in gold mines.

One week after our arrival at Potma/Javas, we were ordered to the soccer field. The commandant of the camp came out and delivered his welcome speech. He told us that we would soon be sent home, although he didn't know the exact date.

"As long as you are here, you will have to work," he told us.

This announcement was not received well by the prisoners. Some whistled and others yelled "No!"

"You will receive good pay and better food."

Some prisoners showed a little interest.

"A store will be opened in the camp stocked with milk, bread, and sugar," he told us. "You will have six-day work weeks. On Sundays, you will be free to do whatever you wish. Soccer teams can be organized and the different nationalities can play against each other."

He also told us there was a library. There weren't many books available, he said, but he would order more if there were enough interest. The commandant urged the prisoners to use the theater in the camp to produce and present plays. He authorized making costumes and whatever else we needed.

More prisoners began showing an interest in working.

"What kind of work is available for us?" someone asked.

"Next to the camp, there is a furniture factory with enough work for 250 to 300 workers," the commandant said. "No previous experience required. They will provide the necessary training on site. The nearby kolkhoz has requested one hundred," he continued. "The collective farm will supply two meals daily. Two more jobs are available; one in the power station, and the other in camp upkeep. In the power station they are looking for stokers for the boilers. The pay is high!"

At that point, most of the prisoners were ready to work.

"Tonight, the narjadchik will contact you, and you can make the arrangements yourselves. If you have any questions, ask the narjadchik or see me if he can't answer your questions," the commandant said.

We were to report for work the following Monday at 8 A.M.

After supper, a medical doctor came into the camp. We had to walk past him and his nurse nude. He inspected us and sent to the right those who were handicapped, too ill, or too old to work in the furniture factory or at the nearby kolhoz.

When the medical inspection was over, he took the names of those who weren't fit for physical work, about fifty prisoners. A physical examination was scheduled for the unfit, who were assigned to camp maintenance and sent home to Hungary with us.

On Thursday evening when the narjadchik came to me, I refused to make a commitment to work. Later, I learned that forty other slaves also refused to work.

From then on, I was called repeatedly to the commandant's office. The camp administration wanted to use me as an example to convince the others to work.

Finally, Gaspar and I decided to join the brigade responsible for chopping wood for the kitchen. We enjoyed each other's company and the pleasant warm weather. But after two weeks, we decided that we had chopped enough wood and quit. We were called into the commandant's office two or three times a day to no avail.

At first, we enjoyed spending time exchanging our experiences with the other prisoners. But after a while, being idle made the time seem to go by slowly. In addition, we were always hungry on the significantly reduced food rations allotted to non-working prisoners. And we felt the need to be busy. So, we reported to the commandant and selected a work assignment in the power station as stokers.

Two stokers worked together in six-hour shifts. At regular intervals, we had to open the boiler doors and shovel coal inside. The heat was unbearable. Our skin burned and by the third day, it cracked and peeled. A couple of days later, it was so bad we had to quit.

The daily summons to the commandant's office became routine again. By this time, he had realized he could only prevail if he found challenging work for us. The camp store needed someone who could organize it and be responsible not only for selling without losing money, but making the hungry customers happy.

"You are the kind of people I am looking for," the commandant said. "You are intelligent, honest and trustworthy. Would you be interested in setting up the store and running the operation?" Would we? Of course! We jumped for joy at this offer and we agreed. It was the opportunity we were looking for.

"You will report directly to me. I want to see the ledger and inventory sheet daily," he said.

We decided to start the next day, which was Thursday, and be ready for business the following Monday. The store would be open every morning for two hours and evenings between 5 P.M. and 8 P.M. We ran the store until our departure in October.

That summer was long and uneventful—except that I managed to send a postcard to my mother in Hungary. And, wonder of wonders, her reply came a few weeks later.

It was only through a stroke of luck and someone's quick thinking that I was able to read my mother's card. The censor, Major Baron, had gone away on vacation and a girl who was acting on his behalf promised to let me read any mail that arrived for me, though she would have to take it back after I read it. Baron returned on mail-delivery day and was ready to take back censorship duty. The girl picked up the cards that had come from the post office and, without censoring them, handed them over to Baron who was standing among the men anxiously waiting for their mail. Baron read out the names on the cards. He read my name, and had I been right in front of him, he would have remembered not to give the card to me. But someone who was a quicker thinker grabbed the card and passed it on to me.

It was September 1955, the first time I received a sign of life from the outside world in seven and a half years, and even longer since I had seen my mother, brother, and sister. The card said they were at home in Papa and in good health.

God must have intervened for me to receive that card with such good news of my family because the guards were doing everything in their power to keep me incommunicado.

The weeks in Potma/Javas passed slowly. Only a few new prisoners arrived each day, and periodically, men and women left for their homelands and freedom.

During the summer of 1955, the Hungarian prisoners organized a soccer team and played several games. Our team beat the Germans and played against the team from one of the neighboring camps. We won the game and took the trophy home. Jointly with the Germans we formed a "culture club" and prepared and presented plays together. They were great successes—despite the women's roles being played by men.

We had our last soccer game on 15 October 1955. The next day, around 4 P.M., the narjadchik came running into our barracks to announce that the Hungarians had to gather on the soccer field in thirty minutes. Shortly, two prisoners brought a table and a couple of chairs. Time crawled as we waited anxiously.

A special delegation from the Kremlin itself had come to see us. I jumped when I saw that General Masslenikov, the "butcher" of Vorkuta, headed the delegation, accompanied by four colonels. They placed on the table a big bundle of papers.

The general walked to the table. "You will leave for Hungary tomorrow and will be turned over to the Hungarian authorities," he announced. "Some of you will receive full amnesty, others will have their cases reviewed and decided by the Hungarian courts. Now, my assistant, Colonel Koslov, will read the names and the group to which each of you belongs."

Colonel Koslov stepped to the table and picked up the sheets of paper.

"Those belonging to the group receiving full amnesty, move to the right. The others should stay where they are."

Utter quiet descended on the field.

Then the colonel began reading the names in alphabetical order. He passed over my name. I knew then that although my years in Red Hell were over, I would now have to face Hungarian Communist Hell. A chill ran through me. I didn't know how much more suffering and humiliation I could take.

When the colonel had read all the names, I looked around and found many of my friends in my group. Less than half, 252, of the Hungarian prisoners would be turned over to Hungarian authorities for re-sentencing. All of my friends in the Apponyi conspiracy case received full amnesty. I was the sole exception because of what I had said more than seven years earlier. After my trial, when I was asked to state my wish, I had answered, "I do not have any wish to be granted by the Soviets, but ask the Almighty to erase this evil Soviet Empire from the face of Earth." This statement was recorded in my file and stayed there throughout my years in prison.

10

Return to Hungary
(1955)

None who have always been free can understand the terrible fascinating power of the hope of freedom to those who are not free.

Pearl S. Buck

That night, I couldn't sleep. In my mind, I relived the time spent in the torture centers of the Communist Hungarian Secret Service located on Andrassy Street and at Hadik Barracks in the most prestigious and elegant district in Budapest.

But I vowed to accept my situation. *Either I die or I come out as a moral victor*, I told myself.

The next morning, everyone was ready to leave. We said good-bye to our friends and walked through the gate. I looked back, knowing that the Soviets' Red Hell would shortly be behind us forever.

At the train station, only a few hundred yards from the camp, there were thirty railroad wagons waiting for us. These wagons did not have cages or shelves. But before we climbed aboard, the captain in charge of the transport ordered those who hadn't been granted amnesty to board first, thirty prisoners to a car. The captain didn't want the two groups to mix. When the group that was to be handed over to the Hungarian authorities had boarded, an NKVD soldier padlocked the cars. It meant we would travel as slaves—no longer slaves of the Soviet Union, but of the Hungarian communists.

Then it was time for the other group to board, but no one moved. The captain tried to convince them to board the train, but they stood firm.

"Take the padlocks off the doors. We are not going until we can board the train the way we want to," the group yelled in unison.

There was nothing the captain could do but order the NKVD soldiers to remove the padlocks. Everyone got off the train and joined their friends, then re-boarded in less than ten minutes.

The captain made a last remark before the train left. "You will receive cold meals—that will be enough until you reach your final destination. Your final destination is Hungary," he continued. "The trip will not take longer than three days."

Then he asked us not to leave the train because he was personally responsible for the transport, though he said, he would allow visitation between cars. Then he took a final count: 550. The train left the Potma/Javas station on its way to Moscow.

The captain was friendly, making social visits to every car. Stations were far apart and the train, which was moving fast, stopped only a couple of minutes at each. The captain used that short time to move from car to car, developing a good rapport with the prisoners. He was interested in our backgrounds, life in Hungary, and our future plans. He didn't want to talk about politics and he didn't want us to compare communism and capitalism for him.

The train arrived in Moscow around 3:30 P.M. that day. The captain announced through a hand-held speaker that we would stop there at least an hour. We could walk around on the platform but we had to be back no later than 4:30 P.M.

I took a walk with Gaspar. We looked at each other and we each knew what the other wanted to say. We decided to use this opportunity for sightseeing in Moscow, knowing that we wouldn't get back in time for the train's scheduled departure. We decided to go downtown, see Red Square, Lenin's Mausoleum, the famous Moscow subway, and the university.

If we finished our tour early enough, we would visit Sasha, whom we knew from the gulag, and his family. Sasha had been a colonel in the Soviet Air Force, a highly decorated fighter pilot with the highest number of kills during World War II. He was arrested on fabricated charges on the order of Beria, the people's commissar for internal affairs, who had been a trusted confidant of Stalin. After Stalin's death, Beria was arrested, convicted, and executed for his atrocities and crimes committed against innocent victims. After Beria's execution in May 1954, Sasha received full amnesty and returned to Moscow where he received a hero's welcome. Shortly after his triumphant homecoming, he was promoted to general. To prove he didn't forget his former comrades in the gulag, he soon sent a postcard through one of the free employees of our mine. We saved this card containing his home address as a treasure.

As we walked out to the street, we noticed several taxicabs parked in front of the station. We stopped at the nearest one and asked the driver the cost of the fare downtown. It seemed affordable, so we hired him. We had no map of the city, so we showed him Sasha's address on the card. He told us Sasha lived only a block away from Red Square. On the way to Red Square, we passed a post office and asked the cab driver to stop.

"We would like to send a telegram to our family," I told the driver.

"Where is your family?" he asked.

"In Hungary," I replied.

"Are you coming from the gulag?" he asked after a brief pause.

When I told him we were, he became even friendlier. He told us his father had died in Vorkuta several years earlier from the cold, hunger, and hard work.

Then he gave us some pointers, telling us what we could do and what we shouldn't do. "Since you don't have passports, avoid the police."

At the post office, we sent telegrams to our mothers. They were surprisingly inexpensive. Each telegram contained the same brief message. "We are in Moscow and heading home, Gaspar and Bela." This way, they would know we were together in Moscow on 16 October 1955.

When we arrived at Red Square, we tried to hand the driver the money for the fare, but he wouldn't accept it. We coaxed him into taking it, saying we would soon be jailed in Hungary where the money would do us no good.

At Red Square, we visited Lenin's Mausoleum, the subway, the university, and the Gum Department Store. Some of the main streets looked a little like those of Western cities, but a hundred feet off a main thoroughfare, it was like taking a step back to the eighteenth century where paved streets became dirt trails.

Soon it was getting dark and was time to head for Sasha's apartment. We walked up to the third floor and easily found the door with the number we were looking for. We knocked after a short hesitation and heard footsteps inside. The door opened and Sasha stood there with a beautiful woman behind him.

"I do not believe my eyes," he exclaimed. "This is the most pleasant surprise in my life. Come in and meet my wife, Marusja."

Sasha and Marusja lived in a one-room apartment approximately twenty-five by thirty feet. They shared the kitchen,
bathroom, and toilet with the other tenants on their floor.

After our initial excitement at seeing each other again, we
discussed our plans. Sasha wanted us to stay for several days as
his guests. He told us he could arrange for us to receive full
amnesty upon our return to Hungary. We didn't accept his offer
because we wanted to return to Hungary with our friends. It
could have taken years for the amnesty petition to work its way
through the slow bureaucratic Soviet system. Meanwhile, we
could be sent to the darkest corner of the Soviet Union and be
left there forever. We agreed to stay overnight.

Meanwhile, as Marusja prepared dinner, Sasha opened a
bottle of vodka. We talked late into the night. Well after midnight, Marusja and Sasha changed into their pajamas and pointed to the freshly made bed.

"You sleep in the bed and Marusja and I will sleep on the
floor," Sasha said.

We protested. Sleeping on the floor in his apartment would
have been better than the best sleeping arrangements we ever
had in the barracks at Inta/Vorkuta. But they were adamant.

"Don't argue about this," Sasha said. "Marusja and I agreed
to this arrangement. The argument is closed."

After the long day, we were exhausted and fell asleep
immediately.

The next morning, we bid good-bye to Sasha and Marusja
and took a taxicab to the railroad station. We purchased tickets
for the Blue Express to Kiev, three hundred miles away. After an
eight-hour journey, we arrived in Kiev at 6 P.M. and inquired as
to the whereabouts of our transport. We were told that it had
left Kiev earlier that morning.

The ticket agent, a young Ukrainian girl named Katyusha,
told us that her shift would end at 7 P.M. and then she would be

happy to help us locate our train. Our train was approaching Lvov, where it would be pulled onto a side-rail for the night. The next train would leave Kiev for Lvov at 6 A.M. and would arrive at Lvov around noon.

Since we had no place to go, Katyusha invited us to her one-room apartment, which was within walking distance of the station. Like most Muscovites, she shared a kitchen and bathroom with all the other tenants on the same floor.

She offered to share her meager supper with us. Before we accepted, we went out to find a store or farm to purchase some food, but since the stores were already closed, we returned empty-handed. She shared her evening meal with us, then offered her bed to us, saying she would sleep on the floor. Since this was not acceptable to us, the three of us ended up sleeping in the same bed.

We had a lively discussion before falling asleep. First, she told us more about herself. She came from a well-to-do Ukrainian family. Her parents had owned a large farm that was taken away by Stalin and made into a state collective farm, a kolkhoz. Her parents were members of the Bander anticommunist group. Because of this, every member of her family was convicted and sent to the gulag. Since she was a young girl at that time, she was left behind and placed with her aunt where she finished her education. The Soviet Railroad Systems hired her as a ticket agent after graduation.

It was then our turn to introduce ourselves. We talked about our past, the gulag, our family, friends, and our dreams for the future. I didn't even have a chance to finish my story before I heard the other two snoring.

The next morning, we got up early and left for the railroad station after breakfast. We purchased tickets and waited for the train that was scheduled to arrive at 7:30 A.M. While Katyusha was distracted, we folded three hundred rubles in a piece of paper and slipped it into her pocket. By the time we had to board the train, she found out that our transport train still hadn't arrived at Lvov, which would give us a chance to catch up with it and rejoin our group.

The train finally arrived. We boarded the clean, luxurious express train that even had a dining car for the three hundred-mile, nine-hour trips. Our fellow passengers, Ukrainians living in Lvov, were an elderly woman, a young girl, and a man in his seventies. All of them were friendly.

It didn't take long for them to figure out that we came from a prison or labor camp. Initially, they were careful about what they said. The communist system didn't foster trust. It frequently used agent provocateurs working for the NKVD who manipulated average citizens into expressing their opinions about the communist system. Then, they turned them over to the NKVD. These agents' favorite "hunting ground" was the Ukraine—it was fertile soil for their activities.

When our fellow travelers found out who we were, they opened up to us. At noon, our new friends invited us for lunch in the dining car, which was as clean as our cabin. The tables were set with spotless white tablecloths, expensive china, and silverware. The menu was a dream come true—fried chicken, lamb, pork, and fish for entrées and fruit or cake for dessert. There was also a good selection of wines. The dinner with wine, dessert, and coffee cost forty rubles per person, plus a fifteen-percent tip. The elderly gentleman insisted that we were his guests and paid the bill.

After lunch, we went back to our cabin and fell asleep. We were awakened about 3 P.M. by the conductor. He said we would arrive in Lvov on schedule at 5 P.M.

Upon our arrival in Lvov, we thanked our Ukrainian friends for their hospitality and rushed to the station manager's office to locate our transport train. After a few phone calls, he tracked it down. The train had left Lvov earlier and stopped twenty miles away. It would continue the following morning.

We had to act fast to catch up with the train carrying the former prisoners. Since there was no scheduled passenger train, our only option was to hire a taxi and leave immediately. After turning our pockets inside out, we found that we only had four hundred rubles left.

Two taxis were waiting for business in front of the station. We approached the first one and bargained with its young driver. He agreed to take us to join our transport train for the princely sum of two hundred rubles. We paid him and climbed in. The poor condition of the bumpy road made the drive a slow one.

In the meantime, the captain in charge of the transport had delayed its departure as long as he could, hoping that the two missing prisoners would turn up before the train arrived at the final destination, Csap, on the Russian-Hungarian border.

We arrived, as the driver had estimated, by midnight and soon found our train. We thanked the driver, who returned to Lvov.

We woke up the captain, who didn't seem to mind when he saw who it was. He was in the wagon by himself and invited us to join him.

"We did not want to leave Russia without seeing your beautiful capital, Moscow," I said before he could ask any questions.

"Where did you spend the two days?" he asked.

"We went sightseeing in Moscow during the day and spent the night at the railroad station," I said.

He said he had notified his superiors who, in turn, contacted the police to request help in finding us.

We described in detail what we did, naturally without mentioning Sasha or our Ukrainian hostess. Since he had no more questions, he sent us to our wagon where we received a warm reception from our friends.

The next morning at 11 A.M., the train left for the five-hour trip to Uzhgorod. Before the train pulled into the Uzhgorod station at 4 P.M., we opened the gate of our wagon and Erwin played an old patriotic song on his beautiful trumpet—one he had made in Inta. The song he chose was perfectly suited to our situation, the weather, the time of day, and our location. The melody and words were sentimental reminders of heroic times in Hungarian history.

As the mountains echoed with the sound of his trumpet, tears rolled down our cheeks, and we turned our faces toward the high, majestic Carpathian Mountains that protectively encircle our country.

> "Ah, graceful silhouette of yours
> The proud fortress of Krasznahorka
> You tower high above the majestic
> Carpathian Mountains.
>
> In the blue deep mist of the late
> Evening darkness.
> The autumn wind swirls around you
> And whispers heroic tales of
> Past glories . . . long forgotten.
>
> Now you are forsaken, empty, and lonely,
> The proud and mighty fortress of
> Krasznahorka."

Uzhgorod is a relatively large city with a population that was half-Hungarian. For many centuries, the city and the region belonged to Hungary. After World War I, it was annexed to Czechoslovakia. During World War II, it was returned to Hungary and at the end of World War II, the Soviet Union occupied and annexed the area. After the annexation, their first activity was to eliminate the "undesirable elements," such as landowners, professionals, former military personnel, and intellectuals. These groups were arrested, convicted, and sentenced to forced labor in the Soviet Gulag. In our camp, there were many prisoners from that area. After 1953, we became pen pals with their relatives and friends with help from the free workers in the mine. From our letters, they had learned of our repatriation and the approximate time of our arrival at Uzhgorod on the way to Hungary. For days, they kept vigil at the station until finally our train rolled in.

They came to the station to greet us with baskets loaded with goodies we hadn't seen in years. Many of them joined us in a long leisurely stroll—we were transported as free Hungarian citizens, even those who didn't receive amnesty, and were free to move about. They stayed with us late into the night and we told them about our long ordeal. After they left, we took the goodies to our wagon and shared them with friends who didn't have anyone waiting for them at the station.

The next morning, the train left early for the last ten miles to Csap.

The Russian railroad is a wide-gauge track system, different from Western systems, so we had to change trains at the border. The reason for the difference is military. Invading armies were forced to change trains at the border, delaying the arrival of troops and supplies to the front lines. During World War II, German troops wasted precious time switching cargo from their Western railroad wagons to Russian ones.

At our arrival at Csap, three-dozen uniformed Hungarian Communist secret servicemen carrying machine guns boarded the train and took positions on platforms outside the cattle cars. They were cruel, hard-core soldiers, trained to enforce the rules of their communist overlords. They were made to believe that we were dangerous criminals and enemies of the Hungarian people. On alert, they were instructed to use their machine guns without hesitation if necessary. None of the guards spoke to us as it was strictly forbidden. Even a smile was considered a punishable violation.

The officers in charge of receiving the returning prisoners were unfriendly and indifferent. The reception procedure was simple. The Russian captain read all the names in alphabetical order and each person called had to board the assigned cattle wagon. As soon as the wagon was filled, the gates were closed and the loading of the other wagons continued until everyone was processed. When the receiving officer was satisfied that no one was missing, he picked up the documents and boarded the luxurious Pullman car reserved for the Hungarian officials.

The process was cool and emotionless. No one said, "Welcome home!"

When the train crossed the Russian-Hungarian border and stopped on the Hungarian side, the secret service agents slapped padlocks on every wagon. Two guards were assigned to each. The former prisoners, now "free" Hungarian citizens, locked in the cattle wagons yelled in unison, "You secret service men! You still hold the power with machine guns. You have not changed since 1945."

The trip to our final destination took less than two hours. Shortly after our arrival, we learned we were in Nyiregyhaza, about 190 miles northeast of Budapest. From the station, buses took us to an abandoned World War II military barracks. In Nyiregyhaza, the arriving former prisoners were separated into two groups. The group that had received full amnesty from the Soviets was taken into the mess hall where tables were set with a glass of wine at each place. The men in the other group were told that their cases would be reviewed. Some would be acquitted and the others re-sentenced according to the Hungarian communist penal code.

"You should not worry because the maximum sentence will not exceed twenty-five days," one of the commanding officers said. "However, all those days will be Christmas days."

Along with the others in the group that hadn't received amnesty, I was thrown into a cattle wagon. The gates were closed and padlocked and the transport began its final leg of the journey. We learned from civilians gathered around the transport train that we were heading toward Jaszbereny, about twenty miles east of Budapest.

Four hours later, our train rolled into a relatively large station at Jaszbereny. One of the prisoners in our wagon who knew the city said we would probably be transferred to a local state prison there.

Shortly after our arrival, large buses lined up near the train. About twenty-five secret service soldiers with machine guns formed a "receiving line" while we were transferred onto the buses. The four-mile journey from the station to the jail took just minutes, and the transfer into the jail cells, with three or four to a cell, went quickly.

The prison at Jaszbereny, an old state-owned and operated facility, was at that time unoccupied, with the exception of a few inmates sentenced to one or two years for minor violations and who were assigned cleaning and maintenance work. My cellmates during the first two months there were Gaspar Szep, a veterinary student; Nick Csomos, a dentist; and Steve Bacsek who had been a supervisor in a textile factory.

Those who had received full amnesty were issued temporary identification cards and given tickets to their hometowns. After they arrived home, they immediately notified the relatives of those of us detained in Jaszbereny. Three of my friends from the Apponyi conspiracy who were also from Papa contacted my mother immediately. They told her I was back in Hungary and in good health, but detained by the secret service. They weren't sure where I was being held, though, so my mother immediately sent a letter to the Ministry of Internal Affairs requesting information.

She received no reply. A couple of days later, when she visited the secret service headquarters, she was told that they didn't know my whereabouts and that I might have left the country. Then she sent letters to the relatives of those friends who were held with me telling them that their son, husband, or other relatives were in Hungary and were being held by the political secret service.

About six weeks later, my mother got the news from the Department of Internal Affairs in Budapest that I was being held at Jaszbereny. Relatives of the detained prisoners set a date to meet at the main office of the prison. Nearly twenty people showed up. The chief of the prison met them and admitted that I was held there. My mother insisted on seeing and talking to me.

"You cannot see him now, but I will arrange a visitation with my superior," the chief offered. "I promise you an answer within two weeks. The answer will be in a form of an official letter."

Since it was getting close to Christmas, my mother knew that the earliest she would be allowed to visit me would be in mid-or late January.

Meanwhile, the days went by fast for me because I had good company. Steve was a great storyteller. He remembered movies he had seen twenty years earlier and gave us two-hour reenactments of the films. Another favorite entertainment was chess. I had a set in the bundle that I had carried with me from the gulag, that I had made in Inta as a gift for my brother. Escorted by a guard—at my request—I brought that set from the storage room to my cell and we played everyday to pass the time and occupy our minds.

Our days there were full. Every morning, we made a schedule of our activities for the day, and adhered to it strictly. A typical day went like this: two hours of exercise including walking, push-ups, and sit-ups; two to three hours of story telling on a rotating basis; playing chess for a couple of hours in the afternoon.

Soon, Christmas of 1955 was around the corner and we prepared a special program for Christmas Eve. We sang "Silent Night, Holy Night," then prayed, and after the celebration, entertained each other by telling our life stories. The guards didn't interfere with our celebration and overlooked our not being in bed by 8 P.M.

Nick and Steve were interested in my flying stories. Nick was a capable politician and an active member of the Small Holders Party. As such, he knew what was going on behind the scenes. He told us the unbelievable story of how Bela Kovacs was kidnapped in 1948 by the secret service and convicted by a Soviet military tribunal without trial to eight years in jail and forced labor in the gulag. The night following his arrest, he was transferred to the headquarters of the Soviet Army, then to Neunkirchen, Austria, then to Lvov, and ended up in Lubyanka, Moscow's central prison, where he was kept in solitary confinement for years.

In addition to good company and interesting stories, we also had good food, which was great compared to what we'd eaten in the gulag.

Medical care, however, was nonexistent. One day, I had a toothache and when I couldn't take the pain any longer, I knocked on the cell door to tell the guard about my excruciating pain.

"Nothing can be done now, but tomorrow you can see the visiting doctor," the guard said.

"I cannot wait until tomorrow. I need help now! Dr. Csomos is a dentist, and he can help," I said.

The guard left, and after what seemed an eternity, returned and escorted Nick and I upstairs to the emergency room. Nick looked around, but couldn't find any medical instruments.

I was desperate. I noticed a large rusty nail lying on the floor. I asked the guard to allow me to take it to my cell and use it to loosen the filling in the infected tooth. It was against prison regulations to have knives, nails, or any items that could be used to cause bodily injury to others or ourselves. But the guard was understanding and allowed me to take the nail to our cell.

By then, the pain was intolerable. I sat on the edge of the bed and began to work at loosening the filling. I had only a small mirror and the rusty nail for tools.

My friends, Steve and Nick, were so interested in my "operation" that they didn't go to bed. Shortly after midnight, I felt the filling loosen. Then Nick took over the procedure and removed the old filling. The pain eased immediately, and the relief was overwhelming. Exhausted, the three of us finally went to bed. When I woke up the next morning, the pain was gone.

One day in mid-January 1956, Nick, Steve, and I each received a letter from our loved ones. A couple of days later, we were notified that secret service officials at their headquarters in Budapest had granted permission for visitation.

Visiting days were arranged so that only one prisoner per cell was permitted a one-hour visit by a relative. I was the first in my cell to receive one. Before the visit, we were told what we could and could not discuss.

I couldn't sleep the night before the visit. Early in the morning, I was taken to a barber to be shaved and readied to meet my visitor. I felt like a human being again for the first time in many months. At 9:55 A.M., the door opened and I was escorted to the small visiting room. A glass wall divided the room, with one chair on each side of it. A small opening in the center of the glass allowed prisoner and visitor to speak to each other.

I arrived first and sat down. Shortly, the door on the other side of the glass opened and a woman walked in. Her hair was pure white. It was my mother, who meant so much to me. Except for the dark hair that had turned white, she hadn't changed; the same kindness shone on her face. We reached through the small opening and held each other's hands as tears ran down our cheeks. For a moment, we were speechless.

Then she found her voice. "We had already buried you. Every year on your birthday I lit candles in the cemetery at your father's grave and said many prayers for you both."

Neither of us spoke for a while. She looked around and when she saw that the guard had left us alone, she continued. "When I picked up your blood-soaked underwear in March 1948, I was convinced that you were executed."

Then she spoke about my sister and brother, who were both home in Papa and healthy—and missed me very much. She also talked about a special relationship that was developing between my sister and my friend and former prison mate, Joco, who had found himself divorced from his wife on his return home. She remarried a high-ranking communist official in the early 1950's. Joco and my sister Magda were planning to get married. She also told me about our neighbors, my schoolmates, and my friends. She reached through the window and grabbed my hands, kissing them hysterically, crying one moment and laughing the next.

When visiting time was over, a secret service agent in civilian clothes came in.

"Lady, the time is up. Say good-bye to your son. You have to leave."

After an emotional final embrace, she collected enough strength to leave. I watched through teary eyes as her small figure left the room.

The weeks after my mother's visit went by quickly. I was taken up for interrogation every day. The interrogators were unfriendly and hostile. After the first session, I learned that the secret service didn't have any information about my case. In Hungary, in 1954 or 1955, Gabor Peter, the chief of the secret service, had been convicted and sentenced to fifteen years in prison. Before his arrest, he burned all the documentation on prisoners who were convicted and sentenced during his tenure. Upon my return, the Russian NKVD didn't send any documentation to the Hungarian authorities. This and the fact that I didn't break down during torture, divulge any information, or confess made the interrogators' job difficult.

In early August 1956, Bela Kovacs, secretary of the Small Holders Party and the minister of agriculture until his arrest in 1948, was transferred to my cell. Here, the strong friendship between us that had developed in the gulag grew even stronger.

During a visit from his wife in July 1956, he was told that he would be released shortly. At the end of August, he was escorted out of the cell a free man. His last words to me before he left were, "Bela, you will follow me shortly." Since he had many friends and acquaintances in the newly formed Hungarian government who wanted him on their side, he was sure he would have enough influence to arrange my release.

In early September, I was escorted to the chief's office where I was given strict orders not to talk about my imprisonment in the gulag and Hungary. Then I was issued a temporary identification card and given train tickets to Papa. The chief said he hoped that I would become a productive member of society in communist Hungary as he shook my hand.

After this "indoctrination ceremony," I was taken to the storage room to pick up the few belongings that I brought with me from the Soviet Union. Then I was escorted to the railroad station to catch the train to west station in Budapest. The train for Papa left from the east station, so I had to use public transportation to get there. Since I had no money, I had to travel without a ticket and I worried that the conductor would have me arrested for traveling without one.

During those first few hours after my release, I felt conspicuous, and found myself looking behind my back, searching for armed guards directing my every move. But the trip to the east station went smoothly. Neither the conductor nor the police stopped me.

Shortly after noon, I boarded my train. I found out that it was an express train to Gyor where I would have to change to yet another train that would take me to Papa.

When the conductor came by to check tickets, he looked at me suspiciously, then at my ticket. "Your ticket is not valid for an express train. You have to pay the additional fare and penalty."

"I only have Russian money, not Hungarian," I said. "I am coming from Jaszbereny and this is the ticket I was given."

It didn't take long for the other passengers in the compartment to figure out that I was a former political prisoner being repatriated. In a spontaneous outpouring of kindness that touched me deeply, they pulled out their wallets and gave money to the conductor to pay the additional fare. It was more than was needed. It took some time for the conductor to realize that this poor guy was coming from a Russian prison, so he had to let him use the ticket he was given.

In Gyor, I changed trains again and began the last leg of my journey. During the short trip, my mind busily planned for my return home. When the train rolled into the station at Papa, I looked around, searching for familiar faces. But there was no fancy welcome for a "traitor" who had fought against the new government established by the Communist Party. I was disappointed.

I left the train and walked on a road so familiar to me, stopping every few steps to rehearse my plan, then change it again. I noticed wet spots on the pavement at my feet. I was crying. But I didn't care what others thought. Emotions had me.

Finally, I was standing at my mother's front door. I hadn't been there in more than eight years—since Christmas Eve 1947.

I knocked and seconds later, the door opened and I faced my beautiful mother. We held each other, speechless, for what seemed like an eternity.

I stepped into the familiar apartment and we began talking. She told me how she had suffered after my arrest. For the first few months, she had traveled once a week to Budapest to deliver my freshly washed underwear, pick up the dirty ones, take them home, wash them, and take them back the following Monday. Then in mid-April 1948, when she came to deliver my clean underwear, she was told to stop bringing it since I wouldn't need it any more. She silently bid me goodbye although she could never truly accept that she wouldn't see me again.

When she arrived home that day, she opened the bag containing the underwear she had picked up and saw that it was blood soaked. She thought I had been killed, and buried me in her mind. But this also gave her a purpose in life—to find my grave, say a prayer there, and light a candle. She kept my bloody, unwashed underwear as a relic.

My mother's several letters to secret service headquarters and the state department went unanswered. Finally, when she received the first and only letter from me, it gave her comfort and some peace of mind just knowing that I was still alive.

As evening approached, my sister and brother came over to welcome me home. We talked late into the night. My sister told me that she and Joco had a small private wedding in Papa shortly after his return from Nyiregyhaza. After their marriage, my sister moved in with Joco, who lived in a small house with his parents in Papa.

After they left, my mother prepared dinner. Shortly after midnight, we were exhausted and retired for the night.

11

The Hungarian Revolution
(23 October 1956)

*. . . the political situation changed significantly in Hungary. What
had begun in 1953 as an intra-party struggle between the Reformists'
National Communist faction and the orthodox, Stalinist faction, combined with a growing ferment among the country's intellectuals, turned
into a nationalist, anti-Soviet revolution on 23 October 1956.*

Over the next few days, I spent considerable time planning
my future. I knew that I would have to move to Budapest to
finish my education. So, after spending several days with my
mother, I left for the city.

During my short stay at home, my brother made arrangements with his dentist friend to examine my teeth, do as much
repair work as he could in the time available, and make
arrangements for the additional work. This meant that I could
see my mother and my siblings when I returned home for
more dental work.

In Budapest, I stayed with my Aunt Jolan until I found a
small, furnished room to rent near her apartment. Aunt Jolan's
apartment was where I had been arrested on 15 March 1948.
She worried that my "hell" wasn't over yet, and I could be
picked up again by the Hungarian Secret Service any time.

I visited the University of Budapest. In 1948, I had missed
exams in Calculus and Strength of Materials because I was

arrested. I looked up the two professors who gave those exams. Since they were members of the old Horthy Regime in Hungary and knew about my arrest in 1948, they welcomed me with open arms. They gave me free books and set times for me to take the exams, which required that I enroll in the engineering department. But to become an engineering student, I had to secure the approval of the Communist Party, which was represented at the university by the student council.

Two days after I submitted my application to study electrical engineering, I found my name on the door of the student council office along with an appointment time for my hearing.

I waited nervously outside the student council office and they called me in five minutes early. The chairwoman and two young men in their early twenties represented the student council. They sat at a long table with a document containing my personal data in front of them. After routine questions such as date and place of birth, father's name and occupation, mother's name, and my political affiliation, they switched to questions about my POW and gulag years.

We talked about my time in the POW camp at Saratov. When the subject of my arrest and conviction came up, I told them I had been released from the Soviet Union, then held by the Hungarian Political Secret Service in Jaszbereny, then released in August as a free Hungarian citizen.

The interview lasted only twenty minutes, the chairwoman asking most of the questions. All three listened intently to my story. Then I was told to wait outside. After a short time, they called me back in and said they had approved my enrollment in the engineering department.

My next task was to find employment. My cousin, Leslie, who was working for Siemens X-Ray Service Organization in Budapest as a technician, spoke to the managing director about me, and my political and technical background. A short time later, the director invited me for an interview and offered me a probationary position starting on 20 September 1956. When my probationary period was over a month later, Siemens offered me a permanent position at a higher salary, which I accepted gratefully, happy that things were working out well.

Unfortunately, shortly after I was hired, the political situation in Hungary changed significantly. What had began in 1953 as an intra-party struggle between the Reformist's National Communist faction and the orthodox Stalinist faction combined with a growing ferment among the country's intellectuals, and turned into a nationalist, anti-Soviet revolution on 23 October 1956.

I walked to work as usual that day; it was only a short distance from my rented room. At work, the day went by fast and was uneventful, but when I arrived home from work, I found out that it hadn't been uneventful for the Hungarian people. When I heard what had happened, I promptly turned around and rushed to the Radio Budapest building to join the protest.

Students of the Engineering School at the University of Budapest had called for a peaceful demonstration. By mid-morning, tens of thousands of people began to move towards the statue of Petofi, a well-known revolutionary poet and historical figure of the 1848 uprising against the Habsburgs. At 1 P.M., the minister of internal affairs forbade the students' march. But when the minister's order was ignored, it was promptly revoked.

So, in a dignified, happy atmosphere, the crowd walked from the statue of Petofi to the statue of Joseph Bem, another Hungarian hero who fought the Habsburgs in 1848 to express solidarity with neighboring Poland's anticommunist movement. Speeches were made, all calling for Imre Nagy's reinstatement as prime minister.

Some of the demonstrators went on to the Parliament building, others to the headquarters of Radio Budapest. The director of Radio Budapest refused to receive the delegation from the crowd, which had requested airtime to broadcast their demands, summarized into "sixteen points."

Demonstrations in the early afternoon were at first entirely peaceful. None of the demonstrators carried arms and no one called for violence. One cry electrified the masses: "Imre Nagy to the government!" Another, more ominous cry was soon heard, however: "Russians go home!" Within hours, that cry was to echo throughout the entire city with increasing intensity while the crowd swelled with a steady stream of newcomers.

Toward evening, Imre Nagy delivered a short, cautious speech at Parliament Square that failed to satisfy his audience. By that time, the red star on top of the parliament building had been extinguished. The mood of the masses began heating up after Erno Gero, the first secretary of the Communist Party, made derogatory remarks about the demonstration in a radio address. His speech added fuel to the fire.

"Down with Gero!" the crowd chanted as they roamed the streets. But the first to come down wouldn't be Gero, but his idol, Stalin, or rather the great statue that had long rankled the Hungarian people.

It was the riots in front of the radio station that evening that marked the decisive turn from protest to outright revolt. The trouble began when the political police guarding the building arrested a delegation that had entered the radio station. The crowd demanded their release and tried to storm the doors. At first, the police responded with tear gas, then they opened fire, killing and wounding several unarmed demonstrators. The crowd, enraged by the killings, stormed the radio station and occupied the lower floors.

Two trucks full of soldiers arrived from Buda across the Danube River, but the soldiers wouldn't fire on the people. Instead, the soldiers began distributing arms to the demonstrators. By that time, the crowd had swelled to thousands as workers, students, and civilians of all types pushed their way to the scene. Machine guns began to rattle on both sides, signaling the beginning of an armed revolution.

By 9:30 P.M., the protesters had toppled the large statue of Stalin in City Park where the church of Regnum Marianum had been razed to make room for the twenty-four-foot statue of Stalin.

In the face of such a large crowd, the secret service was helpless. Army units were called in to protect the Radio Budapest building, the headquarters of *The Party Daily Newspaper*, and a few other office buildings including the Communist Party headquarters. But the army, instead of following orders and attacking the crowd, gave the demonstrators their weapons. And the revolution began that night.

I joined the demonstrators and returned home well after midnight, mentally and physically exhausted.

Everyone felt the freedom of throwing off the yoke of Soviet oppression that evening and the following days. Young and old, educated and uneducated, students and factory workers participated. Interestingly, young children, the "Kids of Budapest" who had been brought up under communism, were the most avid supporters of the movement.

I spent all my free time on the streets and was happy to see that the day I had so long awaited had finally arrived.

The next morning, I went to work early. Worried that I would be taken away by the secret police, the director of Siemens X-Ray Service sent me home. He told me to come back the following day when he would give me further instructions.

Shortly after I got home, my landlady knocked on my door and escorted two men inside, Nick Csomos, my dentist friend from the gulag, and another man I didn't know.

Nick introduced the man as the vice-secretary of the Smallholders Party.

"We need you, Bela!" Nick said. "You have to go to Bela Kovacs' hometown and convince him that he's needed in the new government."

The Communist Central Committee wanted to co-opt Kovacs to its side as minister of agriculture.

"We have a car and a driver at your disposal as long as you need them," Nick added.

Bela Kovacs lived 130 miles from Budapest—a trip that I estimated would take three to four hours. Nick wanted me to leave immediately, but because of an earlier commitment, I couldn't leave until 2 P.M.

The driver agreed to pick me up at my apartment and then left. But Nick stayed behind and we talked about our future. He emphasized several times the importance of Kovacs coming to Budapest and gave me good "ammunition" to use to persuade Kovacs to return.

After Nick left, I packed necessities for three days then walked to my aunt's apartment. The first time I saw her after my release, she told me how much she'd worried about me after I disappeared without a trace and she didn't know for eight years what had happened to me. This time she said, "From now on, I want to know every move you make so your mother and I can track you down if anything should happen to you."

On the second day of the revolution, the Communist Party's Central Committee met in a long session. The Central Committee, after co-opting Nagy and a few of his apparent supporters, recommended to the presidential council that Nagy be appointed prime minister.

By then, Party leaders had requested Soviet military assistance. As Soviet Army units reached Budapest, martial law was declared. The Party labeled the revolution a "Counter Revolution," which rapidly inflamed the situation. The insurgents, sensing the confusion and weakness of the regime, occupied several of the Party's local offices.

Sounding puzzled by the rapid turn of events, Nagy asked the insurgents to trust him and let him proceed toward full implementation of the "New Course." In vain, he also asked them to turn in their weapons. By then, with anarchy ruling the streets, Nagy began to lose his once enormous popularity. The people no longer were thinking in terms of the Party and its factions; socialist legality and the end of the era of the "personality cult" were no longer burning issues. The years of hostility suddenly had found expression in new slogans, one of which could be heard more than any other: "Russians, go home!"

I left my aunt's apartment and headed to where the action was, where I joined one of the groups carrying a Hungarian flag with the communist emblem cut out of its middle.

The group walked in a disciplined manner toward secret service headquarters. We were close to the building when I noticed a large group in the park facing the building. I walked over to the park and saw uniformed secret service men hanging by their feet from the branches of several trees, hands tied behind their backs.

I walked closer to see what was going on and the sight was horrifying. The secret servicemen were dead, their mouths stuffed with large wads of money. Later, I found out that on the first day of the revolution, they were paid in advance for several months. Since they couldn't go home, they carried large amounts of money in their pockets. I turned away, sick.

I decided to go home and wait for my driver. He arrived at the agreed-upon time and we left immediately. We saw Soviet soldiers dug-in alongside the main road. But they didn't stop us or interfere, and the trip was uneventful.

We arrived at Pecs at 5:30 P.M. and it took about thirty minutes to find Bela Kovacs' home, six miles to the northeast. From his family, we learned that Bela was at the headquarters of the Smallholders Party. Piroska, his oldest daughter, offered to escort us there.

When we walked in, Bela was standing on the podium addressing the members of the Smallholders Party. Well over one hundred people filled the room. When he saw us walk in, he stepped down from the podium to greet us. When the meeting was over, he introduced me to the secretary and other officers of the Party and we had a long discussion.

The secretary asked me whether I could obtain small arms and ammunition for the local members of his Party. At first, I was hesitant to make a commitment. Then Bela convinced me that he was an honest, trustworthy anticommunist, and I said I would do my best to get the arms.

After the meeting, Bela invited us to his home. We arrived there at 8 P.M. to find dinner waiting for us. After dinner, when everybody had gone to bed, Bela and I talked in a quiet part of the house and I told him the purpose of my visit.

"Bela, I would like to do it, but my poor health tells me not to accept your proposal," he replied.

I was sorry to hear that he'd decided to retire from politics, but had to accept it since he was in ill health. We went to bed around midnight.

The next morning, I woke up early and went out for a walk. The weather was perfect and I enjoyed the early morning fresh air. Shortly, Bela emerged through the back door and joined me. I sensed that he had something important to tell me.

"Bela, I have decided to go with you to Budapest, provided you stay with me for as long as I need you," he told me.

We left for Budapest shortly after 10 A.M. The trip went smoothly, and when we arrived early that afternoon, we went directly to the Parliament. Bela's daughter, Piroska, had informed Nick Csomos and the Party's Central Committee that we were on our way to Budapest. After a brief reception, Nick took us into a small room in the Parliament used for emergency housing for members of the House. Since it had two beds, I stayed with Bela overnight. Before retiring, Nick described the happenings of the third day of the revolution, 25 October 1956.

The Kremlin had sent Mikoyan and Suslov, two Soviet generals, to Budapest. At Party headquarters, to which they were escorted in Soviet tanks, they ordered the replacement of the Party's first secretary by Janos Kadar, a cautious centrist who had spent several years in jail under Rakosi.

A week earlier, the change would have been seen as a dramatic step, signaling the end of totalitarian rule. But the Hungarian people were no longer paying attention to such cosmetic changes in leadership. Now the change was seen as an empty gesture. What mattered that day was the shooting at thousands of demonstrators in front of the Parliament building.

Secret service officers positioned on nearby rooftops had shot and killed more than one hundred unarmed demonstrators.

The next morning, 26 October, we woke up early and I began a long discussion with Bela. Breakfast was brought in at seven and we continued our conversation while eating.

"I am in good hands now," Bela said to me after breakfast. "If you still want to do what you promised the secretary of the Smallholders Party, that is, obtain and deliver small arms with ammunition, I will not hold you back."

I made sure that he had everything he needed, gave some final instructions to the bodyguard, and left with mixed emotions, sensing that I would never see him again.

On my way home, I developed a plan for obtaining arms and a truck with a driver to deliver them to Pecs. My plan was to contact the Revolutionary Committee, convince its members that I was one of them, and state my request.

I went to the committee's office in the center of Budapest. It didn't take long after I pulled out my temporary identification card to gain their support. They gave me a sealed envelope and told me to go to the engineering department at the University of Budapest, find the colonel assigned to the Revolutionary Committee, and hand him the letter. He would give me arms and get a truck with a driver.

I followed the instructions and found the colonel.

"When do you want to leave for Pecs?" he asked.

"As soon as I can."

"The earliest that I can have everything ready for you is early tomorrow morning."

I agreed to meet him in his office the next day around 8 A.M. Then I walked home. Since my rented room was four-and-a-half miles from the university, it took me almost two hours.

At home, I learned that the twenty-four-year-old daughter of my landlady was seriously injured the previous day at the Parliament. She was shot twice in the leg; one of the bullets did serious bone damage in the lower part of her leg. She was in the hospital emergency room waiting for an available bed.

On the fourth day of the revolution, the Party offered amnesty and called for a cease-fire. It promised a new, more broadly based government. But throughout Hungary, the insurgents began to form revolutionary committees to take over the functions of local governments.

In Budapest, Soviet soldiers seemed less in evidence, but it wasn't clear where they had gone. Prime Minister Nagy was seen leaving Party headquarters and walking over to the Parliament building. His supporters spread the news that Nagy had just freed himself from the influence of his Party's comrades, and was finally beginning to understand what had been happening around him—and would act accordingly.

I was exhausted that day and went to bed early. The next morning after an early breakfast, I took a streetcar to the University of Budapest to meet the colonel. I arrived at his office a few minutes early. As soon as he noticed me, he came out to greet me and said a small pick-up truck was waiting outside.

The truck, covered with a tarpaulin, was loaded with 120 military rifles, five boxes of ammunition, and two boxes of hand grenades. The driver, reading a newspaper in the cab, was ready to leave. I thanked the colonel and left immediately.

We arrived at Bela's house by noon, as planned, since the trip went smoothly. Bela's wife relayed the message that we should deliver the load of arms to Pecs, where the insurgents were based in a high school on the city's outskirts. The secretary of the Smallholders Party was expecting us.

Mrs. Kovacs's directions made it easy to find the school where we met the secretary, unloaded the cargo, and then turned right around and headed back to Budapest.

The poorly equipped Hungarian insurgents in Pecs were resisting Soviet efforts to take over the uranium mines and the airfield, and shooting could be heard from every direction. We had barely left the school when a Soviet soldier and a uniformed Hungarian Secret Serviceman man stopped us.

The secret serviceman asked for our identification cards, and when he noticed that I had only a temporary one, he became suspicious. He took away our identification cards and car keys and herded us to a small room in the basement of a nearby grocery store. They searched us, emptied our pockets, and took our wallets. Then they padlocked the door and left.

The only light in the room came through a small window, which had a wood panel that was fastened to it from the outside. The shooting seemed to be getting closer. It stopped in early evening.

A short time later, we heard steps outside. It was the owner of the grocery store stopping by to check on the store and the basement. Since the door was padlocked, he had to go find tools to open it. From him, we learned that Hungarian soldiers had pushed the Russian soldiers out of the city.

Once we were free, we immediately began walking toward Mecsekalja, to Kovacs' home, and arrived there around midnight. Since the lights were on, we knew it wasn't too late to knock on the door and ask for help. Mrs. Kovacs and her two daughters greeted us. They sensed that something bad had happened to us.

We sat down and told our story. They listened with great interest and offered us a place to stay for the night. We didn't want to risk putting the Kovacs in danger since the Russians and the secret service were after us, so we declined their offer.

After a long silence, Piroska told us she had a plan to discuss with us after dinner. The Kovacs knew we were hungry since we hadn't eaten since early that morning. After the meal and wine, we were ready to listen to Piroska.

She offered to take us to the wine cellar a short distance from the house, where we could stay as long as necessary. Julius, the driver, wanted to return to Budapest. We reminded him of the dangerous situation we were in—the secret service had our identification cards and were looking for us. But we couldn't convince him and he left a short time later.

Piroska gathered up blankets and other bedding to take to the cellar, which consisted of a large storage area and a small, well-ventilated room with a small cot in one corner. Piroska made my bed.

"I'll be back with breakfast in the morning," she said. After she left, I undressed and went to bed.

I woke up early, dressed, and went out for a walk. On the road leading to the Kovacs' house, the outline of a person became visible in the semi-darkness. I stopped and as the figure drew near, I recognized the pretty face of Piroska. I began walking faster.

"I brought your breakfast," she said.

I took it from her and we walked together to the cellar, enjoying each other's company in silence. When we sat down, I asked her to brief me about what had happened in Budapest on the fifth day of the Revolution, 27 October 1956.

She told me that throughout the country, the insurgents had begun to form revolutionary committees, which took over the function of local governments. Prime Minister Imre Nagy still followed, rather than led, our people. Later, he would announce the composition of his new government. As some of the Stalinists were gone, two former Smallholder Party leaders—Tildy and Piroska's father, Bela Kovacs—were offered the posts of minister of state and minister of agriculture, respectively. She assured me that her father was in safe hands.

Armed groups roamed the streets. In Vac, freedom fighters released the political prisoners held in one of the country's largest jails. If anything, the gap had widened between the government and the insurgents.

In the early morning hours of 28 October 1956, the Communist Committee appeared ready to adopt a hard-line approach, calling for an attack by communist Hungarian and Soviet forces against key areas of Budapest controlled by the freedom fighters. Nagy, on the verge of resignation, succeeded not only in canceling the plan, but also in altering the composition of the Party leadership. A six-member presidium took over the function of the Central Committee. Significantly, most

of the die-hard Stalinists were denied positions of responsibility. Nagy finally met a few of the insurgents' demands. He
announced the removal of Soviet military units from Budapest,
dissolution of the hated secret service police, plans to restore
Hungary's traditional emblem, and his intentions to negotiate
with Moscow about the removal of Soviet troops from the
whole country.

Since the situation in Budapest seemed to be improving, I
felt I could do more there than in the wine cellar in Mecsekalja.
But Piroska wanted me to stay at least one more day, so we
spent the next day together strolling outdoors, exchanging
ideas, discussing our hopes for the future, and picnicking under
a shady tree.

The day went by fast and it was time to say a private good-
bye. We both sensed that our paths would not cross again.

The next day, the seventh day of revolution, I woke up
around 5 A.M., feeling restless and depressed. This was my third
day in "captivity" and it reminded me of the years I had spent
in a solitary cell in Lubyanka. As a free citizen of my country, I
didn't have any more earthly goods than I'd had back then. My
total assets were the clothes I wore, which weren't in the best
condition. Both shoes had a large hole on the sole. My pockets
were empty; I hadn't had a cigarette for days—a real punishment for a person who'd smoked for many years. I hadn't had
a bath or fresh underwear for days. In addition, the political situation, which changed from hour to hour, bothered me.

When Piroska brought my breakfast, I told her again why I
had decided to return to Budapest. She listened and agreed that
I should return. I described to her how I planned to make my
way to Budapest.

"The train is not a good choice for many reasons. The only
means left is hitchhiking," she said. "I have a practical solution for you. I've collected food such as flour, potatoes, beans,

vegetables, and lard for the residents of Budapest where there are serious food shortages."

"I have enough food to fill a truck, and I have one with a driver ready to leave," she continued. "There is enough room in the cab for you. And you can leave early tomorrow morning."

During breakfast, Piroska gave me a brief summary of what had happened in Budapest on the seventh day of the revolution. The Party's daily newspaper, *Szabadnep*, in the hands of Nagy's followers, published an editorial titled, "Response to Pravda," which rejected firmly, but politely, Soviet charges that the Hungarian "counterrevolution" was instigated by "British and American Imperialists." The editorial asserted that all Hungarians sought freedom and independence, and once these goals were achieved, everyone wanted to have peaceful and friendly relations with the Soviet Union.

As the government and even the Communist Party thus began to identify with the causes of the revolution, some of the insurgents appealed for an end to the bloodshed. They were not yet prepared to turn in their arms, but they seemed to be gaining a small amount of respect.

I stayed for the rest of the day in the vineyard. I took long walks and sat down and read when I grew tired. Piroska not only took care of my meals, but provided newspapers and other reading material. After dinner, we closed the cellar and walked back to the Kovacs' residence. I took a bath, washed my underwear, and went to bed early.

The next morning, I got up at 5 A.M. and had an early breakfast. I thanked the Kovacs for everything they'd done for me and promised I'd be back. When the time came for the final good-bye, Piroska gave me a package of cigarettes, some matches, and a copy of the latest newspaper.

On the way to Budapest, I read the paper and learned what happened on the eighth and ninth days of the revolution. The

Revolutionary Council claimed the government lacked legitimacy. In the meantime, the political parties of the postwar coalition announced plans for reorganization. One group of armed freedom fighters, after several hours of fighting, had occupied the headquarters of the Communist Party, while another group liberated Cardinal Mindszenthy from detention.

Meanwhile, in the streets of Budapest, hundreds of communists, mainly secret service officers and agents, were lynched or killed. One result was that Party members lost whatever confidence they had to regroup; many took refuge in friends' apartments. Another result was the growing isolation of the most radical elements among the freedom fighters.

The country's new hero was General Maleter, who deserted to the revolutionary forces and opposed the summary executions. Maleter's call for order and support for the Nagy government gained adherents both in Budapest and in the countryside.

On 1 November, the tenth day of the revolution, new Soviet military divisions were reported to have entered the country. Nagy declared Hungary's immediate withdrawal from the Warsaw Pact and the country's neutrality. On behalf of the renamed Hungarian Socialist Workers Party, Kadar voiced the communists' admiration for our "people's glorious uprising" and the Party's full support of "the government's demand for the complete removal of Soviet forces." Then under mysterious circumstances, Kadar and five other like-minded communists left Budapest with Soviet assistance for the Ukrainian City of Uzhgorod.

Unaware of Kadar's disappearance, however, the public was relieved to hear that even the communists had endorsed the government's latest measures, reflecting the almost jubilant mood of the day. The freedom fighters' daily newspaper carried the headline: WE ARE INDEPENDENT! WE ARE NEU-

TRAL! But those who knew of the scope of the Soviet troop movements and of Kadar's vanishing act began to feel that the end might be in sight.

I arrived in Budapest before noon. The driver took me home, handing me several grocery bags filled with food before he left for a poor section of Budapest to distribute the rest.

12

Escape to the West
(2 November 1955)

Because of the urgency of the situation, he did not want to waste precious time and continued. "You have to leave immediately! I hope it is not too late! You don't even have time to go home." He then pointed to the truck outside with a driver in the cab, the engine running, and . . .

I took the bags of food to my aunt, who was happy to see me. I learned from her that two communist secret service officers had come by to see me. She was suspicious and told them that she didn't know my whereabouts and hadn't seen me for several days.

I was scared. I hurried home, paid the rent, changed my clothes, and rushed to Siemens to report for work. The director was in his office behind closed doors. When he heard my voice, he stepped out, grabbed my arm, and pulled me into his office.

"Two men in their thirties in civilian clothes came by at least twice a day during the last three days to see you," he said after closing the office door. "I sensed from the way they questioned me about you that they had a different purpose than a friendly chat. You have to leave immediately! I hope it isn't too late. You don't even have time to go home."

He pointed to a truck outside with a driver in the cab and the engine running. Casually dressed men, women, and babies sat in the truck bed. I quickly counted eighteen people, including two women and two babies. The supposed purpose of their trip was to provide the scheduled maintenance work on X-ray machines at hospitals in the counties of Vas and Zala.

The director buzzed for the secretary and told her to add my name to the work order.

The first hospital was in Zalaegerszeg, 140 miles a southwest of Budapest. I estimated the trip would take four hours, allowing for several rest stops. The director put me in charge of the group. I was to report to the head of the X-ray department at each location, show my work order, and hand over a sealed envelope from the director.

"Your real assignment is to help the group on the truck defect to Austria," he told me.

The group included ten physicians and a girl in her mid-twenties, a Polish medical student, four X-ray technicians, the wife and two small children of one of the technicians, and me.

The director signed the work order, handed it to me, and urged me to leave right away.

As we drove out of Budapest, we saw several looming Soviet tanks and the sounds of shots could be heard from time to time. The trip was uneventful, though, and we were never stopped.

During the trip to Zalaegerszeg, Claire, the Polish medical student, and I sat in a corner of the truck, where we talked about life and philosophized. Since she didn't speak Hungarian, nor I Polish, we conversed in German and developed an intimate friendship.

It was early evening when we pulled up in front of the first hospital. I walked in, leaving the others on the truck, and found the head of the X-ray department. I presented the work order and handed him the sealed envelope. He showed me the living quarters assigned to us and the cafeteria where we would be served meals. Then I went out and got the others from the truck.

After a brief rest, we walked to the cafeteria where we discussed our plan over a welcomed meal. We were to cross the border in two groups. The first group—the ten physicians and the Polish medical student—would cross after dinner that night at 8 P.M. The rest of us would cross the following day.

According to our plan, I would join the first group for the ride to Kormend, fifteen miles from the hospital. Our guide, Ribarics, who lived on the outskirts of Kormend, was the former prisoner I'd known in the gulag. He had helped several people flee Hungary between 1945 and 1948 when he was arrested for it and for some other offenses. After his return home in 1955, he continued helping defectors to supplement his small income. I knew Ribarics as an honest and reliable person.

Ribarics would lead the group on the seven-and-a-half-mile trek toward Austria, where they would stop approximately one hundred yards from the border on the Hungarian side. There, Ribarics would collect his fee and return home, leaving the escapees on their own. I recommended that they walk to Furstenfeld, Austria, nineteen miles from the Austrian-Hungarian border, where a refugee center had been set up for Hungarian freedom fighters, those who were defecting in the wake of the revolution.

After dinner, the driver took me to Kormend to make arrangements with Ribarics to guide us to the border. We found his home easily. I knocked on the door and his face lit up when he opened it and saw me. He invited us into his house. Since it was already late, there was no time for socializing.

"We are looking for someone who can take ten people tonight and the rest of us tomorrow to the border," I said, getting right to the point of my visit.

Since he had no other commitments, he agreed, then told us his fee, and the time he wanted to leave.

"It is now 7:15 P.M. We will be back by 8:30 P.M.," I said.

He asked me to return with the second group the next day no later than 6:30 P.M. We agreed and quickly headed back to the hospital.

When we arrived at the hospital, the first group was assembled and ready to go. We left at 8 P.M. and arrived at Ribarics' house on time. Everyone was anxious to leave for Austria immediately.

Just before we left, Claire, the Polish medical student, said to me, "I would like to join the second group. Would that be possible?"

"Do you have any special reason to delay your departure?" I asked.

She blushed. "I would like to stay with you as long as I can," she said with some hesitation.

I gladly agreed. I sensed her feeling toward me was more than just "friendly," and I was touched. Shortly after the first group left, we returned to the hospital. It was late when we finally went to bed.

The next day went by slowly. We rested and relaxed in preparation for our journey. We left the hospital after dinner and arrived at Ribarics' house in Kormend a couple of minutes before the agreed upon time. He was already waiting for us outside and we set out immediately on our uncertain trek.

The weather was cooperating—mild temperature, a cloudless sky, and no rain in sight. A half moon provided enough light to see the ground in front of us.

There were nine in our group, including two babies, one under a year and the other not quite two. Since the path through the forest was narrow, we had to form a single line with the guide in front, followed by Alex and George each carrying a baby; their mother Susan, and father Greg; my cousin Leslie; Claire; and I at the end. Everyone except me carried a small bag containing toilet items and two or three changes of underwear.

Together, we had enough money to pay the guide and for emergencies. Our only navigational instruments were a compass and a flashlight. The guide was our navigator, taking us in a straight line from Kormend to the border. I had estimated it would take between three and four hours to reach our goal, considering the two babies who slowed our pace, so we'd arrive about 10 P.M.

The narrow path was free of branches and trampled smooth by the many other defectors who had preceded us, so we made good progress. After an hour, we arrived at a pasture where we took a short rest. It had puzzled us as to how Ribarics could lead us in such a straight path. He shared his secret by pointing to a blue ribbon tied to a tree. The markers were fifty feet apart. The "smiling" little blue ribbons and the well-worn path were our lifeline to the border.

Two other men in the group picked up the babies to take their turn carrying them and we resumed our quiet trek. Our guide had warned us that the slightest sound could alert the border patrols nearby, and we risked arrest or even death.

Suddenly, one of the babies began screaming. Cousin Leslie had tripped over a tree stump and dropped her. Her parents rushed to the baby to quiet her and we continued our journey.

After two hours, we arrived at a large open field where we stopped. Ribarics told us the border was only 100 to 150 yards away. We were in the "no-man's land" between Hungary and Austria. We could see the holes where mines used to be.

Ribarics pointed in the direction of Furstenfeld, our final destination. We paid and thanked him and bade him good-bye. He turned around toward home and we watched him disappear in the dark woods. After he left, we took a short rest. The others asked me to lead them, which I agreed to with some hesitation. It hit me that it was a tremendous responsibility to lead a group of nine to freedom.

I moved to the front of the line and we were ready to take our last steps on Hungarian soil.

I soon realized it was easy to walk at the end of the line through a well-traveled path and let someone else navigate. But that was in the past. Left on our own, the navigation became a serious problem. We had to rely on the compass and navigate from point to point. This second leg of our journey was untraveled, and on many occasions we had to walk around trees and bushes, which made us lose our sense of direction. Then we had to reset our course by picking out a new point fifty to one hundred yards away. We also realized that we couldn't keep up the same pace we'd set through the smooth forest path.

I estimated that the best we could achieve through such difficult terrain was two miles per hour. At that speed, the trek to Furstenfeld would take almost ten hours. I was busy trying to think how I could make it easier for my friends when I heard noise from the right. I turned my head in that direction and saw in the semi-darkness the outline of a man. The distance couldn't have been more than twenty yards. He was approaching fast.

When he was ten yards away, it became obvious to me that he was a Hungarian border guard holding a machine gun pointed at us.

"Stop! Who are you? Where are you going?" he yelled.

We froze.

As the group's leader, I answered. "We are Hungarians heading towards Austria."

He pointed his machine gun at us and stopped several feet away. I could see him clearly. He looked about twenty-one or twenty-two years old. His babyish face was stern. I kept my eyes on his face and watched his every reaction closely, trying to gauge what to do next.

Meanwhile, the group was quiet, completely confident in me. The soldier glanced at the group and noticed the two babies and women and his face softened. This was a signal for me that he had human feelings after all and we might be able to make it out of there alive. I began to negotiate with him.

"Look, let us go! We'll give you all the money we have."

He was silent for a few moments.

"Okay, I let you go." He put his gun back on his shoulder.

I collected the money we had, five thousand forints, equivalent to the earnings of a skilled worker for six months.

"Here, I have five thousand forints for you," I said.

The border guard's eyes opened wide and his face lit up. His smile told me that he hadn't seen that much money in his entire life. He took the money and pointed.

"There is a road about one mile this way that is used by the Austrian border patrols. It is a dirt road in good condition and leads in to the highway to Furstenfeld."

We asked him where the other border patrols were.

"You don't have to worry because this is the time for the changing of the guards," he told us.

Feeling safer and close to a free country, we continued our journey. After thirty minutes of walking, I noticed a piece of paper on the ground and bent down to pick it up. It was torn from an Austrian newspaper and had been used as toilet paper. To me, it meant that we were on Austrian soil and we all let out a sigh of relief. A short while later, we found the dirt road, then turned left and soon reached the main road to Furstenfeld.

We continued walking on the highway after a short rest. We were tired, thirsty, and hungry, but knowing that Furstenfeld was within reach gave us the strength to continue. Our pace quickened and soon we passed a road sign pointing to Furstenfeld. The distance was only two miles. We all broke into cheers. Within minutes, lights appeared on the horizon. Shortly after that, we passed the one-mile marker and the "Welcome to Furstenfeld" sign.

Arrows pointed toward a school, indicating that it was the reception center for the freedom fighters. Refugees of other nationalities were welcome there as well, including Claire, who was a Polish national.

It was 4:30 A.M. In the reception center at Furstenfeld, the gym had been converted into a sleeping facility. When we walked in, there were already forty-five to fifty refugees sleeping on the floor, including many children and women. We were worn out and needed rest. We each picked one of the spots on the straw-covered floor that had two folded blankets on it. Before we went to sleep, we had a much needed drink of water.

Since the other refugees had gotten a full night's sleep, they woke up early. Running children awakened us. Sue fed the babies while Claire and I went on a discovery tour to find food and information.

We found a Red Cross representative who told us that after breakfast, temporary identification cards would be issued to us. Then we would be transferred to the central refugee center in Vienna.

Claire and I continued our tour until we found the kitchen where Red Cross personnel were preparing breakfast for the refugees. When Claire told them about our escape and our long walk during the night, they put together a special tray for our group, which we ate in no time.

Later, breakfast was brought for everybody. When we finished, Claire left again to gather more information. She came back with the good news that we could go immediately to the office before it opened and our papers would be processed before everyone else's. If we were lucky, we could be on the train to Vienna early that afternoon.

The processing of our papers didn't take long and we were handed our temporary passports and tickets to Vienna.

We boarded the train shortly after noon and arrived in Vienna at 4 P.M. At the station, buses were waiting to take us to the "Welcome Center," a school on the outskirts of Vienna. There were already several hundred refugees just like us.

We were escorted into a room that could hold about one hundred people. It was half-filled. The room was divided down the middle by a walkway. The straw-covered floor on both sides had blankets on it. Each side had room for fifty refugees. We took our places in the farthest corner of the room.

I spent the rest of the afternoon walking around, looking for relatives, friends, and acquaintances. I found only one person I knew, a fellow political prisoner in the gulag. We had returned from the Soviet Union at the same time. I was surprised and disappointed that I didn't find anybody else I knew.

Meanwhile, Claire had gathered more information and returned with the news that many nations had agreed to accept large numbers of refugees. The United States was at the top of the list, then Canada, Australia, England, Germany, Sweden, and other smaller nations. During processing, we were asked to indicate our first and second choices. Because most of the refugees wanted to immigrate to the United States, there was a six-week wait. For some countries, there was no wait at all.

After dinner, we rushed to the processing office and took our places at the end of a long line. There were about fifty refugees ahead of us in the slow-moving line.

Claire, with her diplomatic, pleasant personality, often found ways to shortcut the tedious bureaucratic system, and she did so again. She left and returned within minutes to lead us into a small office where two clerks were processing papers.

The Lorant family with the babies went first to one of the clerks. I went to the other clerk, who asked for my identification card. When I told her I didn't have one, she went to get her supervisor. When they learned that I had been a political prisoner in the Soviet Union and had spent eight and a half years in the gulag, they decided to order a background check on me.

They made a phone call, and shortly, a police officer came in and put me into a police car. The car stopped in front of a local jail, where the police officer escorted me to a small cell. He locked the door and left. I couldn't figure out what was going on. Memories of the years spent in a solitary cell returned. I began to pace from one corner to the other as I had done in Lubyanka. Around 10 P.M., I stopped and lay down on the cot.

The next morning at 7 A.M., a guard woke me up and shortly breakfast was brought in. I couldn't eat. I was bewildered by what had happened. I wondered, *Am I beginning another long stretch of incarceration? Slavery?*

I was pacing nervously up and down the cell when the door opened and I was taken to a photographer who took my picture. Next, I was taken to a clerk who attached the picture to an Austrian identification card and handed it to me. He opened the door and I walked out.

Outside, Claire and Leslie were anxiously waiting for me. They explained what had just happened. Since I didn't have any ID and because of my political background, the Austrian authorities had to do a background check on me. The request was sent to Budapest, which usually took a week for a reply before they could issue a temporary identification.

Claire had circumvented the bureaucracy again by asking for help from the American Embassy. The clerks there were cooperative, and found my name on the list of people convicted and sentenced to jail and forced labor in the Soviet Union.

The clerk at the Embassy made a phone call and told Claire where I was and requested my immediate release from the Austrian police.

Claire and Leslie arrived just five minutes before I was released. I gave them each a big hug and thanked them for what they had done for me. When I looked at Claire, I saw tears running down her cheeks. I was overwhelmed by their devotion to me and by the quick turn of events.

From the jail, without wasting time, we rushed to the reception center's processing office, again bypassing the long line. A clerk filled out our forms and asked us our preferences. My first preference was the United States. Canada was second. The clerk told us that the wait to enter the United States would be six weeks or longer, but we could leave for Canada in a couple of days.

I gave her the name and phone numbers of the American Embassy staff member whom Claire and Leslie had contacted earlier, and asked her to call him. She called and said I could leave the next day for the United States, but the others would have to wait for their turn, which could take six weeks or longer. I decided to wait or go to Canada rather than leave my friends behind. We mutually agreed not to wait to get into the United States, but go to Canada together.

Meanwhile, Claire found out that refugees wishing to go to Canada needed to contact Ann Kethly, a former Hungarian politician whose office was only a block away. She was the contact person between the Canadian authorities and Hungarian refugees. Together, our group walked over to Ann Kethly's office. I told her about the members of our group—occupational skills, family situations—and asked her to help us immigrate to Canada.

"Your timing is perfect. A ship is leaving from Bremerhaven, Germany for Halifax, Canada in four days," she told us. "If you are interested, I have enough tickets for you."

"We are interested and would like to go," I replied.

Then I discussed Claire's situation with her. Since Claire wasn't a Hungarian citizen, she didn't qualify as a refugee. Ann Kethly said she couldn't do anything for her.

The office issued us tickets for the train to Bremerhaven and for the ship bound for Halifax. The tickets were in our pockets on 24 November but we had to wait until 27 November to take the train.

The three days went by very slowly on one hand and very fast on the other. I spent the entire three days with Claire and they were bittersweet. I didn't want to leave her behind—she and I had grown very fond of each other, had shared many tender moments, and were emotionally attached. But it was impossible to take her with me. We discussed this several times and finally she insisted that I should go, leaving her behind.

She accompanied me to the train station and stayed with me until I boarded. Even at that moment, I was still undecided. I knew the time had arrived to choose between my five friends and Claire. The conductor had already signaled to the engineer to leave. The train began to move, and we embraced. She was sobbing when I jumped on the train, and I struggled with my emotions as I looked at her until she disappeared from my sight. That was the last time I saw her, and I knew we would never meet again.

Claire was a dear, unselfish, caring friend. I sensed that if we had stayed together, we could have developed a long and loving relationship.

I walked back to our train compartment to join my friends and settled down on the seat next to the window that they'd reserved for me. They thanked me for my decision not to abandon them. They understood how I felt about leaving Claire and tried to offer comfort.

The train trip took almost a whole day, stopping at large cities along the way. The first stop was Munich, where we waited for an hour. On the platform, Red Cross personnel greeted us and distributed food, clothing, and other necessities donated by German citizens for the Hungarian refugees. One of the Red Cross employees looked at me, then walked away and returned with an overcoat and a hat. Seeing my worn shoes, she left again and found an almost new pair for me. When I told her the circumstances of my flight from Hungary, she gave me toilet items—a razor, soap, a toothbrush, toothpaste, and a comb. Also, each of us, including the babies, was given ten German marks. In the new clothes, I felt like a new man and all the basics made me feel content. I even had money to buy cigarettes.

Our next stop was Nurnberg where we got sandwiches, hot drinks, and a package of cigarettes. The train made two more stops in Hanover and Bremen. Finally, we arrived in Bremerhaven at noon. At the station, buses were waiting to take us to the port where the ship was waiting for the passengers to board.

The sight of that huge floating hotel filled us with emotion as we realized that the ship was our lifeline toward the fulfillment of our dreams in a new homeland. The name of the ship was *New York*, a luxury liner owned by Greek Line, a Greek shipping company. Ship personnel were German-speaking.

After a medical exam, we were escorted to our cabins in the bottom of the ship. I shared one with my cousin Leslie. The cabin was equipped with two bunk beds. The upper one was hanging on heavy rubber bands used to smooth out the roughness of the choppy water. Leslie took the upper level and I took the lower bunk. What luxurious accommodations!

After getting settled in, we walked around and were impressed by the ship's luxury. During our discovery walk, I met the chef, Hans, who was a couple of years my senior. We had a long chat and developed a friendly rapport.

He had served during World War II in the German Luftwaffe as a pilot, was shot down in 1944, and spent four years in Soviet POW camps. Before we parted, he asked if I had a wish list, and what would be the first three items on it.

"Two changes of underwear, a clean shirt—and the third, a bottle of champagne."

He disappeared and came back with a bag and a bottle of champagne. The bag contained underwear, clean shirts, and a couple of pairs of socks.

After he left, Leslie and I continued our discovery trip. The rest of our group was in the two cabins next to ours. The Lorant family, Sue, George, and the two babies, were in one, and Alex and Greg were in the other.

After everyone settled in, I invited my friends for a glass of champagne. We walked up to the deck, sat down at a nicely set table, asked the waiter for champagne glasses, and divided the contents of the bottle between the six of us. Then we talked about our defection, our luck during the trek, the long night, and the long walk to and our arrival at Furstenfeld. We talked about Claire and the special attachment between us. They sensed that parting from her had been difficult.

The next day, our ship was still in port and we were busy looking for acquaintances. I found only one, a former class-mate several years ahead of me in high school, who was with his wife. Years later, we met again at the University of Toronto, where he was a professor in chemical engineering and I was working towards my degree in electrical engineering. We took great pleasure in seeing each other again and had long interesting discussions.

★ ★ ★

On 4 December1956, the ship left for Halifax. This was an overwhelming, emotional moment and a significant milestone in my life, and in the lives of all the others around me. I felt I was cutting my ties with the past, although I later realized that that wasn't possible.

I was full of energy and ready to start a new life in Canada. The long years of suffering as a POW in the Soviet Union, political prisoner in Lubyanka and in the gulag above the Arctic Circle . . . these were all behind me.

That first night, after everyone retired, I went to the deck to savor my freedom. I knelt down and said a prayer thanking the Almighty for guiding me from Red Hell to a free land. I prayed for the loved ones I left behind in Hungary. When I returned to my cabin to retire for the night, Leslie was already snoring.

The next two days were pleasant, the sea was calm, and we enjoyed the good food and each other's company. We took long walks on the deck and talked about our adventurous escape and uncertain future. We met many interesting people, but due to the lack of a common language, it was difficult to have a conversation.

I met a pleasant African-American medical doctor. Our interest in each other was mutual, but we gave up fast as we realized that the most important element—a common language—was missing. This made me realize how important it was to learn the language of my adopted country. Learning English as fast as I could would be my top priority.

When I found out that the Lorants had an English-Hungarian dictionary, I borrowed it every day for a couple of hours. From Hans, my chef friend, I got a writing pad and set a goal to learn at least fifty English words every day. My first priority, though, was to master spoken English. Since many

English words originate from Latin, my Latin studies in school were a great help. There were times when I learned two hundred words a day.

When I had enough courage to put my English to test, I tried to converse with the African-American medical doctor. It was then that it hit me—the pronunciation of English is a separate science. Knowing a language in written, orthographic form isn't enough. One must also learn to speak it as well. When all else failed, I resorted to paper and pencil and was amazed at how much I understood of what the doctor was saying, though for her, it must have been too slow and boring.

Suddenly, there was a big change in the weather. The friendly face of the sea turned into an angry one. At times, the ship tilted ten to fifteen degrees. Nearly all the passengers became seasick. Many times, I was the only person in the dining room as passengers stayed in their cabins, hoping that lying down would make the choppy sea more tolerable.

I went to the deserted deck one morning to see how it looked outside. The waves washed over the deck and I had to grasp at the railing, holding on for dear life. That was the only time I was seasick. I learned fast what one should and should not do during stormy weather on a ship.

The weather didn't improve until the ship docked at the Halifax pier.

Thus, we arrived to our final destination, Canada, the land where we hoped to find a bright new future and the fulfillment of our dreams.

We were prepared to work hard and overcome roadblocks, secure in the knowledge that we were now free to pursue whatever line of work or profession we chose.

Before I left the ship, I visited Hans, thanked him, and said a final good-bye.

After we disembarked, we filled out forms, went through medical exams, and the routine processing of the Canadian Immigration Service. We took buses to the railroad station where we boarded the train for Toronto. In Toronto, we were housed in the Red Cross "Welcome Center" in the center of the city.

★   ★   ★

My arrival at the Welcome Center closed yet another chapter in my life. I cut my ties with the past and began a new life on this side of the ocean.

But I never forgot and never will forget that my roots are in Hungary, where I left behind my family and friends and many fellow POWs and political prisoners I'd met in the gulag. My years in political prisons, jails in Hungary and Russia, and labor camps above the Arctic Circle shaped me into the man I am today. And although I could never forget the eleven years of my youth that I lost at the hands of Russian and Hungarian communist governments, I don't harbor bitterness or anger against my captors.

In my new homeland, I preferred to focus on the future, and not on the past. I regained my strength and stamina and kept my unwavering faith in the Creator of the universe, looking forward to becoming a productive member of society and making a new life in North America.

Epilogue

Upon my arrival in Canada in 1956, two equally important goals topped my list of priorities—mastering English and establishing a happy home.

On my first day in the refugee center set up for the "Hungarian Freedom Fighters of 1956," I searched the bulletin board for names of friends, acquaintances, or relatives. I couldn't believe my eyes when I found business cards with the name Paul Puky, a former classmate at the Air Force Academy, pinned to the board. I took one and tucked it away in my pocket. Paul, I learned, had immigrated to Canada and settled in Peterborough, Ontario in 1945 at the end of World War II.

In early January, I was hired by a catering company in Bancraft, Ontario as a helper in the employees' kitchen of a uranium mine. The job didn't work out and after a month, with eighty dollars in my pocket, I quit and decided to visit an old friend of mine in London, Ontario. That same morning, I packed my meager belongings and walked to the bus station where I boarded a bus.

I enjoyed the "luxurious" bus ride as the beautiful winter scenery glided by. After two hours on the road, the bus stopped at the terminal of a small city to pick up connecting passengers. I glanced at the sign over the entrance door of the terminal and immediately recognized the city name on the sign: Peterborough. I reached quickly into my pocket, pulled out the card and confirmed that I was indeed in Paul Puky's hometown.

The quick phone call I made to Paul that day triggered a long sequence of events—someone else might call them coincidences—which paved my way and shaped my future. And the one-day stay I had agreed upon with Paul and his wife, Eve, grew into years.

At the insistence of Paul and Eve, I agreed to stay for another day to attend a welcome reception organized by some long established Hungarians for the newly arrived "Freedom Fighters."

Paul and Eve drove me to the reception in their antique Model T Ford. When we arrived, a large group of Hungarians was already there. Paul took me around and introduced me to the old-timers.

I was standing with a glass in my hand near the entrance, conversing with a small group, when a young woman in the company of an elderly lady, I guessed to be her mother, walked in.

As our eyes instinctively met, my heartbeat went up, and a pleasantly warm feeling rushed through my body. Without realizing it, we sent a simultaneous message to each other through our eye contact. The acknowledgment was instantaneous on both sides and we were soon introduced to each other.

Now, it was clear to me why I had extended my stay in Peterborough. It was part of a chain of events that led me to Susan, who has always been beautiful not only outside, but inside as well. She became my best friend and has been my life partner for more than forty-five years.

I learned from my darkest moments in captivity that nothing in life happens by chance—but everything according to God's grand plan. This was proven to me again by my meeting Susan in Ontario. A mathematician using probability calculations would conclude that, considering the long sequence of events, with so many twists and turns in the road, the probability of our meeting was very small—almost zero in mathematical terms.

In Hungary, Susan had been a successful athlete, winning many Hungarian and international competitions in track and field and basketball. We both lived in Budapest in 1948 and could have passed each other on the street. But it took all those years to bring us together in faraway Canada. A coincidence? No!

Three months later, Susan and I were married and our daughter, Lilly, was born in December 1957.

During my first two years in Canada, I worked in several manual jobs. In choosing employment, the two deciding factors were to be able to meet people, thus giving me the opportunity to practice the language, and to maximize my income. I was not afraid of hard work.

After two years, I felt brave enough to consider continuing my engineering education and had enough money for the first year of college.

But another hurdle had to be cleared before I could begin. Because of the political situation under which I had left Hungary so quickly in 1956, I had left all my important documents behind. It would have been dangerous to go back to my apartment to collect my diplomas and transcripts from the Technical University of Budapest. But I needed those documents to enter the engineering department at the University of Toronto.

The Almighty again lent his helping hand. He guided me through the labyrinth and led me to a former schoolmate, Dr. Paul Biringer, who was already a full-time professor in the engineering department at the University of Toronto. I hadn't known this, but one day, I heard Susan and her brother mention Paul's name. They had known Paul in Stockholm where they all lived before immigrating to Canada. Another coincidence? With his help, I was able to enroll as a second-year engineering student. I completed and passed the second year, and each of the next two years was easier than the previous one. I graduated with a degree in electrical engineering.

But financial woes still loomed. Susan's earnings were only enough to sustain our basic daily needs—with only one hundred remaining in our bank account. We didn't know how we would pay for the 650-dollar tuition for the second semester that was due the first week of January. Since we knew that the one hundred dollars wasn't going to make any difference regarding tuition, and since it was the Christmas season, we sent the money to my mother in Hungary. Two days later, grant money in the form of a check for 350 dollars arrived in the mail. The next day, another check for two thousand dollars arrived. Both were for grants I hadn't applied for. Coincidence? Not according to my belief.

In May 1962, I graduated from the University of Toronto with honors, second out of seventy-two in my class. Again, without the guidance of someone higher up, I couldn't have accomplished this by myself.

Immediately after the final exams, IBM interviewed me at their Poughkeepsie, New York facility. The following day, an offer arrived that I couldn't refuse. My starting date was 4 June 1962. Susan and I were jubilant!

My initial assignment was in research and development of magnetic memories. The department was responsible for the development of all memory components for every computer developed by IBM.

Since my family was still in Toronto and I was living in Poughkeepsie, I worked practically around the clock, seven days a week. By the time my family joined me in September, I was well known by my superiors. For my tireless hard work and creativity, I received awards and was promoted to the next level. In the first year, I was advanced to a supervisory position. Initially, I directed the activities of a small group of eight to ten engineers and technicians. Eventually, I was given the responsibility of the entire function.

Through the IBM education program, I earned a Master of Science degree in electrical engineering in 1968 at the University of Syracuse, New York. In the next two years, I completed the requirements for a Ph.D. with the exception of a one-year residency required for graduation.

Between 1962 and 1969, four U.S. patents were issued to me in the field of magnetic memories. I was the invited speaker at numerous international conferences and the author of several articles published in the *Institute of Electrical and Electronic Engineering Journal* (IEEE).

In the early 1970s, monolithic memory technology replaced the old magnetic technology and consequently, my job was eliminated. My new assignment, in another cutting-edge technology, the Large-Scale-Integration (LSI) of logic and memory components, took me to IBM's new site in Manassas, Virginia. Under my technical direction, an interactive design system used worldwide was developed for the LSI components. In this assignment, three additional patents were issued to me, bringing the total to seven.

As a child, I had dreamed of a future as an aviator and as a young man, I won admission to the Hungarian Air Force Academy, graduating in 1944 as a second lieutenant. In 1978, after thirty-five years on the ground, I returned to soaring, my lifelong avocation, and earned the highest award, a Gold Badge with three diamonds. I now own a high-performance sailplane and in it, I soar with the eagles as often as I can. That year, I moved to Burlington, Vermont; in 1981, I moved to East Fishkill, New York; and in 1986, I returned to Manassas.

On 1 July 1987, after twenty-five years of service, I retired from IBM as a senior engineer. In the same year on 26 February, I witnessed the miracle of life with the birth of our grandson, Kyle Bela.

Safe in the United States, I still longed to see my mother, siblings, friends, and relatives again. But for thirty-three years, the Communist government refused to grant me an entry visa to Hungary. In the three decades of my exile, my mother, two siblings, many relatives, and friends were laid to rest.

It wasn't until September 1990 that I was able to return to Hungary, following the collapse of the "Evil Empire." Since then, my wife and I have been making yearly visits there. And I am finally able to pay my respects at the graves of my family and friends who are buried there. I trust that they understand that I wasn't allowed home to bid them a final good-bye, and that thirty-three years of exile wasn't my choice.

On our first visit back to Hungary since I had fled, I received a hero's welcome. I was promoted to the rank of colonel in the newly formed Hungarian Air Force. The Distinguished Freedom Cross for Free Hungary was conferred upon me in 1997. Two years later, in 1999, I was inducted into the Knightly Order of Vitez, the Hungarian knighthood. I was humbled by these honors, but at the same time I was filled with pride and felt redeemed as these honors were bestowed upon me for the sufferings and hardship I experienced while in captivity.

A succession of honors conferred upon me over the years has left me with a sense of high privilege—and a concern for raising future American pilots. In 1997, I founded "Gogos Scholars," a soaring scholarship, which to date has paid for twenty talented youngsters to train as sailplane pilots in Minden, Nevada, one of the world's best soaring sites.

After my retirement, I established an accounting and tax service in Warrenton, Virginia, which is now owned and operated by my daughter, Lilly, and her husband, David Dibble.

★   ★   ★

Now, at the sunset of my life, I find myself revisiting the years that have passed. My life can be divided into two distinct periods—my youth on the "other side of the ocean," and my later years on "this side of the ocean."

In my youth, I was fortunate to be able to study at and graduate from a private high school run under the strict discipline of Catholic monks. In high school, at the Air Force Academy, and at the University of Budapest, I obtained a solid knowledge of mathematics, physics, chemistry, and other subjects required for my profession. I also learned several foreign languages. Latin, Greek, French, and German proved to be enormous assets in countries where I lived—Austria, Russia, Canada, and the United States.

Looking back, I realize the last ten years I spent "on the other side of the ocean" were character—and morale building. The ideas and concepts I studied in high school crystallized and became the foundation for my personal beliefs. First, everything happens in life not by chance, but by design. Human lives are part of the Grand Plan. I witnessed several times during the years in Red Hell that no one can change or even influence the Grand Plan charted out for each one of us, and whatever happens is not by coincidence, but by the will of the Creator. Second, justice always prevails. Good deeds are rewarded and bad deeds are punished. Third, every human being has an earthly mission and nobody departs before it is completed.

After losing a decade of my youth in Red Hell, and narrowly escaping from communist Hungary, I arrived in the land of opportunity, the United Sates of America. Equipped with a solid professional knowledge and high moral standards, I have been able to achieve a successful professional career and a happy family and social life on this side of the ocean.

The credit belongs to the man who is actually in the arena . . . who strives valiantly, who knows the great enthusiasm, the great devotions, and spends himself in worthy cases. Who, at best, knows the triumph of high achievements and who, at worst, if he fails, fails while daring greatly so that his place shall never be with those cold and timid souls who know neither victory nor defeat.

Teddy Roosevelt